Approaches to Teaching the Works of Italo Calvino

Approaches to Teaching World Literature

For a complete listing of titles, see the last pages of this book.

Approaches to Teaching the Works of Italo Calvino

Edited by

Franco Ricci

The Modern Language Association of America
New York 2013

Library of Congress Cataloging-in-Publication Data

Approaches to teaching the works of Italo Calvino / edited by Franco Ricci.
pages cm. — (Approaches to Teaching World Literature ; 125)
Includes bibliographical references and index.
ISBN 978-1-60329-123-1 (cloth : alk. paper) —
ISBN 978-1-60329-124-8 (pbk. : alk. paper)
1. Calvino, Italo—Study and teaching. 2. Calvino, Italo—Criticism and interpretation.
I. Ricci, Franco, 1953– editor of compilation.
PQ4809.A45Z56 2013
853'.914—dc23 2013010257

Approaches to Teaching World Literature 125
ISSN 1059-1133
ISBN 978-1-60329-165-1 (EPUB)
ISBN 978-1-60329-166-8 (Kindle)

Cover illustration for the paperback and electronic editions: Paul Klee, *Garden on Debris*, 1923–24, watercolor and black ink transfer on cream wove paper, mounted on cream card, 268 × 254 mm, Olivia Shaler Swan Memorial Collection, 1943.593, The Art Institute of Chicago. © 2013 Artists Rights Society (ARS), New York.

Published by The Modern Language Association of America
26 Broadway, New York, New York 10004-1789
www.mla.org

CONTENTS

Part One

MATERIALS

The Instructor's Library

Italo Calvino was a prolific and highly successful creative writer, journalist, editor, and essayist. Given his worldwide popularity, the critical literature on him has become an immense and continuously expanding universe of intersecting and overlapping opinions. This body of work includes monographs, collected volumes, convention addresses, special issues of journals, and articles too numerous to list. Nevertheless, there are touchstones along this winding path that are indispensable to the instructor's bookshelf.

Einaudi is the chief Italian publisher of Calvino's fiction. Calvino was employed as an editor by Einaudi until 1983, when the company became enmeshed in legal wrangles; he moved to the Garzanti publishing firm in 1984. Since the author's death in 1985, Mondadori has published his collected fiction (*Romanzi e racconti*), his nonfiction (*Saggi*), a collection of personal and professional letters (*Lettere, 1940–1985*), and *Album Calvino*. A selection of autobiographical writings and pivotal interviews (*Eremita a Parigi*) was also published by Mondadori, who continues to regularly republish Calvino's individual works in its popular Oscar paperback collection.

In this volume we have chosen to use translations published by Calvino's most prolific English publishers, Harcourt Brace Jovanovich in the United States and Lester and Orpen Dennys in Canada, as well as London's Secker and Warburg. Martin McLaughlin has produced two translations of Calvino's most important essays, *Hermit in Paris: Autobiographical Writings* and *Why Read the Classics?* By far the best bibliographic information in either Italian or English has been compiled by Mario Barenghi, Bruno Falcetto, and Claudio Milanini in the third volume of *Romanzi e racconti*. The compilers comment judiciously on Calvino's fiction and nonfiction, as well as his critical works. The bibliography also includes his poetry and his prose works for theater, cinema, music, and the other arts. Giorgio Bertone has an extensive bibliography in his work *Italo Calvino: Il castello della scrittura*; when combined with the above bibliography, it provides a complete list of attributable works by the author.

Good general introductions to Calvino in English include the following monographs: Sara Maria Adler, *Calvino: The Writer as Fablemaker*, an introduction to Calvino's pre-1977 works; Albert Howard Carter III, *Italo Calvino: Metamorphoses of Fantasy*, an engaging work that examines the use of fantasy as Calvino's core; Beno Weiss, *Understanding Italo Calvino*, an informed and personal reading of the author's fiction; and Martin McLaughlin, *Italo Calvino*, a painstakingly precise and illuminating examination of thematic and stylistic questions recurrent in Calvino's work.

More specialized book-length studies are JoAnn Cannon, *Italo Calvino: Writer and Critic*, which examines the theoretical implications of the writer's craft; Lucia Re, *Calvino and the Age of Neorealism: Fables of Estrangement*, which focuses on Calvino's first novel and on ethical issues; Franco Ricci, *Difficult Games*, which explores the psychological and existential anxieties of the author's early stories; Kathryn Hume, *Calvino's Fictions: Cogito and Cosmos*, which traces the metaphysics of Calvino's imaginative structures; and Ricci, *Painting with Words, Writing with Pictures*, which studies the relation of words and images in Calvino's writings.

Several seminal articles are particularly useful in concept-oriented courses that may range from specific critical approaches to broad cultural issues: Teresa de Lauretis, "Narrative Discourse in Calvino: Praxis or Poiesis?," a semiotic analysis that lays the groundwork for future semiotic studies of the author; John Gatt-Rutter, "Calvino Ludens: Literary Play and Its Political Implications," a compelling reading of Calvino's ludic implications; Linda Hutcheon, "Actualizing Narrative Structures: Detective Plot, Fantasy, Games, and the Erotic," a look into the self-reflexive nature of Calvino's most popular fiction, including *Cosmicomics*, *T Zero*, and *Invisible Cities*; Marilyn Schneider, "Calvino at the Crossroads: *Il castello dei destini incrociati*," a structuralist reading of this work; Gore Vidal, "On Italo Calvino," a close friend's and intellectual's purview of the author's career; James Gardner, "Italo Calvino, 1923–1985," a well-reasoned review of Calvino's main themes; Gian Paolo Biasin, "The Surface of Things, the Depth of Words," an anthropological reading of one of Calvino's last works that opens onto politically charges issues of gender and culture; de Lauretis, "Reading the (Post)Modern Text: *If on a winter's night a traveler*," a feminist reading that focuses on absence, duality, and subversion. Finally, to properly situate Calvino's fiction within a modern or postmodern context, I strongly recommend two essays by John Barth, "The Literature of Exhaustion" and "The Literature of Replenishment."

One of the great advantages of the computer age is that a scholar is never more than a click away from being inundated in a sea of information, and the Web offers a good starting point for sources on Calvino. Once one has filtered out the fan-based sites of little critical value and the random offerings, one can certainly use the Internet as a viable teaching and information tool in the contemporary electronic classroom (see in this volume Andrea Dini's excellent critical overview of online sources).

Works by Italo Calvino

Primary Texts

All works listed below were published in Turin by Einaudi except where otherwise indicated; they are presented chronologically, by genre.

Fiction

Il sentiero dei nidi di ragno (1947)
Ultimo viene il corvo (1949)
Il visconte dimezzato (1952)
L'entrata in guerra (1954)
Fiabe italiane (1956)
Il barone rampante (1957)
I racconti (1958)
Il cavaliere inesistente (1959)
I nostri antenati (1960)
La giornata d'uno scrutatore (1963)
La speculazione edilizia (1963)
Marcovaldo ovvero le stagioni in città (1963)
Il sentiero dei nidi di ragno (with pref.; 1964)
Le cosmicomiche (1965)
Ti con zero (1967)
La memoria del mondo e altre storie cosmicomiche (1968)
Gli amori difficili (1970)
Le città invisibili (1972)
Il castello dei destini incrociati (1973)
Se una notte d'inverno un viaggiatore (1979)
Palomar (1983)
Le cosmicomiche vecchie e nuove (Milan: Garzanti, 1984)
Sotto il sole giaguaro (Milan: Garzanti, 1986)
La strada di San Giovanni (Milan: Mondadori, 1990)
Prima che tu dica "Pronto" (Milan: Mondadori, 1993)
Tutte le cosmicomiche (ed. Claudio Milanini; Milan: Mondadori, 1997)

Nonfiction

Una pietra sopra (1980)
Collezione di sabbia (Milan: Garzanti, 1984)
Lezioni americane: Sei proposte per il prossimo millennio (Milan: Garzanti, 1988)
Sulla fiaba (ed. Mario Lavagetto; 1988)
Perché leggere i classici (Milan: Mondadori, 1991)
I libri degli altri: Lettere, 1947–1981 (ed. Giovanni Tesio; 1991)
Eremita a Parigi: Pagine autobiografiche (Milan: Mondadori, 1994)

Collected Works

These volumes were published in Milan by Mondadori in the series I Meridiani.

Romanzi e racconti, 3 vols. (ed. Mario Barenghi and Bruno Falcetto; 1991–94)
Fiabe italiane (pref. Mario Lavagetto; 1993)
Saggi, 2 vols. (ed. Barenghi; 1995)
Album Calvino (ed. Luca Baranelli and Ernesto Ferrero; 1995)
Lettere, 1940–1985 (ed. Baranelli, introd. Milanini; 2001)

Translations in English

Fiction

Adam One Afternoon (trans. Archibald Colquhoun and Peggy Wright)
The Castle of Crossed Destinies (trans. William Weaver)
Cosmicomics (trans. Weaver)
Difficult Loves [and] *Smog* [and] *A Plunge into Real Estate* (trans. Weaver)
If on a winter's night a traveler (trans. Weaver)
Invisible Cities (trans. Weaver)
Italian Folktales (trans. George Martin)
Marcovaldo; or, The Seasons in the City (trans. Weaver)
Mr. Palomar (trans. Weaver)
"Numbers in the Dark" and Other Stories (trans. Tim Parks)
Our Ancestors (trans. Colquhoun)
The Path to the Spiders' Nest (trans. Colquhoun)
The Road to San Giovanni (trans. Parks)
Time and the Hunter (trans. Weaver)
Under the Jaguar Sun (trans. Weaver)
"The Watcher" and Other Stories (trans. Weaver)

Nonfiction

The Literature Machine (trans. Patrick Creagh)
Six Memos for the Next Millennium (trans. Creagh)
The Uses of Literature (trans. Creagh and William Weaver)
"The Written and Unwritten Word" (trans. Weaver)

Calvino and the Internet

Andrea Dini

> You ask me for a biographical note—something that always embarrasses me. Biographical data, even those recorded in the public registers, are the most private things one has, and to declare them openly is rather like facing a psychoanalyst. (Calvino, "By Way" 339)

In this age of blogs and social media, Calvino's 1980 appeal to a justified restraint in narrating one's personal (and public) life almost comes as an outmoded, unheard-of proposition. Yet, ironically, numerous versions of his biography can be found on the Internet decades later. Any search of Italo Calvino will yield nearly three million results, including images, videos, books, blogs, and discussions, and, once commercial sites selling Calvino's books are eliminated, most of the remaining pages are linked by one, significant factor: a biographical summary or a biobibliographic profile.

To stop at the threshold of an author's curriculum vitae is, after all, the byproduct of nonspecialized literary information online. Paul Goring, Jeremy Hawthorn, and Domhnall Mitchell, in their guidelines for undergraduate literature students, note that literature information online often limits itself to

> when a writer was born and died, what he or she wrote, and perhaps [to] a few standard excerpts from their works. Frequently, the pages are put there by fans—people who are interested in a particular writer, but who do not always have original or useful things to say about her or him. . . . [W]hat you will get is a brief biography taken from a printed text, a list of books, some photographs and perhaps a few short summaries. (113)[1]

This scenario perfectly applies to Italo Calvino, limiting the scope of pedagogically relevant Web-based activities to approach his works: issues of copyright exclude (or should exclude) primary texts from appearing in full online, leaving space for fillers or rewriting of standard pieces of information from printed materials or links to secondary sources, mostly from the popular press. When primary texts appear in lengthier form, they often come from an undocumented source. Pertinence and reliability are always at stake.[2] Even narrower searches, by titles of Calvino's works, yield somewhat similar outcomes in Italian or English (summaries, a handful of academic papers, syllabi, links to articles from the popular press).

Despite the disheartening situation of randomness that these Web pages seem to embody, some notable exceptions do exist. Although online resources for Calvino can only be used as ancillary components to a printed bibliography, *ancillary* does not equal *negligible*, and they can certainly spark in-class debates of various kinds.

First and foremost, to profit pedagogically from what is available on the Internet, instructors must teach students how to adopt a critical thinking approach to electronic secondary sources on Calvino's works. As a preliminary task, students must be taught how to identify a site's credentials when the accessed page does not come from an official (institutional) source, by locating the following pieces of information: author or Web master (affiliation, organization, or host site organization, etc.); type of materials (summaries of works, personal reflections, transcripts from other identifiable critical sources, journal or newspaper articles); and pertinence to an in-class discussion or written analysis of Calvino's opus. Once students have assessed a Web site's target audience, they will be able to frame its contents in terms of how relevant or trustworthy they might be for a study of the author.

One course component in my Senior Seminar in Literary Research is evaluating Internet literary sources. In online research, as with any library research of printed materials, students need to be exposed to a variety of sources and be asked to choose between different versions of the information provided, making informed decisions on what to use and, in the process, developing a critical eye. Sites on Calvino often contain multiple, divergent versions of biographical data (compare, e.g., *Wikipedia* pages in Italian and in English with the profiles on *Italica*, on the site for the Associazione Nazionale Partigiani d'Italia [ANPI], or even on Todd Comer's *Outside the Town of Malbork*).[3] Calvino's Internet biography is therefore a good starting point for a twofold examination: one internal, in which students come up with the most complete, pertinent, and reliable portrait or assemble their own, and one external, in which students learn how to compare and evaluate possible embedded points of view in critical materials that disguise themselves as factual—as in biographical accounts. The same exercise may apply to the works mentioned in every profile. Students are also invited to reflect on the omissions, on the possible reasons why some works are not included or just briefly outlined, when in other profiles a significant amount of lines is devoted to the works. This activity is useful for evaluating how summaries of any kind represent interpretative, not just neutral information. The results from my classroom have been encouraging. Students start discussing Calvino's critical reception as represented by these Internet sources directly (even without being aware of it at first), and they begin to contextualize his works (or historicize, if you will), tying them down to his biography, and consider his writings as the product of a specific historical context while they keep interrogating their universal qualities—Calvino's message today.

Institutional sites like *Italia Libri*, *Italica*, *Rai.it* and *Rai.tv*, and *ANPI* contain the most stimulating materials, all in Italian, on Calvino. *Academia.edu* has also become a reliable electronic source of scholarly papers on Calvino that have been published in literary journals or in books. With the exception of *Calvino e i libri*—a project from *scuola media* ("middle school") students that reinterprets Calvino's career through *Lezioni americane* (with his memos on exactitude, quickness, lightness, and so on taken as a key to his works)—other sites in Italian are mostly disappointing for our academic purposes. Comer's *Outside the Town of Malbork* contains the best material in English, although it still seems equally outdated. Sites are put up by fans, who often are not conversant with any recent scholarship in Italian or in English on the author.

Institutional sites also may offer an unbalanced image of the author, with a bias that seems to come with the language and tradition of the institution they are the result of. Italian sites privilege the writer's production up to the late 1950s, to then concentrate on *Se una notte d'inverno un viaggiatore* (1979; *If on a winter's night a traveler*). Most of their discussions and summaries are geared toward defining the realistic (or neorealistic) qualities in Calvino's texts, discussing their fairy-tale elements, or examining the writer's political engagement between 1945 and the early 1960s, between *Il sentiero dei nidi di ragno* (*The Path to the Spiders' Nests*) and "La giornata d'uno scrutatore" ("The Watcher"). They tend to stick to his relationships with other Italian writers, like Cesare Pavese and Elio Vittorini, and to escape his formalistic, Oulipo-related period. Calvino's contribution to the debate on postmodernism or the influence of postanalytic philosophy on his thought (e.g., Nelson Goodman and Thomas Nagel) is usually not mentioned. Anglo-American sites, on the contrary, tend to underline the late production from *Cosmicomiche* on, with greater emphasis on *Città invisibili*, *Se una notte d'inverno*, *Lezioni americane*, and Calvino's connections to John Barth and Jorge Luis Borges, among others. Not surprisingly, even biographical accounts continue to strike a discordant note, in the way this or that title is emphasized, devalued, or reevaluated within a particular period.

These aspects constitute a potential field of discussion on Calvino's reception by two literary traditions: by accessing these pages, conceived for different audiences, any Internet user interested in the writer may end up with two rather divergent ideas of who Calvino was or what his production was like. If we were to rely, for example, on the portrait given by Paul M. Willenberg's *In Calvino Veritas: The Critical Calvino Page*, the Calvino we would know would just be a champion of postmodernist thought. Student are therefore invited to explore how (and possibly why) summaries of the same works diverge, by contrasting, whenever possible, Italian and Anglo-American Web sites, to finally report to the class their inferences on what kind of writer certain sites propose to the public audience. I assign Rebecca West's "L'identità americana di Calvino" to clarify some issues pertaining to his popular yet nonetheless critical reception.

The main reason I use the Internet for Calvino is to listen to his voice. The RAI sites *Rai.it* and *Rai.tv*, for Italian television and radio, and *Italica*, "a RAI International website devoted to Italian language and culture," remain pivotal for any approach to teaching Calvino that advocates using multimedia sources as integration to printed materials. The writer materializes on-screen to become an indelible memory.

On *Rai.it*, a special twentieth-anniversary section on Calvino includes five video clips of interviews with him made in 1968, 1979, 1981, and 1983. Each video clip (in *RealPlayer* format; mediocre video quality, excellent audio) is accompanied by a partial transcript, which enormously facilitates the design of pre- and postviewing activities. I introduce these clips toward the end of a module devoted to Calvino, when most of the assigned readings and in-class discussions have already shaped students' ideas on what kind of writer he was and what his place is in the Italian literary canon. On *Rai.tv*, students can find longer and perhaps more interesting clips (uploaded between September and October 2008), and the overall quality of the site is superior to that of *Rai.it*. The site also features more video clips—ten instead of five—ranging from Calvino's reflections on the role that Vittorini had in his work (and separate videos on Stendhal or Galileo) to discussions of books such as *Palomar*, *Cosmicomiche*, and *Se una notte d'inverno un viaggiatore*. Especially useful is an interview in which Calvino discusses the lack of introspection in his stories and novels. Of all the online contributions dedicated to the writer, *Rai.tv* is perhaps the most useful.[4]

To activate students' background knowledge and ease the overall comprehension of each segment, at both the linguistic and the content levels, previewing materials include the following:

- vocabulary glosses (in the target language or in English)
- data sheet with factual information on the works or the topics being discussed in the clips
- written questions taken from the interview's transcript, to be preliminarily discussed in class as group work, in the light of what students know of the writer's works and habits

This last piece normally raises valid questions with regard to what students perceive are Calvino's values for literature, culture, and the use of one's language. Class discussion is immediately resumed as a follow-up (postviewing) activity. I ask students to read, print, and bring to class all transcripts. I also assign further selected readings, from Calvino or from secondary sources, about the interviews' topics, expanding on those already assigned for previewing activities.

Both pre- and postviewing phases can therefore be conceived as departure points for further exploration of Calvino's beliefs on literature and for using additional texts or excerpts from his writings. His interviews with Gregory Lucente and with Guido Almansi, for example, pair well with discussion of Calvino's antipsychological stance in character portrayal and *I nostri antenati*; *Palomar*'s story "Del prendersela coi giovani" can be compared with the clip "Gli errori in commune" (in *Italica*'s multimedia section, curated by Barbaro), in which Calvino discusses relationships between generations; excerpts from *Lezioni americane* can help address his philosophical and literary legacy in the twenty-first century (in debates of whether his recommendations have been met).

By the end of these lessons, students should see how complex this deceptively easy-to-read writer is or how difficult it is not to take into account national literary traditions, points of view, or bias when attempting to decipher his works and his reception critically. At this point, perhaps, a more coherent view of Calvino's works and legacy will have taken shape. Perhaps, too, students will have been captivated by his elusive silences (the ones we noticed on his pages, by his restraint), while his uncertainties and his stuttering during the interviews are witness to his attempts at finding the most precise word to express thoughts, to clarify his vision of his firm advocacy of humanistic values. The rest is up to them, the student-readers.

NOTES

[1]I strongly recommend the chapter "Guide to the Use of Electronic Media" (Goring, Hawthorn, and Mitchell 101–32) to instructors who want to include electronic media in their courses. The guide is an excellent aid in defining (and narrowing) students' Web searches; it clearly illustrates how to browse the Web and evaluate primary and secondary sources, assessing issues of reliability, pertinence, and authority. By assigning the whole chapter, instructors will save a significant amount of class time having to explain basic concepts of what reading an electronic text really means or how to conduct a successful search. This chapter also plainly explains how to search electronic databases, e-journals, and other electronic resources for print sources. For Calvino, in addition to *JSTOR* and the *MLA International Bibliography*, the Italian-based *Italinemo*, edited by Marco Santoro, can be a valuable resource for students with a good command of Italian. The site, in operation since 2000, includes, as of 2012, 120 literary journals, with more than 1,900 issues and 41,000 reviewed articles.

[2]To date, no official Web site has ever been put up or edited by Calvino scholars fluent in both Italian and English or with an academic affiliation. Despite the many Italo Calvino home pages that come up during a search, no comprehensive site has been published with an academic audience as its target, which limits the scope of how relevant to the study of Calvino's works such a home page can be. The natural comparison in the field of highly successful online enterprises is the rigorous format followed by the prestigious *Journal of Gadda Studies*, edited by Federica Pedriali and officially housed at the University of Edinburgh. The journal, in soliciting and publishing noteworthy contributions, aims to disseminate Gadda's texts and scholarship. We can only hope that in the near future similar initiatives will be taken for Calvino to fully exploit the range of secondary sources on the author, given that copyright laws prohibit his primary texts from being reproduced in electronic form.

[3]I have included *Wikipedia* among the pages I ask my students to check for a simple fact: students use *Wikipedia* as an Internet resource, whether or not it is considered a trustworthy source and even if their instructors might frown on this choice. The exercise in comparison I assign for electronic sources (coupled with biographies published in print) can be a useful way to assess *Wikipedia*'s limitations both for the Italian and the English versions of Calvino's biography and summary of his works. Perhaps instructors can directly address in the classroom what *Wikipedia* is and how it functions, underlining the problematic aspects of an "open" authorship.

[4]The clips from *Rai.it* and *Rai.tv* are generally downloadable (by right-clicking on the link) through *Internet Explorer* or *Firefox* and can be distributed to students by e-mail

as attachments, posted on course management systems for easier access or guided listening, or used directly in *PowerPoint* presentations by the instructor. Video scripts can be printed or distributed if not all students have Internet access. *Italica* has a subsection of monographs on Calvino within its "Grandi narratori del '900," offering students quite a few critical pages on the writer, from an accurate biography to critical summaries of main works (*Il sentiero dei nidi di ragno*, *I nostril antenati*, *Se una note d'inverno un viaggiatore*) and even a few games. A special multimedia section contains links to some of the interviews found on *Rai.it* and *Rai.tv*.

CALVINO ON THE WEB

Recommended Multimedia Resources

Barbaro, Patrizio, ed. "Grandi narratori del '900: Italo Calvino: Multimedia." *Italica*. Rai Intl., 2001. Web. 26 Dec. 2012. <http://www.italica.rai.it/argomenti/grandi_narratori_900/speciale_calvino/multimedia.htm>.

Calvino, Giovanna, ed. "Audio Special: Celebrating Italo Calvino." *New York Times*. New York Times, 31 Oct. 1999. Web. 26 Dec. 2012. <http://www.nytimes.com/books/99/10/31/specials/calvino.html>. Free site registration is required.

Calvino, Italo. "Intervista a Montezuma." 1974. *Radiomillevoci*. Rai, n.d. Web. 26 Dec. 2012. <http://www.radiomillevoci.it/ramfiles/makesmil.php?idc=670>.

———. *Marcovaldo, ovvero le stagioni in città*. Read by Marco Paolini, to the music of Tanit. Full Color Sound, 2006. CD.

———. *Ultimo viene il corvo*. Perf. by Gabriele Lavia. 1977. *Radiomillevoci*. Rai, n.d. Web. 26 Dec. 2012. <http://www.radiomillevoci.it/ramfiles/makesmil.php?idc=475>.

"Calvino Italo." *Il Narratore Audiolibri*. Il Narratore, 2006. Web. 26 Dec. 2012. <http://www.ilnarratore.com/autori/idx/8/Calvino-Italo.html>. Includes preview links to audio files for *Marcovaldo*, *Le città invisibili*, and *Racconti* available for purchase.

"Italo Calvino." *Maestri del 900. Rai.tv*. Rai Intl., 2012. Web. 26 Dec. 2012. <http://www.rai.tv/dl/RaiTV/programmi/page/Page-fe492284-6035-44ca-bf19-28c8882c0881.html?set=ContentSet-ab4854b0-9ff7-428ca155-ad5c0a4b47b4&type=V>. Includes the following interviews: "Italo Calvino—*Le cosmicomiche*," "Mi chiamo Italo Calvino," "Italo Calvino—Se un giorno d'estate un narratore," "Calvino e le narrazioni primitive," "Calvino e Galileo," "Calvino e Stendhal," "Calvino e Palomar," "Calvino e l'età dell'uomo," "Calvino e l'introspezione," and "Calvino e Vittorini."

Web Pages in Italian

Biga, Francesco. "Italo Calvino, il partigiano chiamato 'Santiago.'" *La patria indipendente* 1 (2006): 29–31. *Associazione Nazionale Partigiani d'Italia*. Web.

26 Dec. 2012. <http://www.anpi.it/media/uploads/patria/2006/1/29-31_BIGA.pdf>.

Calvino e i libri. Liceo Manzoni and Istituto Regionale di Ricerca Educativa Emilia Romagna, 2000. Web. 26 Dec. 2012. <http://kidslink.bo.cnr.it/irrsaeer/calvino2/>.

Di Stefano, Renato. "Italo Calvino (1923–1985): Copertine." *TecaLibri*. TecaLibri, n.d. Web. 26 Dec. 2012. <http://www.tecalibri.info/C/CALVINO_COP.htm>. Includes links to the main works (including a transcription of the first page of each work).

Franchi, Gianfranco. "*Le cosmicomiche*." *Lankelot*. Lankelot, July 2003. Web. 26 Dec. 2012. <http://www.lankelot.eu/index.php/2006/11/14/calvino-le-cosmicomiche/>.

Innocenti, Orsetta. "'A occhi straniati': La Resistenza secondo Calvino." *La patria indipendente* 2 (2003): 38–39. Web. 26 Dec. 2012. <http://www.anpi.it/media/uploads/patria/2003/2/38_39_Innocenti.pdf>.

———. "I *Racconti della Resistenza*: Realizzata la volontà di Calvino." *La patria indipendente* 5–7 (2005): 30–31. *Associazione Nazionale Partigiani d'Italia*. Web. 26 Dec. 2012. <http://www.anpi.it/media/uploads/patria/2005/7/30-31_INNOCENTI.pdf>.

"Italo Calvino." *Associazione Nazionale Partigiani d'Italia*. 2006. Web. 26 Dec. 2012. <http://www.anpi.it/donne-e-uomini/italo-calvino/>.

"Italo Calvino." *Minimum Fax*. Minimum Fax, n.d. Web. 26 Dec. 2012. <http://www.minimumfax.com/libri/scheda_autore/322>.

"Italo Calvino." *New York Times*. New York Times, n.d. Web. 26 Dec. 2012. <http://topics.nytimes.com/topics/reference/timestopics/people/c/italo_calvino/index.html>. Compiles news about Calvino, including commentary and archival articles (e.g., interviews, book reviews).

"Italo Calvino." *Wikipedia*. Wikimedia Italia, 15 June 2006. Web. 26 Dec. 2012. <http://it.wikipedia.org/wiki/Italo_Calvino>.

"Italo Calvino–Aldo Palazzeschi." *L'angolo di Violetta*. Violetta, n.d. Web. 26 Dec. 2012. <http://www.violettanet.it/poesiealtro_autori/CALVINO.htm>.

"Italo Calvino (1923–1985)." *Italia Libri*. Italia Libri, 2000. Web. 26 Dec. 2012. <http://www.italialibri.net/autori/calvinoi.html#Top_of_Page>.

Italo Calvino 1923–1985. *Rai.it*. Rai Intl., n.d. Web. 26 Dec. 2012. <http://www.cittadini.rai.it/dl/portali/site/articolo/ContentItem-c63b02c2-9db9-4fc8-affb-fc91cb659d1b.html>. Includes links to Calvino's biography and bibliography, selected interviews and television appearances, and useful Web resources.

Monego, Marina. "*Marcovaldo*." *Lankelot*. Lankelot, Apr. 2005. Web. 26 Dec. 2012. <http://www.lankelot.eu/index.php/2006/10/26/calvino-marcovaldo/>.

———. "*Il sentiero dei nidi di ragno*." *Lankelot*. Lankelot, May 2005. Web. 26 Dec. 2012. <http://www.lankelot.eu/index.php/2006/08/24/calvino-il-sentiero-dei-nidi-di-ragno/>.

Monego, Marina, and Enrico Campofreda. "*Ultimo viene il corvo.*" *Lankelot*. Lankelot, May 2005. Web. 26 Dec. 2012. <http://www.lankelot.eu/index.php/2009/01/20/calvino-italo-ultimo-viene-il-corvo/>.

Monopoli, Elena, Katia Nobbio, and Francesco Troiano. "Grandi narratori del '900: Italo Calvino." *Italica*. Rai Intl., 2001. Web. 26 Dec. 2012. <http://www.italica.rai.it/argomenti/grandi_narratori_900/speciale_calvino.htm>. Includes links to Calvino's biography, summaries of selected works, and televised interviews (see Barbaro).

Piu, Antonio. *Italo Calvino*. Piu, n.d. Web. 26 Dec. 2012. <http://www.italo calvino.it/>.

"*Il sentiero dei nidi di ragno.*" *Italia Libri*. Italia Libri, 28 Nov. 2000. Web. 26 Dec. 2012. <http://www.italialibri.net/opere/sentierodeinididiragno.html#Top_of_Page>.

Settimelli, Leoncarlo, ed. *Canzoniere partigiano*. *La patria indipendente* 10 Apr. 2011: n. pag. Web. 26 Dec. 2012. <http://www.anpi.it/media/uploads/patria/2011/Inserto_Canzoniere_Partigiano_1.pdf>.

Web Pages in English

Comer, Todd. *Outside the Town of Marlbork*. Comer, 15 June 2009. Web. 26 Dec. 2012. <http://www.italo-calvino.com/>.

"Italo Calvino." *Wikipedia*. Wikimedia, 1 June 2006. Web. 26 Dec. 2012. <http://en.wikipedia.org/wiki/Italo_Calvino>.

Liukkonen, Petri. "Italo Calvino (1923–1985)." *Pegasos*. Maintained by Ari Pesonen. Kuusankosken kirjasto, 2002. Web. 26 Dec. 2012. <http://www.kirjasto.sci.fi/calvino.htm>.

"Science-Fiction and Fantasy Works by Italo Calvino." *Great Science-Fiction and Fantasy Works*. Owlcroft, n.d. Web. 26 Dec. 2012. <http://greatsfandf.com/AUTHORS/ItaloCalvino.php>.

Weaver, William, and David Pettigrew. "Italo Calvino, the Art of Fiction No. 130." *Paris Review* 124 (1992): n. pag. Web. 26 Dec. 2012. <http://www.theparisreview.org/interviews/2027/the-art-of-fiction-no-130-italo-calvino>.

Part Two

APPROACHES

Introduction

Italo Calvino

Italo Calvino was born on 15 October 1923 in Santiago de Las Vegas, Cuba, where his parents, both botanists and agronomists, were working in a floriculture station. He died of cerebral hemorrhage on 19 September 1985. At the time of his death he was the most popular and most translated contemporary Italian writer in the Anglo-American world. His writing has been internationally praised for its imagination, humor, and technical virtuosity. He holds a place in the ranks of writers such as Roland Barthes, Jorge Borges, and Gabriel García Márquez.

His continuing popularity is reflected in the number of courses outside Italian studies in which his works are taught. In settings as diverse as literature courses in Romance languages, comparative literature courses, and seminars in architecture, Calvino has become a touchstone for instructors interested in the panoptic nature of his work and the ever-expanding purview of his thought.

To read Calvino is to engage in a veritable how-to of reading literature and understanding contemporary culture. He approached the task of literature as an admiring apprentice, always eager to learn the latest technique and appropriate the latest critical thought to place himself squarely in the latest trend. He was, in a sense, an opportunistic writer, using his talent to create the occasion for fame, using his fame to situate himself at the forefront of literary popularity, so that he could continue to experiment with new modalities in a *mise en abyme* tour de force reminiscent of the self-reflexive philosophical machinations of his most curmudgeonly character, Mr. Palomar. His fiction engages a broad spectrum of complex ideas, themes, critical perspectives, and narrative styles that may appear daunting for even the most seasoned instructor. Yet beyond the variegated topics and evolving ideological substratum, Calvino's writings present an unmistakable signature: love for literature and faith in the civilizing power of the literary experience. For Calvino, literature is the ultimate culture-bearing artifact that both contains and constructs a culture's genetic code. In this light, the writer is a cultural operator who sustains tradition while promoting change, conserves long-held beliefs while advancing progressive notions. Literature is the space that explores those inherent human qualities that define the human species.

Calvino's popularity rests on his ability to transform a culture's speculative theory into entertaining literary practice. Perhaps no other works are such user-friendly, conscious examples of the major critical and scientific streams of the past fifty years. No other works are so much a part of the historical milieu while at the same time apart from the ideological and critical trappings that would limit both interpretation and reception. Like the tightrope walker who graces the cover of the Italian paperback edition of *I racconti* (Turin: Einaudi, 1958), Calvino walks a tenuous critical-creative line above the fray.

He began writing fiction in 1941, at the age of seventeen. He was a precocious as well as a prolific writer, dedicating his time to short stories, novels, critical essays, and newspaper articles. His fervid imagination produced works that parodied medieval chivalry (the trilogy *I nostri antenati* [*Our Ancestors*], which includes *Il visconte dimezzato*, *Il barone rampante*, and *Il cavaliere inesistente* [*The Cloven Viscount*, *The Baron in the Trees*, and *The Non-existent Knight*]); questioned the efficacy of social realism (the 1940s short war stories but also the 1950s social vignettes that include "La formica argentina," "La giornata d'uno scrutatore," and "La nuvola de smog" ["The Argentine Ant," "The Watcher," and "Smog"); voyaged into the farthest reaches of outer and inner space (*Le cosmicomiche vecchie e nuove* ["Cosmicomics Old and New"]); and probed the minutiae of daily existence (*Marcovaldo*). His dedication to the gnoseological potential of literature compelled him to expand the reading horizon to include scientific hypotheses (*Ti con zero* [*T Zero*]), number theory (*Le città invisibili* [*Invisible Cities*]), tarot cards as conceptual schemes of representation (*Il castello dei destini incrociati* [*The Castle of Crossed Destinies*]), consciousness and psychophysical identification (*Palomar* [*Mr. Palomar*]), narrative theory (*Se una notte d'inverno un viaggiatore* [*If on a winter's night a traveler*]), and the sensuality of sentient experience (*Sotto il sole giaguaro* [*Under the Jaguar Sun*]). In the later part of his career, Calvino explored the relation between words and images and wrote ekphrastic essays, short stories, and descriptions of museum collections and artworks (*Collezione di sabbia*, as well as a long list of prefaces to artworks and published creative essays and articles on art). At his death he was preparing Charles E. Norton Lectures to be delivered at Harvard University. These essays explore the significance of cultural values expressible in a human language and were published posthumously in what has become a seminal work, *Lezioni americani: Sei proposte per il prossimo millennio* (*Six Memos for the Next Millennium*). The essays, taken together, remain faithful to the subtending poetics that generate all Calvino's work: a close attention to style, a minimum of story, popular themes, structure as an integral part of the meaning of text, and visuality as a medium for literary exchange.

It is a measure of Calvino's extraordinary critical acumen and uncommon historical awareness that, from his early neorealist tales to the metanarrative and exploratory modes of his later fiction, the writer can be said to reflect the major literary and cultural trends of the second half of the twentieth century. He remains one of its most respected writers. At once unique and challenging yet popular and accessible, Calvino carries a fame that rests on his ability to fuse esoteric cutting-edge hypotheses with the pleasurable activity of storytelling. His works are characterized by a willful mixture of reality, fantasy, allegory, irony, and fable, all interwoven with speculative science and philosophical inquiry, that leads into novel conceptual pathways. He has explored subjects ranging from the absurdity of the human condition; to space and time; to the relation of mind and body; to concepts of mapping and projection, identification and empathy; to the nature of writing. Calvino believed in the ability of humankind to win despite existentially conditioning obstacles. While coaxing his readers into ever-expanding dimensions, he never lost sight of this basic humanity, never lost faith in the redemptive potential of intelligent human beings reading intelligent literature.

Teaching Calvino

Approaching Calvino can seem a daunting task, given the range of topics, meanings, and applications that he brought to his writing. His work spans a wide gamut of themes that include folktale, fantasy, chivalry, social and political allegory, and cosmological fiction, while his style reflects a theoretical experimentation that toys with structuralism, semiotics, deconstruction, reader response, narratology, minimalism, and phenomenology. The essays in this volume address both the protean stylistic capacity of Calvino as well as the diachronic evolution of his themes.

Assembling the volume made it clear that instructors teach Calvino for a variety of reasons. He is one of the better representatives of the poststructuralist literary school of contemporary Western culture. An indefatigable intellectual in the purest sense, he shares insights that lead readers down the meandering paths of world literature, science, philosophy, literary criticism, and cultural studies. Yet he is easily accessible, grounded in everyday commonality and in the desire to develop interesting and popular story lines. Instructors enjoy his sunny and constant irony, his seductive narrative structures, his incredibly careful thinking through of philosophical questions, his inventiveness, and his intelligence. I was impressed by the variety of non-Italian courses that include Calvino on their syllabi. Many are courses in creative writing, but others are undergraduate courses on translation, literary criticism, architecture, ethics, and world literature.[1] Calvino is usually situated among authors like Nabokov, Borges, Lightman, Ponge, Kafka, Woolf, Palazzeschi, Eco, Morrison, García Márquez, and Tabucchi. Graduate courses include seminars on comparative literature (European, North and South American, Asian), detective fiction (Pynchon, Borges, Perec), self-referential literature (*Don Quixote*, *Madame Bovary*, *Jane Eyre*, *Pale Fire*, *Tristram Shandy*), play, gender, reader response, folktales, and numerous other esoteric topics. Most often, however, Calvino figures in the classroom as a touchstone, an excellent way of introducing larger literary problems that span cultures and epochs and provide material for common philosophical, cognitive, epistemological, and theoretical issues.

I found most rewarding the contributors' enthusiasm for Calvino's work and his ability to enliven and invigorate their students' responses to literature.

Students seem inspired by his stories. Whether tackling ideologically laden neorealist settings or postmodern topics so light that they become invisible, students are usually beguiled by the author's unpredictable content and shifting structures. A recurring comment I gleaned from questionnaires for this volume was that instructors found that their students genuinely enjoy reading Calvino, especially his postmodern work. As unexpected personal responses supplant traditional expectations, students find pleasure in their active participation in the text and their evolving engagement with it. They thus reexamine their notions of what constitutes a complete text, as well as their own place within the literary experience.

In short, Calvino teaches students a very important concept: the quest for knowledge does not end at the edge of the written page. His work examines how we receive, develop, and communicate knowledge and seeks to provoke analysis of the certainties we take for granted. Whether students have a background in the humanities or the sciences, his stories encourage them to develop new analytic skills as well as new knowledge and understanding of both practical and metaphysical topics. Because Calvino's lifelong ambition was working with the modes of knowing in both the arts and the sciences, his words encourage students to engage critically with their society, history, language, and culture. As Joseph Francese responded to the questionnaire, "Students are encouraged to focus on key ideas and issues in human experience, to appreciate the roles of knowledge and values in shaping and understanding human behavior, to emphasize the responsibilities and opportunities of citizenship, to see the importance and the value of the creative arts, to think about important issues that occur and re-occur among peoples in an increasingly interconnected, interdependent world."

In university courses that have increasing enrollments and decreasing depth of coverage and that bring together a broad cross-section of the student body, our primary goal as instructors must be enhancing students' ability to think critically and self-interrogate. Calvino's penchant for questioning boundaries—his impatience with facile categories, disdain of conditioning ideologies, and delight in playful experimentation—make his work a wonderful, often whimsical, vehicle for advancing the pedagogical aim of delighting while instructing.

Rationale for the Volume

This volume is intended for teachers who are already familiar with Calvino and have addressed theoretical concerns in their courses as well as for teachers who are relatively new to the author's works and could use mapping of his variegated universe. The volume's sections divide the essays into areas that focus on general themes and cultural contexts, address theoretical issues, and provide practical classroom applications. The essays are directed at those who teach Calvino at the undergraduate and graduate levels. They are situated—appropriately, given the protean nature of Calvino's work—at the crossroads of several disciplines, including literary studies, language pedagogy, science, humanism, the visual, the architectonic, and the teaching of writing. Regardless of the approach or theme, the intention of each essay is pedagogical, with an eye toward empowering the instructor with innovative, enjoyable, and workable classroom strategies.

Calvino is particularly suited for use in college courses as an example of differing or developing critical discourses. Because of the political and ethical dimensions of his writing, his merits as a literary innovator, and his wide breadth of literary adaptation, instructors often use his works for comparative analysis between authors or cultures and for studies in literary aesthetics. The volume is thus useful to nonspecialists as well as to non-Italianists who wish to include Calvino in either general-interest culture courses or specific literature and criticism courses. The essays also provide a snapshot of contemporary critical thought by presenting the wide variety of creative strategies employed by the author. Although readers will see Calvino from different perspectives, the contributors maintain a fundamental notion of his writing project: that literature, more than any other medium, is both inspirational and practical in that it brings new dimensions to political, social, artistic, stylistic, linguistic, and, as in this volume, pedagogical issues.

As editor of this volume I hope to inspire a shift in perspective on Calvino as well as an invigorated sense of renewed engagement with his work. Toward this end, I asked contributors to think critically about their modalities of production in the classroom, about how their teaching strategies are tools for both the comprehension and the production of meaning in the classroom. I then asked them to develop exercises for practical application and development that teach students to think outside the proverbial box.

All contributors voiced the need to teach today's students that reading and writing can be a creative and joyful experience. Students need to be invited into another realm, to visualize the world as the author describes it, to decipher the inscriptions made in their minds; they need to learn, through one of the most visually committed writers of the twentieth century, that literature can be an eye-opening experience. The essays in this volume reflect the sense of play, the unpredictable content, the protean shifts of style, and the adept technical skill that are the hallmarks of Calvino's writing. They offer a panoply of angles and attitudes that springs from an intimate knowledge and working relation with the material discussed. Each contributor finds pleasure in teaching Calvino, and all are dedicated to helping their students experience the delight of reading literature by using Calvino in their respective courses, an end heartily endorsed by Calvino himself.[2] It is thus Calvino's own penchant for pursuing "a different perspective, with a different logic and with fresh methods of cognition and verification" that inspires the essays in this volume (*Six Memos* 7).

NOTES

[1]One of the most fascinating courses I have encountered was a graduate studio in architecture conducted by Robert M. Beckley and Rodney Parker in December 1989 at the University of Michigan's College of Architecture and Urban Planning. In the studio course, Architecture: The Creation of an Invisible City and Its Artifacts, each of the eleven student designers used Calvino's *Invisible Cities* to generate ideas for the creation of a sixth city. The new cities explored the elusive concept of what constitutes a city by interpreting the knowledge, insights, and ideas accumulated by Calvino. The resulting designs were a marriage of the intimate relation between the written word and architectural spaces.

[2]"È sempre con curiosità e speranza e meraviglia che il giovane, l'operaio, il contadino che ha preso gusto a leggere, aprono un libro nuovo. Sempre così vorremmo che venissero aperti anche i nostri" 'It is always with curiosity, hope, and marvel that a youth, a worker, a farmer that has found pleasure in reading, opens a new book. We hope that our books will always be opened with the same enthusiasm' (*Pietra sopra* 18; my trans.).

The Figure of the Intellectual in Calvino's Early Fiction

Eugenio Bolongaro

Throughout his life, Italo Calvino devoted a great deal of energy to reflection on what it means to be an intellectual in contemporary Western society. One of my objectives as a Calvino scholar has been to demonstrate that this reflection is central not only to Calvino's essays but also to his fiction. This focus is particularly evident during the first phase of his career, which spans from the publication of *Il sentiero dei nidi di ragno* (*The Path to the Spiders' Nests*) in 1947 to the appearance of "La giornata d'uno scrutatore" ("The Watcher") in 1963. This is the period I discuss here.

Approaching Calvino's fiction as a meditation on the role of the intellectual immediately presents a difficulty: our students, especially in North America, have only a vague notion of what the term *intellectual* actually means. Therefore the first item on the agenda must be to provide the context they need to understand this term.

The Historical Context

I begin my discussion of the figure of the intellectual in Calvino's works by asking every student in the class to define *intellectual*. This exercise typically reveals a wide range of opinions, providing me with the opportunity to make two fundamental points: the word *intellectual* refers to complex clusters of phenomena that have stubbornly defied any single theoretical definition, and the most useful way to come to grips with the meaning of the term is to consider its history. We must examine how *intellectual* first emerged and developed in the literary cultures of France and Italy, the two intellectual traditions that are most pertinent to a discussion of Calvino's works.

Historically, the key event in the development of the modern notion of the intellectual was the Dreyfus Affair.[1] The dramatic circumstances surrounding Alfred Dreyfus's conviction and final rehabilitation allow me to shift the debate from a conceptual definition to the practical significance of the figure of the intellectual. Victor Hugo's courage in denouncing the French army, his ability to rally the support of a large section of the French cultural elite (artists, scientists, et al.), and his final success in exposing the truth and vindicating Dreyfus's innocence are an inspiring but also sobering narrative. Truth triumphed, but the affair deeply divided the country, and it is important to stress that the term *intellectual*, in its modern meaning, was born under the sign of that division. For the opponents of Dreyfus's rehabilitation, *intellectual* was synonymous with *meddler* or *traitor*, an insult leveled at Hugo and his allies. When the accusations by the intellectuals were vindicated, however, the term began to be used with pride to signify a commitment to truth and justice against the hypocrisy of the establishment. As a result of its birth in division and controversy, the word has led a double life as a term of respect (especially among the politically progressive) and as a term of contempt (especially among the politically conservative).

At this stage the class is ready to focus on the Italian cultural tradition, and Antonio Gramsci can be introduced. Before exploring Gramsci's ideas, I find it helpful to present some key biographical facts, such as his involvement in the radical political activities of the worker's movement in Turin; his founding of the Partito Comunista Italiano, the Italian Communist Party; his opposition to fascism, which led to his imprisonment and premature death in 1937; and finally the publication of his *Prison Notebooks* after the end of World War II.[2] It is then important to connect Gramsci to Marxism and explain that his originality as a Marxist consisted primarily in his focus on the importance of culture in the revolutionary overthrow of capitalism.

One of the central components of Gramsci's thought on culture was his theory of the role of intellectuals. The basic tenets of this theory can be summarized as follows:

One is not born an intellectual; one becomes an intellectual through formal education.

No matter what their particular occupations may be—government official, lawyer, scientist, writer—intellectuals have the social function of articulating and reproducing the ideology of the dominant class, which, in capitalism, is the bourgeoisie.

Revolution (i.e., the overthrowing of the bourgeoisie) can be successful only when intellectuals revolt against bourgeois ideology and use their skills (e.g., the capacity for rational thought, objective knowledge of the

> world) to help the proletariat in its struggle to seize power and transform society.

I open discussion of this theory of intellectuals by pointing out how Gramsci politicizes culture, which, in his view, can serve the interests of the dominant class or challenge those interests. The choice is in the hands of the cultural producers, that is, the intellectuals, who become vanguard figures in the struggle for social change. For Gramsci the choice facing them was clear. Following Marx, he thought that the bourgeoisie, tainted by its exploitation of other human beings and blinded by its privileges, was unable to produce true knowledge. Yet as it struggled against its own oppression, the proletariat could potentially speak for all oppressed humanity and, ultimately, articulate universal human values. Intellectuals were educated to uphold such universal values (e.g., truth, objective knowledge) and could remain loyal to them only by allying themselves to the proletariat. In Gramsci's view, therefore, the commitment to human progress entailed fighting alongside the working class. For this reason, the Partito Comunista Italiano relied heavily on his ideas to rally the support—the commitment—of Italian intellectuals to its political agenda.

It is important to explain to students why, in the immediate postwar period, Italian intellectuals found so appealing the idea that they should have a strong political role. The country had suffered a humiliating military defeat and endured a vicious civil war. Fascism, which was responsible for both these tragedies, was completely discredited. It had also been responsible for the persecution of many progressive intellectuals, while it tolerated conservative intellectuals as long as they did not take a political position against the regime. The reaction against fascism, then, led young intellectuals to reject the old cultural establishment, whose noninterference with political power was seen as a betrayal. In the words of Elio Vittorini, one of the most influential figures of the period, Italy needed a "new culture" that was not afraid to set the political agenda and fight for humanist values such as democracy, truth, and justice. Gramsci's theory provided a robust theoretical legitimation for the kind of activism that intellectuals like Vittorini advocated. But the Gramscian idea of commitment raised a crucial issue: How could a political agenda be productively connected to an aesthetic agenda? How could a synergy be established between being a good Communist and a good artist? This issue is precisely what troubled Calvino and set in motion his meditation on the role of the intellectual.

Figures of the Intellectual: Kim, Cosimo, Amerigo

Calvino's early fiction contains a number of characters and situations that allow the author to present and explore the committed Gramscian intellectual, that is, a Marxist intellectual struggling alongside the proletariat for a socialist revolution. I direct students to three exemplary figures: Kim in *Il sentiero dei nidi di ragno* (*The Path to the Spiders' Nests*), Cosimo in *Il barone rampante* (*The Baron in the Trees*), and Amerigo in "La giornata d'uno scrutatore" ("The Watcher"). I then ask students to reflect on how these figures are problematic and how they express a crisis that deepens over time to the point that in "The Watcher" Calvino is led to reexamine the foundations of the Gramscian commitment that defined the post–World War II Italian intellectual.

Kim: The Intellectual and Hope in the Utopian Future

Kim appears in chapter 9 of *The Path to the Spiders' Nests*. This late arrival, about three-quarters of the way through the narrative, marks a sudden shift in style. The perspective from which the story is told changes. Pin, the boy protagonist, is almost forgotten, as the narrative focuses on Kim, the commissar who has come to inspect the partisan band before an important battle, and the mood changes. The war, no longer the grim but exciting adventure tale that Pin sees, becomes a disturbing human experience that Kim attempts to analyze with clinical detachment. Students who have begun to think about the role of the intellectual grasp how this moment of self-reflection and analysis functions in the novel.

There can be little doubt that in chapter 9 Calvino wants the reader to pause and reflect. So far in the novel, we have seen events from the perspective of a child, an outlook that, however engaging and refreshing, is inherently limited and deforming (thus the mix of fantasy and realism). But the time has come to go beyond Pin's horizon. Kim provides the vantage point from which the Resistance can be confronted in all its real complexity (and in the remaining chapters of the novel, this complexity will confer on Pin's experience a new and deeper meaning). Kim becomes the prototype of the committed intellectual: he is using his knowledge and analytic skills to help us understand the full historical significance of the struggle, which Pin cannot grasp. Yet the task that Kim undertakes is fraught with difficulties, and Calvino carefully identifies them.

Kim tries his best to fulfill his role as the ideological leader of the partisans. Yet as he examines the situation, he becomes hesitant. He hoped that the Resistance would forge a new sociopolitical consciousness among the partisans, but he has to admit that the historical significance of their actions still escapes most of them. He is not yet able to grasp fully that significance himself. In the end, Kim confronts the gap between revolutionary ideology and reality. But his commitment to the cause remains, yielding hope—hope that the Resistance will at least initiate the long process of individual and social change that is needed. At the end of the chapter, Kim achieves a kind of serenity, but more from his love for Adriana than from a rigorous application of his Marxist ideology.

The historical and political importance of this ideological stance in 1947 Italy should be emphasized. Through Kim, Calvino challenges the myth of the Resistance as the crucible in which the Italian nation was reforged and achieved a progressive consensus. He depicts the Resistance instead as a first, tentative step on the way to revolution and socialism. He also challenges the easy populism that the notion of commitment often masked. The narrow ideology that has become part of Kim's intellectual apparatus seems inadequate to the reality of the situation. Yet there is a kernel of hope, a utopian element that rescues Kim from disillusionment. The conditions of possibility for this utopian dimension are a central theme in the elaboration of the next figure of the intellectual we encounter in Calvino's early work.

Cosimo's Utopia: The Intellectual and the Necessity of Distance

Approaching *The Baron in the Trees* from the perspective of the figure of the intellectual is especially pertinent not only because Cosimo, the protagonist of the novel, is such an intellectual but also because many narrative elements that might seem secondary and peripheral (e.g., the Gian dei Brughi episode) reveal a deeper significance when seen in this light. Virtually all the episodes express Calvino's reflection on the role of the intellectual. The way Cosimo speaks to his father shows his coming of age:

> "Buongiorno, signor padre."
> "Buongiorno figlio." . . .
> "Sai che un tratto del bosco è di nostra proprietà, ereditato dalla tua povera nonna Elisabetta buonanima?"
> "Sì signor padre. In località Belrìo. Vi crescono trenta castagni, ventidue faggi, otto pini e un acero. Ho copia di tutte le mappe catastali. È appunto come membro di famiglia proprietaria di boschi che ho voluto consociare tutti gli interessati a conservarli."
> "Già," disse il Barone, accogliendo favorevolmente la risposta. Ma aggiunse: "Mi dicono sia un'associazione di fornai, ortolani e maniscalchi."
> "Anche, signor padre. Di tutte le professioni, purché oneste."
> "Tu sai che potresti comandare alla nobiltà vassalla col titolo di duca?"
> "So che quando ho più idee degli altri, do agli altri queste idee, se le accettano; e questo è comandare." (*Il barone* 145–46)
>
> "Good day, my lord father."
> "Good day, son." . . .
> "Do you know that part of the wood is our property, inherited from your poor grandmother, the late Lady Elizabeth?"
> "Yes, my lord father. In the Belrio area there are thirty chestnuts, twenty-two ashes, eight pines, and a maple. I have copies of all the surveyor's maps, and it was as a member of a family owning woods that I tried to collect together all those with a common interest in preserving them."
> "Ah yes," said the Baron, giving this answer a favourable reception. "But," he added, "they tell me that it is an association of bakers, market-gardeners and blacksmiths."
> "Them too, lord father. Of all professions that are honest."
> "Do you realize that you could lead noble vassals with the title of Duke?"

> "I realize that when I have more ideas than others, I give those others my ideas, if they want to accept them; and that to me is leading." (*Baron* 178)[3]

The first key point in this exchange is Cosimo's acknowledgment of the bond of family and community. His rebellion challenges his father's reactionary ideology but does not seek to sweep away the past. Cosimo wants to change the world but does not think that the first step toward change is destruction. Second, he bases his claim to authority on reason and empirical knowledge. His conduct is guided by accurate information of the land he wants to protect (the type of trees, the maps). He is indifferent to the claim of status, displaying an egalitarian attitude typical of the Enlightenment. Finally, he makes it clear that the only power he wishes to wield is that of persuasion: his weapons are words and ideas. Cosimo sees himself as an intellectual whose function is to make knowledge available to the community so that the community itself may take action. This role is at the heart of his utopian vision, and we should note the gap between his stance and the Gramscian ideal of a committed intellectual acting as a militant component of the party machine. Cosimo, like Kim, is keenly aware of the gap between himself and those whom his words and deeds address. Unlike Kim, however, he does not bemoan this condition but rather sees it as essential to fulfilling his role as an intellectual.

The necessity of distance for the intellectual is implicit from the start: that Cosimo chooses to live in the trees indicates that the role he wants to play requires him to be at the edges of the social world rather than in the thick of it. In the final chapters of *The Baron*, his leap into oblivion as he grabs the rope of a hot-air balloon and disappears into the sky reaffirms the imperative of distance: even in death he will not be subsumed in the community he served all his life. This stoic ethical stance, rather different from Kim's hope in human connection and love, reflects a changed historical conjuncture. Calvino finished writing *The Baron* in February 1957 (Barenghi 1329), a few months after Soviet tanks invaded Hungary, putting an end to the Hungarian Revolution. At that moment, many Italian intellectuals felt compelled to leave the Partito Comunista Italiano. Calvino too quit the party. The ending of *The Baron* seems to suggest that intellectuals must rediscover the imperative of distance from their political masters to preserve the utopian aspirations that are at the core of any true commitment. And yet this distance also signals the loss of a home for the intellectual, a painful loss as the writer faces the challenge to strike an independent path through an increasingly complex, disappointing, and treacherous political reality. The difficulty of meeting this challenge is the subject matter of our next text, "The Watcher."

Amerigo: The Rebirth of the Intellectual

"The Watcher" is not an easy work to teach.[4] One key challenge is to help students appreciate the complex texture of the narrative, specifically the ambivalent relation between the authorial voice and Amerigo, the protagonist of the novel. Amerigo is a flawed character whose stances are presented at times in a deeply sympathetic and at times in a severely critical light. This oscillation is an integral part of Calvino's meditation on the role of the intellectual.

Like the author, Amerigo is a Communist and a scrutineer at the polling station in the mental institution that provides the setting for the novel (i.e., the Cottolengo). Insofar as "The Watcher" elaborates fictionally Calvino's real experiences, the authorial voice is sympathetic to the protagonist, whose political affiliation is vindicated by the electoral fraud he is bearing witness to; nevertheless, Amerigo also reveals the sclerosis of commitment in early 1960s Italy. Once a rallying cry against a hypocritical cultural establishment, commitment has become for him the excuse for toeing the party line, surrendering to political expediency and opportunism. Then the authorial voice distances itself from the protagonist and exposes mercilessly Amerigo's intellectual pretensions and the false subtlety with which he avoids taking any uncomfortable political position. The revolutionary activist has become the defender of a comfortable status quo.

This complex modulation of proximity and distance between the authorial voice and the protagonist is exemplified by the passage in which Amerigo attempts to define what it means to be a Communist (*La giornata* 14–15; "*Watcher*" 7–9). Students may find daunting this seemingly endless single sentence, punctuated by no fewer than nine parenthetical asides. It is therefore an excellent place to start a sustained analysis of Amerigo's way of thinking. Note, for example, the metaphors that mark the beginning of the long digression: reality appears to Amerigo as an artichoke, a gluey mass, a damp sponge—images that underscore a labyrinthine but ultimately empty or coreless structure that he is incapable of negotiating. Throughout the passage, he moves from one opposition to the other in a pathetic mimicry of dialectical thinking. Every statement, every image is qualified by a kind of opposite that produces ambiguity rather than dynamic contradiction and resolution (e.g., Amerigo ponders whether he became a Communist because of his affinity for "razionalismo settocentesco" 'eighteenth-century rationalism' or "l'avanzata del proletariato socialista" 'the advance of the socialist proletariat,' because of "le contraddizioni interne della borghesia" 'the inner contradictions of the bourgeoisie' or of "l'autocoscienza della classe in crisi" 'the self-awareness of the declining class'). In such passages, Calvino delivers a double message: Amerigo is doing his best in a bad situation, but at the same time his capacity for self-deception is staggering; he is fundamentally a good person but also someone who no longer possesses any desire to challenge his preconceptions.

The intellectual sclerosis of the protagonist of "The Watcher" is depicted with a deepening irony, until, in chapter 12, Amerigo comes face to face with a surreal vision of human suffering. He accompanies the presiding officer of the polling station into a wing of the asylum that holds inmates so severely disabled and malformed that they can barely be recognized as human. This encounter shocks him out of his complacency, reawakening in him an authentic sense of the value of life and human dignity. The sudden epiphany is simple but fundamental: "l'umano arriva dove arriva l'amore; non ha confini se non quelli che gli diamo" 'Humanity reaches as far as love reaches; it has no frontiers except those we give it' (83; 64). The parabola of Gramscian commitment ends here. Both Amerigo and Calvino return to the bedrock of values in which the notion of commitment was rooted, values that include human fellowship, solidarity, and generosity. These values provide the ethical standpoint from which to reconsider the relation between politics and literature and the danger of allowing a tired revolutionary rhetoric to deaden our sensitivity to present suffering. In "The Watcher," Calvino does not abandon hope in the future, in the value of literature, and in the role of the intellectual in helping bring about a better world. Yet he comes to a clear understanding that the role of the writer is first of all a cognitive and ethical one. The claims of suffering are first and orient our understanding; all political projects must be rooted in the commitment to always renew that understanding. This new kind of commitment is informed by a keen sense of human fragility, by sensitivity rather than enthusiasm, by doubt rather than hope.

A careful analysis of the figures of the intellectual in Calvino's early fiction will help students realize that the crisis from which Amerigo emerges constitutes a criticism of the theory of commitment adopted by progressive Italian intellectuals in the aftermath of World War II. Calvino and his generation embraced the Gramscian ideal of a militant political life in the service of the working class. They then discovered that too often this ideal spawned a subordination of intellectual practice to political expediency. Over time such subordination tended to become a habit of mind, engendering passivity and intellectual laziness. Calvino broke out of this habit by confronting the bedrock of what it means to be human and founding on that bedrock a sensitive and careful understanding of the role of the intellectual. Such understanding would inspire all his subsequent writing. Indeed, *Mr. Palomar*, the author's last work published in his lifetime, is an excellent example of this continued preoccupation, as well as a fascinating foil to "The Watcher."

NOTES

[1] See Derfler for a recent discussion in English of the affair.

[2] For a useful introduction to Gramsci in English, see Ransome.

[3] All quotations from *The Baron in the Trees* are from the translation included in *Our Ancestors* (77–284).

[4] For an excellent overview of this complex work, see Federicis.

Calvino's Essays

JoAnn Cannon

Italo Calvino was not only a prolific writer of fiction, he was also a perceptive and articulate essayist whose writings elucidated the craft of fiction. In his numerous essays spanning a forty-year period, from 1945 to 1985, he delved into the art of storytelling and its function in society. What emerges from a reading of Calvino's essays, from *The Uses of Literature* (*Una pietra sopra*) to *Six Memos for the Next Millennium* (*Lezioni americane*) and countless occasional essays, is both an articulate analysis and an eloquent defense of storytelling, an activity that Calvino depicts as constitutive of all human society. He often conjures up the scene of the primitive storyteller surrounded by a captive audience: "It all began with the first storyteller of the tribe" (*Uses* 3). By evoking this scene, Calvino underscores the universality of storytelling, as if to suggest that storytelling signals the very passage from nature to culture. This essay focuses on a series of questions posed in his essays, all concerning the function of literature in society: What is the use of storytelling? What is the role of the writer? What is the role of the reader? What are the right and wrong political uses of fiction? Why read the classics? For whom do we write? What is the relation between literature and science, between literature and philosophy, between literature and history? Students at all levels—literature majors and nonmajors, undergraduates and graduates—can profit from reading Calvino's essays while pondering such questions. Whether one agrees with his answers is of secondary importance. In fact, it is useful to point out to students that his ideas on these questions evolved over the years. The key point is that Calvino's essays lend themselves to open-ended discussion in which the instructor may explore with students fundamental questions regarding the value of literature while encouraging the development of their critical thinking skills.

Many of Calvino's essays can stimulate discussion of the role of the writer in society. In "Right and Wrong Political Uses of Literature," Calvino describes the shifting aspirations of post–World War II Italian writers: "During the fifties, Italian literature, and the novel in particular, aspired to represent the ethical and social conscience of contemporary Italy" (*Uses* 91). He then explains the gradual shift away from politically committed literature in Italy. His works undoubtedly follow this pattern. In his 1985 essay "Lightness," in *Six Memos for the Next Millennium*, the author returns to the question of the writer's role in society. Citing the good intentions of every young writer of the immediate postwar generation to "represent his own time" (3), he nonetheless advocates the subtraction of excessive "weight" from writing. The essay perfectly traces the evolution of his thinking on the subject of literature's responsibility: "Whenever humanity seems condemned to heaviness, I think I should fly like Perseus into a different space. I don't mean escaping into dreams or into the irrational. I mean that I have to change my approach, look at the world from a different perspective . . . with fresh methods of cognition and verification" (7). He argues that the lightness he advocates does not suggest an escape from the world but rather a participatory detachment. He draws on the myth of Perseus to depict the poet's ideal relation to the world. He identifies a host of writers whose lightness he admires: Lucretius, Ovid, Cyrano de Bergerac, Guido Cavalcanti, Milan Kundera, Eugenio Montale, Jonathan Swift, Giacomo Leopardi, and Franz Kafka. Only by raising himself above the weight of the world can the poet-philosopher "find the strength to change the face of reality" (*Six Memos* 27). This essay, in conjunction with "Right and Wrong Political Uses of Literature," lends itself to consideration of several questions: What is the artist's responsibility to society? Is it the author's role to effect social change? If so, how does the author effect change? What are the means specific and particular to the author?

These two essays also provide helpful study questions as students approach Calvino's fiction. Students may, for example, be asked to use his concepts of lightness and weight in literature to shed light on his 1957 novel *The Baron in the Trees* (*Il barone rampante*) or his 1963 story "The Watcher" ("La giornata di uno scrutatore"). *The Baron in the Trees* serves as an allegory of the poet's role in society. In the figure of Cosimo Piovasco di Rondò, Calvino attempts to resolve the tension between writing and social commitment, between contemplation and action, that haunted him throughout his career. Like the idealistic baron who lives out his life in the treetops, the writer, Calvino suggests, is apparently exiled in a never-never land far from everyday reality. Yet the writer's distance from society is paradoxically portrayed as a necessary condition for true commitment. When Cosimo's brother meets Voltaire in Paris, the philosopher asks, "But is it to be nearer the sky that your brother stays up there?" The brother replies, "My brother considers . . . that anyone who wants to see the earth properly must keep himself at a necessary distance from it" (144).[1] The writer must maintain a critical balance between distance and engagement. Calvino makes this point clear in the introduction to *Il barone rampante*, when he suggests possible readings of Cosimo's detachment from the world: "L'uomo che vive sugli alberi. È un'allegoria del poeta, il suo modo di essere nel mondo. E, più in particolare, è un'allegoria del 'disimpegno'? Oppure, al contrario, dell'impegno?" 'The man who lives in the trees? He is an allegory of the poet, of his way of being in the world. Is he an allegory of lack of commitment or rather of commitment?' (qtd. in Calligaris 53; my trans.). Calvino undoubtedly supports the second interpretation. Only with the proper distance can the artist commit to understanding society. A similar question may be asked of Calvino's "The Watcher," a story dealing with a poll watcher in post–World War II Italy. Students may be asked to summarize his definitions of lightness and weight and to comment on the balance between these two characteristics in "The Watcher." Discussing these critical and fictional works together leads students to question their assumptions about the writer's role in society.

As students consider the author's essays, which were written from the mid-1940s until his untimely death in 1985, they may see how his ideas concerning the role of literature evolved over time, while his conviction of literature's abiding importance in society remained constant. Several essays are particularly useful in this regard. In "Two Interviews on Science and Literature," Calvino shifts his focus from fiction as the ethical conscience of society to fiction as a means of mapping the world. He defines literature, and Italian literature in particular, as a modeling activity that is as valuable as if not more valuable than philosophy on the one hand and science on the other. He outlines what he calls the "deep-rooted vocation in Italian literature," from Dante to Galileo to Leopardi: "the notion of the literary work as a map of the world and of the knowable" (*Uses* 32). In "Philosophy and Literature," he characterizes the relation between philosophy and literature as productively adversarial. He contends that the most fruitful intellectual climate is one in which literature, science, and philosophy call one another into question. His admiration for writers like Jorge Luis Borges, Lewis Carroll, and Raymond Queneau—writers who view philosophy as "a stimulus to the imagination (*Uses* 47)—reveals his relation to philosophy, science, and speculative thought in general. Whether used as a topic for an oral presentation, as background reading for a final paper, or as a source of study questions, these essays serve to open students' eyes to the role of literature and the arts in the broad context of speculative thought. Students from the sciences, who may have a view of literary study as equivalent to escapism, come to appreciate the utility of literature as articulated in Calvino's essays.

Many of Calvino's essays serve as valuable interpretive keys to his literary works. In "Exactitude," the third essay in *Six Memos for the Next Millennium*, Calvino draws a parallel between the discoveries of modern science and the ability of fiction to provide cosmological models. He maintains:

> This taste for geometrical composition, of which we could trace a history in world literature starting with Mallarmé, is based on the contrast of order and disorder fundamental to contemporary science. The universe disintegrates into a cloud of heat, it falls inevitably into a vortex of entropy, but within this irreversible process there may be areas of order, portions of the existent that tend toward a form, privileged points in which we seem to discern a design or perspective. A work of literature is one of these minimal portions in which the existent crystallizes into a form. (69–70)

The conception of fiction as a privileged space in which the randomness of life is contained and negated by artistic form permeates Calvino's essays and informs his fiction. I have assigned this essay to students as they read one of his most intriguing fictional texts, *Invisible Cities*. The city described in "Exactitude" epitomizes the tension "between geometric rationality and the entanglements of human lives" (71). Like many of the cities described to Kublai Khan by Marco Polo in *Invisible Cities*, Eudoxia perfectly captures the tension described in "Exactitude." Calvino's Marco Polo distinguishes between the chaotic city and the tapestry in which may be found the true form of the city. In the open-ended conclusion of the Eudoxia chapter, Marco Polo contemplates the possibility that the formless city represents the "true map of the universe . . . just as it is, a stain that spreads shapelessly" (*Invisible Cities* 97). Calvino's project in *Invisible Cities* seems to alternate between mapping "minimal portions in which the existent crystallizes into a form" and confronting complexity, formlessness, and disorder.

Use of the image of the labyrinth links Calvino to other twentieth-century writers, including Borges, Carlo Emilio Gadda, and Alain Robbe-Grillet. The Borgesian library of Babel, "in which the same volumes are repeated in the same disorder (which repeated, would constitute an order, Order itself)," figures the systematicness toward which literature strives ("Library" 88). Calvino and Borges share the desire to embed disorder within a larger design. Calvino's essay "Cybernetics and Ghosts" (*Uses*) elaborates on the relation between literature and the labyrinth and serves as an interpretive key to the concluding story of *T Zero*, "The Count of Monte Cristo." In Calvino's version of Dumas's classic, Dantes and Faria seek a map revealing the way to escape from the Castle of If. Dantes's modus operandi is in direct opposition to Faria's. Faria proceeds by trial and error, under the assumption that an escape exists. Dantes imagines that the castle is a perfectly constructed labyrinth: "there exists a perfect fortress, from which one cannot escape; escape is possible only if in the planning or building of the fortress some error or oversight was made" (157). In the story's conclusion, the two characters search for the means of escape in the manuscript on Dumas's desk. The model of the Castle of If is undoubtedly a metaphor for the "map of the world and of the knowable" that all Calvino's protagonists seek (*Uses* 32). I sometimes assign my essay "Italo Calvino: The Last Two Decades" to clarify the points of contact between Calvino's essays and those fictions that fall into the category of literature of the labyrinth, including "The Count of Monte Cristo."

Calvino was a voracious and perceptive reader whose strong readings of Dante, Ovid, Boccaccio, Flaubert, Borges, Cavalcanti, Kundera, Gadda, Galileo, and countless other writers have much to teach us about the role of literature. Calvino linked each of these writers to one of the literary values (lightness, quickness, exactitude, visibility, multiplicity, and consistency) that he would bequeath to the next millennium. In *Six Memos for the Next Millennium*, the Charles Eliot Norton Lectures that he was to have delivered at Harvard University in 1985, he deftly captures the essence of a wide range of writers from antiquity to the present day. He admires the lightness of Ovid, Dante, and Cavalcanti. He values the quickness of Borges and Galileo, the conciseness that causes Calvino to "dream of immense cosmologies, sagas, and epics all reduced to the dimensions of an epigram" (51). The hypernovel of Perec, the polyphonic multiplicity of *Finnegans Wake*, and the "encyclopedism" of Gadda exemplify the multiplicity he cherishes (106). I have often included selections from *Six Memos* in introductory comparative or world literature courses taught in English. In each case I ask students to give an oral presentation summarizing the key points of a Calvino essay. His "Why Read the Classics?" is useful in comparative or Italian literature classes. The author outlines the possible definitions of a "classic," including a book that is "treasured," a book that provides new surprises on rereading, a book that "has never finished saying what it has to say," a book that helps you "define yourself," and a book that bears the traces of previous readings (*Uses* 128). The essay lends itself to oral presentations leading into broad-ranging discussion of the subjectivity of literary value, the sociology of reading, canon formation, and reader-response theory. I have asked my students to use Calvino's various definitions of a classic as a point of departure to reflect on their personal reading experiences. The instructor may draw on this insight into students' previous reading to shed light on new works under discussion.

One assignment has been particularly effective in eliciting cogent oral presentations, lively classroom discussion, and perceptive final papers. Calvino was one of the most articulate and convincing proponents of the idea that the reader plays an active and pivotal role in producing the literary text. Many of my students have chosen to focus on the essay "Cybernetics and Ghosts," in which Calvino, in a lively and accessible fashion, sees literature as a combinatory game. Like the "first storyteller of the tribe," he draws on and combines a limited number of prefabricated elements or narrative functions. After entertaining the notion that authors might be replaced by computers, he proceeds to his main point. He focuses not on the genius of the author but on the contribution of the reader:

> [T]he decisive moment of literary life will be that of reading. In this sense, even though entrusted to machines, literature will continue to be a "place" of privilege within the human consciousness, a way of exercising the potentialities contained in the system of signs belonging to all societies at all times. The work will continue to be born, to be judged, to be destroyed or constantly renewed on contact with the eye of the reader. (*Uses* 15–16)

Students generally find this articulation of the reader's role in fiction to be both appealing and empowering. The idea that the student has an active role to play in generating the meaning of the text goes a long way toward dispelling the passivity typical of many undergraduates confronted with a bewildering or "foreign" text. Students may subsequently see this conception of the role of the reader dramatized in one of Calvino's most fascinating experimental fictions, *The Castle of Crossed Destinies* (*Il castello dei destini incrociati*), a text easily taught in conjunction with "Cybernetics and Ghosts." Students may read the entire text of *The Castle of Crossed Destinies* or be assigned the framing story,

"The Castle," and selected chapters that form the intersecting tales. The authorial note with which the volume concludes elaborates on the combinatory qualities of fiction. Many of my undergraduate students have chosen to write their final papers on the relation between this novel and Calvino's essays on literature as combinatory game. They have drawn on his "Cybernetics and Ghosts" and on the authorial note appended to *The Castle of Crossed Destinies* to explicate the fictional text. Another option is to assign the preface to *Italian Folktales* (*Favole italiane*), in which Calvino further elaborates on the "infinite variety and infinite repetition" of Italian folktales and outlines the limited number of elements from which all folktales are constructed. His work on this subject may then be placed in the broad context of formalist and structuralist analysis. Secondary readings may include Vladimir Propp's *Morphology of the Folktale* and Maria Corti's "Le jeu comme génération du texte: Des tarots au récit" ("The Game as Text Production: From Tarot Cards to the Story").

Calvino's critical essays are also extremely useful in upper-division literature courses in Italian. The author was a keen observer of the Italian literary scene of his generation. As a reader for Einaudi, he reviewed and approved manuscripts by Italy's most prominent contemporary writers. Students interested in Italian narrative of the second half of the twentieth century should be referred to Calvino's *I libri degli altri* ("The Books of Others"), which contains a selection of his reader's reports and letters to over three hundred writers, including Beppe Fenoglio, Carlo Cassola, Leonardo Sciascia, Natalia Ginzburg, Lalla Romano, Mario Rigoni Stern, Giorgio Manganelli, Carlo Levi, Anna Maria Ortese, Primo Levi, and Andrea De Carlo. This volume provides a perceptive and fascinating overview of the main currents in postwar Italian fiction.

In short, the instructor may make use of Italo Calvino's essays to stimulate discussion of the classics of Western literature, to identify and address fundamental questions of literary criticism, to shed light on writers and literary trends of the second half of the twentieth century, or to enhance the reading of individual literary texts. In each of these cases, Calvino's essays serve as a stimulating point of departure and provide a valuable tool for developing students' critical thinking skills.

NOTE

[1] All quotations from *The Baron in the Trees* are from Colquhoun's 1959 translation.

Calvino's Scientific Humanism

Guy P. Raffa

Italo Calvino's lifelong engagement in his fiction and criticism with scientific discourses and ideas provides an exciting opportunity for teachers and students to examine the role of interdisciplinarity in contemporary culture, particularly the interrelation of humanities and sciences in education and the arts. Calvino's "cosmicomic" tales—nearly all composed in 1963–68 and appearing in *Le cosmicomiche* (1965), *Ti con zero* (1967), and *"La memoria del mondo" e altre storie cosmicomiche* (1968)—are the most direct and concentrated product of his scientific imagination. In these wonderful stories Calvino reversed the usual direction of science fiction by imagining not the future of the universe but rather its origin and early stages, and he did so in the most fantastical way, by creating molecular protagonists and other primordial and prehistoric actors who possess full human consciousness. Calvino, who praised Galileo as Italy's greatest writer of prose (*Pietra sopra* 186–87), naturally took a keen interest in humankind's first ventures into outer space, an expression of the heated competition between the Soviet Union and the United States for military and scientific supremacy. He closely followed events in the "space race," from the first artificial earth satellites (*Sputnik 1* and 2, launched by the Soviet Union in 1957, and *Explorer 1*, launched by the United States in 1958) and the first human beings in space (Yury Gagarin soon followed by Alan Shepard in 1961) to the pursuit of President Kennedy's dramatic proposal (made in a speech to Congress on 25 May 1961) to put an astronaut on the moon (and bring him safely back to earth) before the end of the decade—a feat accomplished by the crew of *Apollo 11* in 1969. Calvino viewed the new understanding of the universe gained from satellites and human spaceflight as a benefit not only to science but also to the imagination and language of creative writers (*Pietra sopra* 182–83). Images transmitted from space certainly influenced his perception of the moon (Bucciantini 113), as seen in his description of the celestial body as "buccherellata, corrosa, logora" 'full of holes, corroded, worn' from its exposure to "tempeste cosmiche" 'cosmic storms' ("Molle luna" [*Ti con zero* 18]; "Soft Moon" [*T Zero* 13]).

Several of Calvino's other major literary texts, notably *Le città invisibili* (*Invisible Cities*) and *Palomar* (*Mr. Palomar*), also show signs of the author's penchant for seeking inspiration in science and mathematics. Taught in the original Italian or in translation, his works are illuminated by discussion of their scientifically informed content and structure at the same time that they offer insightful commentary on issues significant to both literature and science. One such issue, the dialectic of order and chaos, has received ample scholarly attention (Antonello 192–99; Cannon, "Italian Postmodernism"; Harris; Pilz, "Complexity"; Raffa, "'Io amo'"; Ricci, *Painting* 157–90; Sbragia), and it has proved fruitful in my undergraduate courses that feature a work by Calvino. These courses are a topics course on literature and science, a course on Italian civilization, a course for Italian majors on recent Italian fiction, and a first-year honors seminar titled Composition and Reading in World Literature. As a reader and teacher of Calvino's works, and from the responses of my students to the cosmicomic stories and *Invisible Cities* in particular, I have found that his predilection for narrative ideas and forms influenced by scientific paradigms signals not a retreat from sociopolitical concerns and human interactions but rather his commitment to a scientifically informed humanism that enhances the ability for literary works to speak to the heart as well as to the mind.

I regularly feature the story "Cristalli" ("Crystals"), from *Ti con zero*, in my courses to present in an economical and entertaining manner one of Calvino's most powerful statements on the evolving paradigm of order and chaos in science and in culture at large. Written in a week in 1967, "Crystals" anticipates what James Gleick calls in his 1987 best seller the "new science" of chaos. Calvino's compact yet complex narrative also gives full imaginative support to one Italian critic's provocative claim that "si potrebbe abbozzare una storia delle civiltà seguendo il vario modo in cui esse si sono rappresentati ordine e caos" 'one could sketch a history of civilizations by following the changing way they represent order and chaos to themselves' (Segre 153; my trans.). By pairing "Crystals" in comparative courses with other texts containing rich representations of the order-chaos theme—Lucretius's *On the Nature of Things*, Mary Shelley's *Frankenstein*, Primo Levi's *The Periodic Table*, and Tom Stoppard's *Arcadia*, to give four examples—an instructor may use this claim to introduce a series of related questions for an essay topic or class discussion: How do these very different authors represent ideas of order and chaos? How do the ideas relate to one another, and what values can we attach to them? What role do order and chaos have in creation and creativity, human agency, ethics, aesthetics, and knowledge?

The order-chaos theme in "Crystals" unfolds according to the divergent perspectives of two characters who are present (as molecules) at the creation of the universe and who meet up again as man and woman in modern New York City: Qfwfq, the first-person narrator, whose palindromic name reflects the symmetrical world he seeks, and his romantic interest, Vug, whose earthy, primal-sounding name embodies her attachment to the world as it is, flaws and all. In a lively "he said, she said" debate on the beauty of crystals, Qfwfq and Vug live up to their names (and conform to the conventional gendering of order and chaos) as his praise for the repetitions and regularities of the crystals is countered by her admiration for their imperfections and impurities (*Ti con zero* 41–45; *T Zero* 33–37). Yet Calvino complicates the classical opposition between good-masculine-order and bad-feminine-chaos by calling into question the usual privileging of orderly values over their chaotic counterparts in "Crystals" and by reversing the gender roles in "Senza colori" ("Without Colors"). In this story, it is Qfwfq who looks for differences and breaks in the homogenous order of things, while the female Ayl embraces uniformity and stability (*Cosmicomiche* 61–74; *Cosmicomics* 51–60).

The contrasting perspectives of Qfwfq and Vug in "Crystals" provide insight into other issues that often arise in class discussion of Calvino's work. For instance, Qfwfq's desire for a perfectly symmetrical, totalizing crystal, countered by Vug's celebration of variations and irregularities among proliferating crystals, underscores a difference between structuralist and poststructuralist philosophical positions (Harris 68). This theoretical tension in Calvino's story serves as a valuable point of contact with works by Umberto Eco (Stephens; Viano; Raffa, "Walking"), an author frequently paired with Calvino in Italian literature courses. Qfwfq and Vug also offer ample material for competing narratives in the history of science: Qfwfq's position accords with fundamental assumptions of classical (Newtonian) science, including linear proportionality and reversible time, whereas Vug's insistence that order goes hand in hand with such typically chaotic values as asymmetry and imperfection puts her in dialogue with the scientific paradigm shift popularized as "chaos theory" (Pilz, "Complexity" 429) and more technically defined as the study of "nonlinear dynamics" or "dissipative structures" (Prigogine and Stengers 12–14; Lorenz 161–63; Hayles 8–9). My students and I find it useful and exciting to put Calvino's representation of order and chaos into scientific context by visiting the Center for Nonlinear Dynamics at our school, the University of Texas, Austin (a virtual tour of the center's research is available at http://chaos.utexas.edu/).

In the scientific model adopted by Calvino as a metaphor for literary writing, the order that emerges from chaos is inherently unpredictable. He exploits this unpredictability to great effect. The concrete, mundane world of human affairs becomes poignant and meaningful when glimpses of it arise unexpectedly, seemingly out of place in literary realms of fantasy and abstraction. This is certainly true in the cosmicomic stories, several of which rely on the element of surprise to intensify the reader's emotional response to recognizable human interactions (e.g., in *Cosmicomiche*, "Tutto in un punto" ["All at One Point"], "Sul far del giorno" ["At Daybreak"], "Lo zio acquatico" ["The Aquatic Uncle"]). In "Crystals" these interactions occur in seven episodes that provide a slice of life in New York City: a train from New Jersey into Penn Station, a subway ride, a journey by automobile on Second Avenue, dinner in a twenty-fourth-floor restaurant, a Tiffany's display window, a beach on Staten Island, and a downtown photography studio. "Crystals" comes to a close in this studio as Qfwfq listens to a record by Thelonious Monk, a popular American jazz musician who toured Europe (including Italy) with his quartet in the early 1960s. I play a track or two from *Blue Monk* (recorded in 1963–64) for my students. The music not only helps illuminate the order-chaos theme in "Crystals" but also serves to introduce a broader discussion of the interrelation of order and chaos in jazz (repeated rhythms and chord progressions, improvised riffs) and, with additional musical samples (selected by my students), in other forms of music as well.

The city, as seen in the nuanced depiction of New York in "Crystals," is the image that best captures the creative tension in Calvino's fiction between "razionalità geometrica e groviglio delle esistenze umane" 'geometric rationality and the entanglements of human lives' (*Lezioni* 70; *Six Memos* 71). When I teach *Invisible Cities*, I therefore have students find and analyze evidence of how the "geometric rationality" of selected cities interrelates with the lives of their inhabitants. The city of Zaira, to give one example, is presented in terms of "relazioni tra le misure del suo spazio e gli avvenimenti del suo passato" 'relationships between the measurements of its space and the events of its past' (18; 10). The lines and trajectories of Zaira's spatial geometry (lamppost height, line strung to a railing, the tilt of a window's guttering, a gunboat's firing range, rips in a fishing net) are intimately connected to the lives of the city's inhabitants as well as to actions of their pets and foreign enemies: a hanged usurper, the queen's nuptial procession, a fleeing adulterer, a slinking cat, and finally three old men who provide narrative coherence by tying the gunboat to the usurper to the adulterer to the queen. Thus Zaira "contiene [il suo passato] come le linee d'una mano" 'contains [its past] like the lines of a hand' (18; 11), a felicitous observation that my students and I use to gloss other cities and places both in Calvino's textual universe and in our own lives.

While science per se hardly dominates *Invisible Cities* thematically (as it does many cosmicomic tales), the overall structure of the work is informed by scientific-mathematical ideas. Calvino claims that *Invisible Cities*, published in 1972, is the work in which he managed to say the most, not only because he exploited the narrative possibilities of a single symbol (the city) but also because he succeeded in building "una struttura sfaccettata in cui ogni breve testo sta vicino agli altri in una successione che non implica una consequenzialità o una gerarchia ma una rete entro la quale si possono tracciare molteplici percorsi e ricavare conclusioni plurime e ramificate" 'a many-faceted structure in which each brief text is close to the others in a series that does not imply logical sequence or a hierarchy, but a network in which one can follow multiple routes and draw multiple, ramified conclusions' (*Lezioni* 70; *Six Memos* 71). The table of contents of *Invisible Cities* shows how the text is structured according to a combinatorial poetics, a mathematically informed technique in vogue with Oulipo (Ouvroir de Littérature Potentielle), the experimental Parisian group with which Calvino was affiliated in the late 1960s and early 1970s. The fifty-five cities described by Marco Polo are assigned to eleven categories (five cities per category) and are arranged in nine chapters (ten cities in chapters 1 and 9; five cities in chapters 2–8). Following a precise pattern, new categories are introduced as old categories are exhausted in the chapters until all five cities in all eleven categories have made their appearance (Mengaldo 409–11; Ossola 242–48; Milanini 130–31; Palmore 25–30).

By allowing for multiple points of entry and encouraging readerly initiative in the production of order and meaning, the "many-faceted structure" of *Invisible Cities* generously lends itself to creative assignments and class activities. I often begin discussion of the text by asking students to think of a metaphor for their reading experience ("Reading *Invisible Cities* is like . . ."). Memorable answers include putting together a jigsaw puzzle and playing gin rummy. After my students have read most or all of the text, I teach them the concept of *mise en abyme* by asking them to identify an image, from the text or not, that best represents the work as a whole. Whether responses are obvious (a chessboard, a labyrinth) or subtle (a grammatical sentence, a geometric fractal), students arrive at greater understanding of the text through attempts to explain their choices.

Because each city both stands on its own and is intratextually related to other cities, I like to assist my students in the identification and analysis of important images, themes, and issues by devising process-oriented games that honor the combinatorial spirit of *Invisible Cities*. As the first stage of this activity, I assign cities to students by opening the book to random pages or by having them pick cards indicating cities by category and number (e.g., "Cities and Desire" 3) and I then pose questions: How does the city under examination (in this case, Despina) represent its category (desire)? How does it relate to other cities in its category thus far? Students also consider how well their city fits into a different category (e.g., memory), and they look for patterns suggesting the need to invent new categories—reversals, opposites, hope, despair, surprise, and so on. I expand this activity into a team-oriented game by dividing the class into groups and instructing each team to find as many cities as possible that match one (or more) of the new categories. For a writing assignment based on *Invisible Cities*, I ask students to imitate Marco Polo by using their imagination and experiences to create invisible cities of their own, either cities or towns where they have lived (Houstonia, San Antoniana, Dallasavia, and Austina are Texas favorites) or places of pure fantasy. My students frequently single out *Invisible Cities*, and this activity in particular, as their favorite part of the course.

Consistent with the scientific and philosophical rethinking of chaos (and the values attached to it) as the "womb of life, not its tomb" (Hayles 100), Calvino's fiction can serve as a catalyst for creative chaos not only in scholarly work but also in the classroom. Ultimately, his understanding of chaos and order as fluid entities capable of productive reciprocity is but one example of his exquisitely dialectical imagination. He excels at showing how areas of thought often viewed in opposition to each other, such as science and literature, function like the two halves of his "visconte dimezzato" 'cloven viscount': dangerous when they are cut off from each other and must operate in isolation, beneficent when their interdependency is recognized and they work toward a common goal. For teachers and their students, Calvino's writings transform another dichotomy into a fruitful partnership by fulfilling the promise of literature to delight and instruct.

Open Encyclopedias: Teaching Calvino's Works from a Comparative Perspective

Anna Botta

> Quella che prende forma nei grandi romanzi del XX secolo è l'idea d'una enciclopedia *aperta*, aggettivo che certamente contraddice il sostantivo *enciclopedia*, nato etimologicamente dalla pretesa di esaurire la conoscenza del mondo racchiudendola in un circolo. Oggi non è più pensabile una totalità che non sia potenziale, congetturale, plurima.
>
> (Calvino, *Lezioni* 113)

> What tends to emerge from the great novels of the twentieth century is the idea of an *open* encyclopedia, an adjective that certainly contradicts the noun *encyclopedia*, which etymologically implies an attempt to exhaust knowledge of the world by enclosing it in a circle. But today we can no longer think in terms of a totality that is not potential, conjectural, and manifold. (Calvino, *Six Memos* 116)

The Charles Eliot Norton Lectures that Italo Calvino was supposed to deliver at Harvard University the year he died (1985) are one of the most outstanding and original examples of comparative literary criticism ever written.[1] In these lectures, displaying an agility of reasoning similar to the *discorrere*, or "discursive style," he so much admired in Galileo Galilei's prose, Calvino as critic freely and lucidly draws together works belonging to different national literatures and disciplines, bringing into dialogue the humanities and social sciences, antiquity and the modern world, his own writing as well as *i libri degli altri*, or "other people's books." It is therefore not surprising that his *Six Memos for the Next Millennium* can be used, among other things, as a source for countless syllabi of comparative literature courses. The lectures are configured in a way that invites us as teachers to develop the many literary, philosophical, and scientific maps hinted at by him. It is as if the discussion of each of the authors or texts branches out into an open network of relations and nodal points that we are asked to connect creatively beyond national or disciplinary boundaries. His mental connections display the same agility and levity that characterized his celebrated fable making, his special gift that almost forty years earlier prompted Cesare Pavese to call Calvino "lo scoiattolo della penna" 'the squirrel of the pen' (273; my trans.).

The undergraduate course I teach in comparative literature, Open Encyclopedias, is listed in the Smith College catalog under the general heading "Studies in the Postmodern Novel." The twentieth-century narratives we read in the course, however, challenge the notion of the novel both as a literary genre with specific formal characteristics and as a fictional form distinct from scientific or philosophical writing. After Northrop Frye's *Anatomy of Criticism*, an influential study of the encyclopedic impulse governing literary forms and modes since antiquity, a tradition in criticism developed for studying encyclopedic narrative. Edward Mendelson, for instance, identifies seven major, and voluminous, works belonging to that genre (Dante's *Commedia*, Rabelais's five books of *Gargantua et Pantagruel*, Cervantes's *Don Quixote*, Goethe's *Faustus*, Melville's *Moby-Dick*, Joyce's *Ulysses*, and Pynchon's *Gravity's Rainbow*) and claims that "encyclopedic narratives all attempt to render the full range of knowledge and beliefs of a national culture, while identifying the ideological perspectives from which that culture shapes and interprets its knowledge" (1269). While Frye views the encyclopedic impulse as cyclical and ahistorical, Mendelson insists on the particular historical junctures that made it possible for works written at the margins of their cultures to be recognized ex post facto by their audiences as national encyclopedias and to take on the status of literary monuments.

In presenting my course as a study of open encyclopedias, I take a comparatist approach that is not grounded in a particular literary genre or national approach but that instead insists, as does Calvino in the passage cited above, on the oxymoronic quality of the expression "open encyclopedias." Despite their complexity as well as their aspiration to make sense of our world (their epistemological goal), such fictions do not intend to contain the multiplicity of the world in a single circle (etymologically *encyclopedia* derives from the Greek *enkyklios*, which means "encyclical" [i.e., covering the full circle of arts and sciences], and *paideia* ["education"]). Rather, they attempt to represent the centrifugal force of that complex network of relations, both in effect and *in potentia*, that continually destabilizes our sense of having comprehended the world (etymologically, *cum* and *prehendere* means "to encompass together"). Mr. Palomar—Calvino's alter ego, who defines himself as "ghiotto degustatore d'enciclopedie" 'hungry taster of encyclopedias' (*Saggi* 2: 1797; my trans.)—comments that the challenge of today's encyclopedias is to represent "un sapere sempre più difficile da tenere insieme, con al centro un *anthropos* sempre meno sicuro del suo antropocentrismo" 'a knowledge that is increasingly difficult to hold together, with at its center an *anthropos* increasingly less certain of his anthropocentrism' (1800; my trans.). A similar perplexity is shared by Calvino's friend the writer Raymond Queneau, who, at the outset of his own encyclopedic enterprise (*Encyclopédie de la Pléiade*, published by Gallimard starting in 1956), quotes Robert Oppenheimer: "There have always been many more things to be known than a man can possibly know. . . . Yet, until our times, diversity, complexity, abundance had never so clearly challenged any hierarchical order and simplification" (111; my trans.). How can a novel or a work of fiction be said to be an encyclopedia? Can stories be told in an encyclopedic format? My course analyzes twentieth-century narratives that, sometimes even in very small formats, claim to give us—at least as a possibility contained in their formal structure—the totality of our knowledge while simultaneously denouncing the inadequacy of our epistemological paradigms and pointing to the illusion of such an enterprise. By introducing us to new ways of understanding the encyclopedia's fundamental dichotomy (how to unify knowledge while guaranteeing its multiplicity), these narratives also offer a kind of weak epistemology, one that can be placed alongside contemporary scientific and philosophic discourses. In this age of skepticism toward any totalizing metanarrative (what Lyotard calls "les grands récits"), the narrative function, even if limited to local "petits récits," or "small narrative units," nevertheless gets affirmed as one of our major epistemological tools, "as a mode of thinking fully as legitimate as that of abstract logic" (Jameson xi). The grand challenge faced by literature today, writes Calvino, is "il saper tessere insieme i diversi saperi e i diversi codici in una visione plurima, sfaccettata del mondo" 'to be capable of weaving together the various branches of knowledge, the various codes, into a manifold and multifaced vision of the world' (*Lezioni* 110; *Six Memos* 112). The narrative function enables the works of literature analyzed in our course to demonstrate their encyclopedic hybridity while also reflecting on the type of knowledge required to understand it.

I begin my course by introducing the criteria that guided Jean Le Rond d'Alembert and Denis Diderot in designing their *Encyclopédie ou Dictionnaire raisonné des sciences, des arts et des métiers* (1751–80), a work that embodies the Enlightenment's commitment to systematized knowledge. Its distinguishing characteristic, what makes it modern, is the awareness of its founding contradiction. On the one hand, it claims that human knowledge can be synthesized and fixed into an objective and homogeneous system. On the other, it recognizes that the criteria for any selection are subjective and attempts to maintain a system flexible enough to accommodate new kinds of heterogeneity and changing forms of experience. The tension, writes Alfredo Salsano, is "tra conoscenze sempre in divenire e il tentativo di unificarle secondo un progetto esplicitamente o implicitamente strutturante" 'between the continuous development of knowledge and the attempt to unify it according to a project that is explicitly or implicitly structural' (4; my trans.). The comparative reading of a few selected passages from d'Alembert's *Preliminary Discourse* and Umberto Eco's chapter "Dizionario vs enciclopedia" ("Dictionary vs. Encyclopedia") should make students begin to reflect on the differences and similarities between the modern and postmodern encyclopedic projects. For instance, I ask them to comment on the position of the subject in these two distinct discourses of knowledge. Although d'Alembert is aware that the tree of human knowledge (*arbor scientiae*) is an arbitrary system, he believes that "the encyclopedic arrangement of our knowledge . . . consists of . . . placing the philosopher at a vantage point, so to speak, high above this vast labyrinth" (*Preliminary Discourse* 47). In the *Encyclopédie*, besides dominating over the tree, the subject is also the proud creator of a system that is supposed to be in conformity with human faculties. On the contrary, for a postmodern thinker such as Eco, "the tree of genera and species, the tree of substances, blows up in a dust of *differentiae*, in a turmoil of infinite accidents' ("Dictionary" 68) and "rigenera ad ogni passo il labirinto (delle differenze)" 're-creates at each step the labyrinth (of differences)' ("L'antiporfirio" 76; my trans.).

The postmodern subject has lost the Enlightenment's self-confidence; it finds itself trapped in a labyrinth of incertitudes where epistemology is characterized by instability. As Calvino writes, we live in a time when "il sapere non si lascia circoscrivere in un circolo, ma forse solo in un vortice o cratere o nube d'esplosione" 'knowledge does not let itself be circumscribed by a circle, but only perhaps by a vortex or a crater or a cloud of explosion' ("Ed ora"; my trans.).

We next turn to "Multiplicity," in Calvino's *Six Memos*. I ask my students to comment first on how Calvino connects his definition of *open encyclopedias* to literary works (traditional novels, hypernovels, short stories) and then to investigate our current understanding of the terms *encyclopedia* and *narrative*. How do we go about reading them (consultation versus linear reading)? Can the encyclopedic inventory be devised as a dynamic and flexible structure (such as *Wikipedia*)? Can narrative be considered a valid epistemic technique? Before we address these questions with textual examples, I ask students to familiarize themselves with the table of contents of Calvino's *Invisible Cities* and read its first section together with Georges Perec's essay "Think/Classify." I then ask them to report on their reading: How are the two texts constructed? In which ways are they "open" and how do they challenge our traditional reader's expectations? Or, more specifically, how does Calvino's fictional work manage to be a finely structured text while presenting itself as an unbound atlas of all possible cities, even cities not yet imagined or realized? What use does Perec's philosophical essay make of the traditional encyclopedic feature, alphabetical order? How does Perec go about presenting his nonsystematic thoughts after he has chosen deliberately "to preserve the hesitant and perplexed character of [his] shapeless scraps and to abandon the pretense of organizing them into an article with a beginning, a middle and an end" (185)? Throughout the course, I also encourage students to challenge their linear reading practices, especially with Perec's *Life: A User's Manual*.

Once these preliminary and preparatory arguments are well grounded, I have my students read two nineteenth-century literary works as forerunners of postmodern open encyclopedias: Gustave Flaubert's *Bouvard et Pécuchet* (1880) and Herman Melville's "Bartleby, the Scrivener" (1863). What do such "scriveners" tell us about the legibility of the world and the possibility to represent its totality? In what way do their adventures in knowledge belong to the certainties of the nineteenth century yet also predict the skepticism of the twentieth? The two works also illustrate the paradoxical closeness of two opposite intellectual attitudes, curiosity and skepticism, and suggest how the intention of being exhaustive may in fact lead to complete silence.

In the following weeks of the course, we read fictional works by Calvino (*Invisible Cities* and *Mr. Palomar*), Jorge Luis Borges (stories from *The Garden of the Forking Paths* in *Ficciones*, *The Aleph*, and the story "The Analytical Language of John Wilkins"), Perec (*Life: A User's Manual* and "*Species of Spaces*"), Enrique Vila-Matas (*Bartleby and Co.*), and Thomas Pynchon (*The Crying of Lot 49*), together with excerpts from theoretical texts by Gilles Deleuze and Félix Guattari (*A Thousand Plateaus*), Michel Foucault (*The Order of Things*), Jean-François Lyotard (*The Postmodern Condition*), and Warren F. Motte, Jr. ("Clinamen Redux"). Such a reading list is of course not exhaustive of what I consider to be open encyclopedias. Time constraints, my personal literary preferences, and my academic training all affect the selection process. The list is a possible sample and an invitation for other teachers to read narrative works by different authors (or different works by the same authors) as manifestations of the postmodern encyclopedic impulse.

Regardless of the works read, it is important to have students understand that in a sense we as readers in the postmodern era are experiencing the condition of the emperors described by Calvino at the beginning of *Le città invisibili* (*Invisible Cities*). The age of reason and its empire over the world have given way to the desperate recognition that all we are left with is the crumbling away of past certitudes and scientific explanations:

> Nella vita degli imperatori c'è un momento che segue all'orgoglio per l'ampiezza dei territori che abbiamo conquistato, alla malinconia e al sollievo di sapere che presto rinunceremo a conoscerli e a comprenderli; un senso come di vuoto che ci prende. . . . [È] il momento disperato in cui si scopre che quest'impero che ci era sembrato la somma di tutte le meraviglie è uno sfacelo senza fine né forma. (13)

> In the lives of emperors there is a moment which follows pride in the boundless extension of the territories we have conquered, and the melancholy and relief of knowing and understanding them. There is a sense of emptiness that comes over us. . . . It is the desperate moment when we discover that this empire, which had seemed to us the sum of all wonders, is an endless, formless ruin. (5)

Paradoxically, it is just such a moment of epistemological impasse that stimulates the storytelling of Calvino and the other authors of open encyclopedias. Believing in the power of literature to connect the disparate discourses of our times, they offer an alternative to the rigid schema of scientific or philosophic systems that have failed us. With them, we enter, to use Borges's expression, "the Celestial Empire of Benevolent Knowledge" ("Analytical Language"). Literature assumes the ambitious task of mapping postmodern knowledge through the development of unstable networks and open systems that constantly verge on the unintelligible. Marco Polo's storytelling is presented at the outset of *Invisible Cities* as one such intellectual enterprise: "Solo nei resoconti di Marco Polo, Kublai Kan riusciva a discernere, attraverso le muraglie e le torri destinate a crollare, la filigrana d'un disegno così sottile da sfuggire al morso delle termiti" 'Only in Marco Polo's accounts was Kublai Khan able to discern, through the walls and towers destined to crumble, the tracery of a pattern so subtle it could escape the termites' gnawing' (13–14; 5–6).

Inspired by the subtle tracing of Marco Polo's patterns, I organize the syllabus of my course around six thematic areas conceived as permutational nodes, which each of the assigned texts intersects and combines in a different way: multiplicity/unicity, order/chaos, saturation/void, infinite/infinitesimal, taxonomies and collections, metaphors. I supply students not with an interpretive grid but with an exclusively operational system that will allow them to circulate between ever-changing configurations of creative interpretation. Like the six memos proposed by Calvino, four of these headings are abstract concepts, each viewed in tension with its respective opposite, thus urging the students to investigate each as a movable point over a spatial continuum, one that necessarily entails a dialectic relation between two extremes. As Calvino reminds us, Flaubert wrote in 1852, "ce que je voudrais faire, c'est un livre sur rien" 'what I would like to do is a book about nothing' (qtd. in *Lezioni* 111; *Six Memos* 113), even though the French author then proceeded "to devote the last ten years of his life to the most encyclopedic novel ever written, *Bouvard et Pécuchet*" (*Six Memos* 113). Similarly, the challenge facing many sciences today, such as the science of complexity and chaos theory, is to account for "order out of chaos," to show how determinism and chaos can be linked in a meaningful way if we consider their complementarity (Pilz, *Mapping*).

The other two nodal points I ask students to consider are taxonomies and collections and, finally, metaphors. A disproportionate number of characters in the fictions we analyze are either collectors (e.g., Bartlebooth in *Life: A User's Manual* and Pierce Inverarity in *The Crying of Lot 49*) or people who indulge in other forms of taxonomic activity (e.g., Cinoc in *Life: A User's Manual* and the narrator of Borges's "Tlön, Ubquar, Orbis Tertius"). Both in *Life: A User's Manual* and in *"Species of Spaces,"* Perec's narrators elaborate time and again long inventories of objects and activities (e.g., enumerating all the verbs associated with the action of moving in and out of a new house). Encyclopedias are conceived from just such efforts at listing. As Roland Barthes reminds us:

> [I]nventory is never a neutral idea; to catalogue is not merely to ascertain, as it appears at first glance, but also to appropriate. The *Encyclopedia* is a huge ledger of ownership . . . to appropriate is to fragment the world, to divide it into finite objects subject to man in proportion of their very discontinuity: for we cannot separate without finally naming and classifying, and, at that moment, property is born. ("Plates" 26–27)

Cataloging, building inventories, and classifying are both spatial and conceptual practices; they arrange entities in space and, by arranging, assert a form of learning that is based on mastering the object. When reading these authors, students should be guided by the following questions: In what ways do postmodern open encyclopedias repeat this characteristically modern will to dominate the world through reason (what Heidegger calls "calculative thinking") while asserting a different kind of thinking, one that does not try to capture the world into a rigorous logic grid but instead opens the world up to a "releasement" toward its objects (Heidegger's *Gelassenheit*) and a new way of experiencing them? How do inventory (systematics, classification) and invention (the ceaseless renewal of knowledge) combine to produce this form of postmodern epistemology? A possible way to approach such a paradoxical enterprise is to replace the static concept of the grid with the dynamic activity of connecting. The fictional and theoretical works we read in our course speculate about connection as the characteristic human endeavor. We need to narrate; we feel the necessity of creating and perceiving significant patterns in what we read and do. Lyotard views our self as "a nodal point of communications," as "a post through which various kinds of messages pass" (15). If postmodern authors are still susceptible to the scrivener's old dream, to copy the world within a single book, they also understand that book to be a provisional and unstable constellation, suspended between order and chaos.

After discussing these questions, students should now be prepared to investigate the key metaphors that are used to represent knowledge. Since metaphors inform and are informed by our conceptual paradigms, they are symptomatic of paradigm shifts. In the shift from the modern to the postmodern paradigm, for instance, it is particularly interesting to study how tropes—such as the tree, the labyrinth, the map, the network, the rhizome, and the puzzle—are used to denote either the organization of knowledge, information, and logic or their counterparts, chaos, noise, and illogical aporias. Although for d'Alembert the tree is cast as a positive model of order and simplification out of the dark labyrinth that threatens to engulf the eighteenth-century philosopher, postmodern authors prefer to use more complex models of knowledge, those that also account for discontinuities, paradoxes, and multidimensionality and remain open to changes and reconfigurations. The labyrinth thus becomes a positive trope, as does the rhizome, with its disordered growth or, as in Perec, the paradoxical puzzle whose last piece does not fit into its appropriate space (*Life*).

Much like Perec's enigmatic puzzle, my course does not leave students with the satisfaction of having surveyed postmodern knowledge full circle and covered it exhaustively. I prefer to leave them, and the readers of this essay, with the image of Mr. Palomar's dream. After a day spent in reading an encyclopedia and puzzling over how to construct "un discorso globale che scorra attraverso la discontinuità delle singole voci in ordine alfabetico" 'a global discourse that runs through the discontinuity of the single entries in alphabetical order' (*Saggi* 2: 1797; my trans.), Mr. Palomar falls asleep and dreams of drinking his encyclopedia as if it were a raw egg: "Attraverso un buchino fatto con uno spillo, tira su tutto il tuorlo. No, al centro del tuorlo c'è lui stesso, come già gli avvenne prima della nascita, che divora dal di dentro il contenuto dell'uovo e del mondo" 'Through a small hole made by a pin he sucks up the yolk. No, at the center of the yolk he finds himself, as it already happened before he was born, devouring from within the egg's and the world's contents' (1800; my trans.). There is no way of closing the circle of our knowledge; we are necessarily implicated in an endless process of learning from which the subjective and the objective cannot be disentangled. The more homogeneous and familiar the contents of our encyclopedia appears, the less open it remains to the heterogeneity and the alterity of the world that surrounds us.

NOTE

[1]The lectures were published posthumously, first by Harvard University Press as *Six Memos for the Next Millennium* (translated by Patrick Creagh) and later by Garzanti as *Lezioni americane*.

From Fiction to Theories: Calvino's Art of Narration and Literary Theories

Rocco Capozzi

On the cover of *The Name of the Rose* Umberto Eco muses that what cannot be theorized must be narrated. After much theorizing, he finally chose to narrate semiotic, philosophical, narratological, and other literary issues. This practice is, in essence, one that Italo Calvino exploited in many of his works, reasoning and theorizing through the use of images (see Belpoliti; Ricci, *Painting*), scientific principles, and ideology and finally narrating through the use of words. An analysis of his fiction confirms that he considered for years the theory as well as the nature and role of literature. This essay discusses strategies for teaching narratology and literary theories in the fiction of Calvino. Its overriding argument is that the study of literary theory does not have to be difficult—it can be fun for students if it is discussed with entertaining narratives. Calvino's works provide the perfect vehicle for illustrating theoretical discourse.

A general introduction provides students with an overview of Calvino's production, emphasizing his fiction from the 1960s to 1979. Subsequent lectures focus on basic notions of *écriture*, metafiction, the death of the author, authorial presence, verbal signs, semiotics, intertextuality, and postmodern narrative strategies. The syllabus should include relevant Calvino essays and a selection of passages from the works of Vladimir Propp, Roland Barthes, John Barth, Gérard Genette, Umberto Eco, Ferdinand de Saussure, Charles Sanders Peirce, Lubomír Doležel, Nelson Goodman, J. L. Austin, Wolfgang Iser, and Fredric Jameson to accompany the readings of the novels and short stories of Calvino. Moreover, selections from most recent critics (such as Markey, Hume, Ricci, Belpoliti, Bolongaro, and Benedetti) will serve as a guide in illustrating different approaches to reading him.

Reading Calvino can be a highly entertaining and rewarding experience for students seeking to understand fiction that is interdisciplinary, encyclopedic, and loaded with notions of literary theories. One reason for choosing Calvino as a touchstone for a course on literary theory is that he seems to have preceded the literary critics who popularized the literary theories used to analyze his stories. The relation of fiction and structuralism, semiotics, self-reflexive narrations, *ars combinatoria*, author and reader relationships, interdisciplinary strategies, word-and-image relations, encyclopedic writing, and postmodernism are merely a few examples of theoretical strategies that Calvino seems to have preempted in his works. To emphasize this point, it is helpful to place his essays beside his fictions, thereby encouraging students to understand the theorist, essayist, and writer. It is important to underline throughout the course that Calvino the fiction writer is never divorced from Calvino the essayist; his fabulous stories, rich with allusions to literary theories, are closely related to his theoretical work.

Selections from Calvino's *The Uses of Literature*, *Hermit in Paris*, and *Six Memos for the Next Millennium* may be used as the platform to launch discussions on theories and practices in his work. By deconstructing these works, students enter the writer's laboratory and better understand the master at work. In this way, Calvino's bookshelf (his favorite authors) is discussed alongside the theoretical shelf that Calvino envisions for his readers (see his "Per chi si scrive? (Lo scaffale ipotetico)" [*Pietra sopra* 159–63]). *Six Memos for the Next Millennium* is especially useful because he refers back to his own essays and fiction as well as to the novels of other writers (from Dante and Boccaccio to Cervantes, Flaubert, Valéry, Perec, and Gadda) as he discusses a variety of narrative strategies. The five lectures— "Lightness," "Quickness," "Exactitude," "Visibility," and "Multiplicity"—complement one another in their discussion of the art of writing and reading fiction. Just as important, the memos are an excellent testimonial to the author's lifelong faith in the artistic and social role of literature.

"Lightness" and "Multiplicity" are most useful to students as they study Calvino's applications of *écriture*, intertextuality, and metafiction in his craft. Lightness and multiplicity are also qualities that Calvino admires in the works of classical writers like Ovid (see *Hermit in Paris*; Introduction [*Metamorfosi*]). Furthermore, students should be made aware that the notion of lightness for Calvino is about imagination, fantasy, and intellect and, above all, concerns the art of creating visual images and illustrating ideas. He says it best: "I would like to be Mercutio. Among his virtues, I admire above all his lightness, in a world full of brutality, his dreaming imagination . . . a Don Quixote who knows very well what dreams are and what reality is, and he lives both with open eyes" (*Hermit* 234). Writing, in short, is a self-reflexive (but not narcissistic) experience that exposes the act of narrating for what it is: the art of using words to create possible worlds. Barth recognized Calvino's overall spirit of lightness as he praised the author's wonderful weightless sense of fantasy ("Literature of Replenishment").

At this point one could approach Calvino's experimentation with literariness, *écriture*, and metafiction. A brief history of his contact with French critics during his prolonged Parisian sojourn in the 1960s adds breadth to the course's theoretical frame. Attention should be drawn to authors such as Roland Barthes, Algirdas Greimas, Gérard Genette, Alain Robbe-Grillet, Raymond Queneau, Georges Perec, and Michel Serres. Calvino's fondness for open systems related to literary structuralism and semiotics also increased as Calvino became interested in the works of Roman Jakobson and Claude Lévi-Strauss in conjunction with Barthes's notion of explosive chains of signifiers. In Jakobson, Calvino found an excellent bridge between Russian formalism and Saussurean and Peircean semiotics and structural linguistics. At this time, he was also examining the novels of great masters such as Jorge Luis Borges, Robert Louis Stevenson, Vladimir Nabokov, John Barth, and Thomas Pynchon. In this era, his already strong encyclopedic competence was expanding rapidly, and studying it can help students likewise expand their competence in postmodern theory.

The polyvalent stance of the author, his embracing of and skepticism toward theory, should be highlighted at this juncture. The best indication of his reluctance to completely endorse any one literary theory or trend is evident in some of his most quoted essays, like "Il mare dell'oggettività" ("The Sea of Objectivity") and "La sfida al labirinto" ("The Challenge to the Labyrinth") in the journal *Il menabò de letteratura* and "Cibernetica e fantasmi" ("Cybernetics and Ghosts") and "I livelli della realtà ("The Levels of Reality in Literature") in *Una pietra sopra* (*The Uses of Literature*). His fundamental belief in the role of literature remains that of challenging the "labyrinth"—that is, the chaos, the prison, the hell of reality surrounding us—with fantasy, imagination, and reason. For Calvino fantasy and imagination are never a means of evading reality but, rather, instruments of vision(s) of reality. In short, instead of approaching and confronting reality head-on (and relying on techniques of mimesis), he preferred constructing mental images and metaphors of contemporary reality as labyrinths, hell, prisons, and paradoxes. Examples can be found in the last four stories of *T Zero*, in which the narrators focus on the processes of perceiving and understanding sociocultural and existential issues rather than attempt to solve them. Furthermore, instead of narrating quests for truths in the tradition of the *grand récit* (Lyotard), Calvino chooses a type of cerebral fiction (or metafiction) characterized primarily by metaphysical, deductive, or phenomenological *petit récit* that we see illustrated in *Invisible Cities*, *Cosmicomics*, and *Mr. Palomar*.

Once this theoretical arc of the course has been completed, the instructor may pass to a practical application of the information. I usually select specific passages from Calvino's fiction that illustrate a variety of literary theories that interested Calvino and were in vogue when the stories were written. Instructors should choose passages that best illustrate the technique they wish to cover and that have both pragmatic applications and theoretical importance. This exercise allows students to perform a close analysis of Calvino's work in relation to applicable criticism, literary theories, and terminology.

"Multiplicity," for example, works well in relation to intertextuality. Selections from *Cosmicomics* and *T Zero* can be used in discussions of semiotics, structuralism, Lacanian desire, engagement, neorealism versus *nouveau roman*, and the notion of repetition and difference. *Invisible Cities* and *The Castle of Crossed Destinies* can be analyzed in terms of *ars combinatoria*, *enchassement*, nonlinear narratives, structuralism, semiotics, and repetition and difference. The overall topic on intertextuality can be illustrated through passages from *Invisible Cities* (with echoes of, for example, *Arabian Nights*, Marco Polo's *Milione*, Cortázar's *Hopscotch*, and Coleridge's "Kubla Khan") and *If on a winter's night a traveler*—indisputably, metafiction at its best—which leads to discussions on essay novels, Borgesian fiction, incipits, authorial intrusions, open works, hybrid novels, hyperfiction, playing cat and mouse with readers, and reader-reception theories.

The course wishes to illustrate that while Calvino indulged in structuralist, semiotic, and postmodern theories, he never did so to excess. He steadfastly maintained a salutary distance while often preempting and preceding the very literary theorists who popularized these linguistic and aesthetic theories. Most important, by closely analyzing the novels and short stories of Calvino as vehicles for theory, students come to fully appreciate his unmatched skills in the art of *docere et delectare*. I have written elsewhere about Calvino's notion of entertainment as a serious business, but it was Maria Corti who best summarized the writer's talent in exploiting literary divertissement in relation to *The Castle of Crossed Destinies*, stating that in this ingenious composition "Calvino scherza sapientemente" 'Calvino jokes wisely' (*Viaggio* 184; my trans.). Indeed, he played so sagely with serious fabulations that he deserved Johan Huizinga's definition of a *homo ludens*.

Proceed with Caution: Teaching Symbolism and Intertextuality in Calvino's Fantasy Novels

Andrew Martino

In his essay "Intertextual Irony and Levels of Reading," Umberto Eco argues that texts produce at least two kinds, or "levels," of readers. He calls the first-level reader a "semantic reader" and the second-level reader a "semiotic or aesthetic reader." In each case, the text presupposes a certain type of reader, just as the reader comes to presuppose certain types or genres of texts. As Eco explains:

> To put it bluntly, the first-level model reader wants to know what happens, while the second-level model reader wants to know how what happens has been narrated. To find out how the story will end one usually just has to read the text once. To become a second-level model reader one has to read it several times, and some stories have to be read countless times. (223)

As teachers of literature, we are charged with guiding students toward a path that will enable them to become second-level readers. This type of reader is not limited to literature only; it is important that students understand the meaning and implications of textuality beyond the printed page. That is, by training them to advance to second-level readers, we are teaching our students to become more thoughtful and perceptive readers of the world around them, a world that is now constantly bombarding us with information. In short, we are training them to think critically.

Italo Calvino's heraldic trilogy, *Il cavaliere inesistente*, *Il visconte dimezzato*, and *Il barone rampante* (*The Nonexistent Knight*, *The Cloven Viscount*, and *The Baron in the Trees*), offers an excellent introduction for students to the complexities of second-level reading.[1] Published throughout the 1950s, the trilogy constitutes a wonderful excursion into a textual labyrinth of the modern world. It raises contemporary issues surrounding Cold War politics, such as the arms race and the clash of ideologies—specifically, the place of communism in postwar Europe. Moreover, the trilogy marks Calvino's shift from neorealism to fantasy and more postmodern narrative styles. His use of postmodern intertextuality, the encyclopedic elements of contemporary reality, anticipates the coming of the World Wide Web. First-level readers tend to reduce these novels to fanciful stories or, at best, tales for children. An approach from this perspective implies two things: we need not take seriously the literature we are reading, and we can derive nothing practical (not to mention historical) from the reading of fantasy. Such a literal reading is neither accurate nor critical. How do we, then, guide our students to discover meaning and the intricacies of Calvino's work?

What follows are strategies I have used in my classes that have helped students become second-level readers.

The accessibility of Calvino's writing makes his work far less likely than others' to intimidate students as they first encounter theory. His novels and stories are not only fun to read but also testaments to what Calvino calls "multiplicity," or encyclopedic narratives. The encyclopedic nature of our world is the prime point I try to impart to my students in a contemporary literature class. As Calvino explains in his lecture "Multiplicity," collected in *Six Memos for the Next Millennium*:

> What tends to emerge from the great novels of the twentieth century is the idea of an *open* encyclopedia, an adjective that certainly contradicts the noun *encyclopedia*, which etymologically implies an attempt to exhaust knowledge of the world by enclosing it in a circle. But today we can no longer think in terms of a totality that is not potential, conjectural, and manifold. (116)

The possibility of reading a potentiality of such literature becomes dependent on the connections one makes with the world outside the text. One makes such a connection (at least in part, but in no way superficially) through excursions into symbolism and intertextuality. When teaching the trilogy, I always place a copy of "Multiplicity" on reserve. If time does not permit all the students to read this essay, a group might present it to the class as an oral report along with or in place of the oral report topics mentioned below.

Oral reports become the backbone of our excursion into Calvino's trilogy and serve as a basis for final papers. In the past, students have used everything from traditional oral reports (reading from note cards, displaying a poster or two) to *PowerPoint* presentations to short one-act plays to a mock game of *Jeopardy*. One year a group of students produced a very sophisticated mock documentary on the character Cosimo. This documentary was a takeoff of the popular *E! True Hollywood Story* and showed a considerable degree of creativity as well as intertextuality.

After providing a brief introduction to Calvino, I ask my students to write a short (one-to-two-page) initial reaction to his texts that will give the rest of the class some sense of how they receive him early on. This class exercise has proved to be extremely useful. Generally I have found my students to be more forthcoming when asked to prepare something in writing than when I just go around the room and have them discuss the texts on the spot. Once that task is completed, I divide the class into smaller groups. Each group is assigned an aspect of the trilogy to research and present to the rest of the class; usually there are four or five groups. For *The Nonexistent Knight*, I assign research on Charlemagne, the Knights of the Round Table, and the notion of chivalry; for *The Cloven Viscount*, sections of Plato's *The Symposium* and Machiavelli's *The Prince* and sometimes Robert Louis Stevenson's *Dr. Jekyll and Mr. Hyde*;[2]

for *The Baron in the Trees*, chapters from Voltaire's *Candide*. Each group then presents their topic of research to the rest of the class during the appropriate stage in our discussion. The aim of this activity is to get students to work in groups and to put into practice the problem of intertextuality. As tempting as it is to monopolize the conversation, it is always more constructive to foster discussion among the students. In this sense, I tend to function more as a moderator of discussion than as a traditional lecturer.

Allowing students to assume responsibility for initiating class discussion makes them more likely to come to certain revelations about the text for themselves. I try not to color their reading of a text, because such a pedagogical practice is ultimately destructive of the activities of reading and thinking. This group project is a subtle way for me to get students to discover the text without feeling pressured to pursue only those avenues they think I want them to explore.

Traditionally I have taught *The Nonexistent Knight* as a fable on the practice of writing itself. There is a wonderful connection between storytelling and cartography in this book. Furthermore, students can identify with Sister Theodora's penance: "I who recount this tale am Sister Theodora, nun of the order of Saint Colomba. I am writing in a convent, from old unearthed papers or talk heard in our parlor, or a few rare accounts by people who were actually present" (34). The similarities among Sister Theodora, the students, and the act of research (preferably library research) do not go unnoticed by students. Rarely have I had to point out the symbolic gesture of writing as discovery. Most of my students make that connection easily. Whenever a student becomes actively engaged in the critical reading of a text, such as identifying aspects of his or her own life in the text or the characters, I feel richly rewarded. Sister Theodora's writing as penance and world building should not be passed over in class discussion. In my experience, it is beneficial to spend time on the complex characterization of the narrator: a nun whose penance is to write the story (to turn words into pictures, to capture time) of a nonexistent knight. Several possibilities present themselves for discussion, such as writing as artifact—if something is not, or cannot be, written down, does it exist? The parallels among the narrator, Agilulf, and the student provide possibilities for rich and engaged discussion on writing as a means of knowledge production. On several occasions students have spent time outside class constructing maps that illustrate various references they find in their reading. The maps sometimes take the form of time lines and color-coded transparencies that depict literary time periods and their correspondence to Calvino's text.

The Cloven Viscount, the companion novella to *The Nonexistent Knight*, features not only an investigation into the duality of humanity but also a powerful meditation on the uses and abuses of power. I have found that students are willing to engage in a sophisticated discussion of this text once certain groundwork is laid. For example, an early discussion of the text prompted them to list desirable personality traits on one side of the blackboard and undesirable traits on the other. Some of the desirable traits we came up with were loyalty, honesty, and bravery; some of the undesirable traits were pompousness, meanness, jealousy, bossiness, and crudeness. I ask students to think about themselves and their friends and family when compiling this list, to personalize their reading. We move on to discuss the duality of human nature. As with our opening discussion of *The Nonexistent Knight*, we undertake these activities as a sort of preface to discussing the text. I bring in chapter 17 of Machiavelli's *The Prince* ("On Cruelty and Clemency"), a text that considers whether it is better for a ruler to be loved or feared. I also bring in the famous speech by Aristophanes in Plato's *The Symposium*, which discusses the splitting in half of man and each half's searching for the other. When applied to *The Cloven Viscount*, these two texts provide interesting examples of intertextual reading.

I have also asked students to break up into four groups to take on the role of a legal team and either defend or prosecute both halves of Viscount Medardo. The subject would be the abuse of power, making use of both the bad side's behavior as well as that of the good side. Each group is assigned one half of Medardo and charged with either defending or prosecuting that half. I give the groups time to prepare and then have them make their case before the rest of the class, which serves as a jury. This exercise tends to engage students in profound ways. It provides them with a forum in which to air their views of the characters, and it gives them a chance to role-play, which is fundamental to active learning. Moreover, it affords them the opportunity to devise and implement an important critical task—namely, building a sound rhetorical argument. As students come to realize, a good argument cannot be made without support; that is, preparing a good case forces them to do their homework and engage the text in ways not possible in a traditional lecture-format class.

If teaching the entire trilogy, I ask students to read *The Baron in the Trees* last. Because I find this the most complex book of the three, I spend the most time on it. This text is difficult for students to navigate, so I tie our reading of it to something they can apply to the world beyond the classroom. The novel offers as an excellent starting point for a discussion on the role of the intellectual and what it means to be an engaged citizen. A close reading of *The Baron in the Trees* can also help students approach the concepts surrounding civic engagement, currently a popular topic in higher education. I have had my classes explore the implications of civic engagement in both the city (Paris as an intellectual capital) and the periphery (Ombrosa as a place where the people are fundamentally tied to the land). Thus students explore the ways civic engagement can be used in urban and rural settings. *The Baron in the Trees* could be valuable in a service-learning course. What Cosimo teaches us about responsibility to oneself, one's land, and one's family can provide a rich and powerful experience for non-English majors who may be taking a literature class as part of a general education program.

An engagement with the text by way of civic engagement also demonstrates to students the power of literature outside the classroom. *The Baron in the Trees* can be read as a text about responsibility and what we can do with knowledge of the natural world. A little knowledge, however, can be a dangerous thing. Chapter 12 presents us with the dangers of reading while still retaining a Romantic image of the storyteller and the reader. Like the other texts in the trilogy, it celebrates the power of the human imagination to contribute to the greater good.

Finally, for the student to take away an appreciation of intertextuality and the complexities of critical reading and active learning, Calvino provides a path that is far less intimidating than those offered by many other authors and theorists. His fiction, particularly his fantasy novels, lends itself to multiple readings that can serve as a resonant way for students to approach second-level readings that transcend disciplinary boundaries. Calvino's texts are not only literary but also are philosophical, sociopolitical, historical, at times mathematical, and cultural. With the turn in the academy toward a more interdisciplinary and civic-minded education, Calvino engages us in the intricacies of intertextuality and symbolism on an unintimidating level. What he teaches in his fantasy novels, and what I try to get across to my students, is the plurality of the world. The fantasy novels provide a wonderfully readable site from which to engage encyclopedic contemporary reality.

NOTES

[1]The complete trilogy is available in *I nostri antenati* and in English translation in *Our Ancestors*. Here I cite from Colquhoun's 1977 combined translation The Nonexistent Knight *and* The Cloven Viscount and his 1959 stand-alone translation *The Baron in the Trees*.

[2]Since Stevenson's text is a prime source for *The Cloven Viscount*, instructors may want to consider showing a film version of the story in class. Yet, because the text is so short (fewer than one hundred pages), I always encourage a group to read it and then present it to the rest of the class.

Autobiography, History, and Writing in Calvino: Toward an Ethics of the Subject

Massimo Lollini

One of the most striking features in Calvino's works is a conception of writing that is strictly connected to an ethical vision of subjectivity and autobiography. This writing promotes an understanding of the necessity, artificiality, and incompleteness of human subjectivity. I teach courses on Calvino in Italian and in translation, for undergraduate and graduate students, in a seminar format (fifteen to twenty students). In my course Literature and Testimony in the Twentieth Century, I teach a unit focused on two autobiographical works that represent crucial moments of Calvino's life and literary career: *Il sentiero dei nidi di ragno* (*The Path to the Spiders' Nests*) and *La strada di San Giovanni* (*The Road to San Giovanni*). Students appreciate the intellectual and philosophical dimension of his autobiographical texts, which can be explored by focusing on self-reflective passages. His reflections are particularly suited for comparative literature courses and have important implications for contemporary theory and pedagogy regarding an ethical view of autobiography and subjectivity.

This course studies how the idea of emptiness, usually associated with Eastern philosophy, is also present in some crucial aspects of Western philosophy and literature. Taoist texts establish the role of emptiness as the necessary condition and premise for an effective meditation and action.[1] Hollowness, emptiness, and bareness have the function of removing the obstacles to pure meditation and action. An ethical attention to the role of emptiness also traverses Western tradition. In *Apology* 21d-e, for example, Socrates declares that the wisdom he practices had no conceit of knowledge and that for this reason the Delphic oracle considered him the wisest of men (Plato, *Last Days*). In Plato's *Theaetetus* 210d, Socrates compares maieutic art to the practice of midwifery since he cannot create any offspring but can only assist his interlocutors to become aware of their false beliefs, to articulate and work out their own ideas.

The beliefs of Eastern and Western philosophies concerning emptiness are embodied in the autobiographical works of Calvino. The writer-witness does not want to conceptualize his action because he realizes that autobiography and personal testimonies are not just a way of representing historical events from an individual point of view but also a way to appreciate the limits of historical narration and subjectivity. To become able to appreciate these limits means to develop a special attention to the act of writing as the fundamental gesture responsible for creating the idea of truth and subjectivity in Western culture. Calvino's autobiographical works develop a fundamental "ethics of writing" that can establish a fruitful dialogue with contemporary theory and Western philosophers, including Jacques Derrida, Maurice Blanchot, Emmanuel Levinas, Paul Ricoeur, and Carlo Sini.[2] The ethics of writing explores the limits of symbolization while paying attention to the emptiness of form. It explores that which we cannot conceptualize in and by writing: the void that surrounds the written page and the artificial and incomplete human subjectivity created through writing.

Three autobiographical texts by Calvino are particularly relevant to this approach. I use them as part of a teaching unit in two courses, Literature and Testimony in the Twentieth Century and Autobiography and History in Italo Calvino. Two of the texts, "Ricordo di una battaglia" ("Memories of a Battle") and "La poubelle agrée," were published in the posthumous collection entitled *La strada di San Giovanni* (*The Road to San Giovanni*). The third is the 1964 introduction to Calvino's autobiographical novel *The Path to the Spiders' Nests*.

"Memories of a Battle" and Calvino's Ethics of Writing

"Memories of a Battle" was first published in *Il corriere della sera*, the best-selling Italian newspaper of the time, on 25 April 1974. This narrative was conceived as a contribution to the national holiday celebrating the 1945 liberation of Italy from fascism and Nazism. Calvino had fought with the Italian Resistance against Nazism and fascism from February 1944 to the end of the war in 1945. In "Memories of a Battle," he recalls the battle of Baiardo (a small town close to San Remo, in northern Italy) that took place on 17 March 1945. A member of the Communist Party, he participated in this battle under the partisan code name Santiago.[3]

In the opening paragraph Calvino recalls how for a long time he was convinced that the memories of his Resistance past would remain the same in the present and be available to him at any moment. Yet, thirty year later, when the moment to remember and celebrate the past has come, he cannot recall his experience in the Resistance in its wholeness. Instead the past appears to him hidden "nell'umido letto di sabbia che si deposita nel fondo del torrente dei pensieri . . . seppellito da miliardi e miliardi di altri granelli" 'in the damp bed of sand deposited on the bottom of the stream of thought . . . buried under billions and billions of others grains' (*Strada* 75; *Road* 77). I ask my students to think of the possible meanings of this image of the sand composed of billions of tiny grains of sand; then, through guided questions and further readings, I help them realize the crucial value of this metaphor in Calvino's imagery. I receive good answers to my questions after having them read his *Six Memos for the Next Millennium*. They find there the image of sand in a clear and effective paragraph on writing:

> Comunque tutte le "realtà" e le fantasie possono prendere forma solo attraverso *la scrittura*, nella quale esteriorità e interiorità, mondo e io, esperienza e fantasia appaiono composte della stessa materia verbale;

> le visioni polimorfe degli occhi e dell'anima si trovano contenute in righe uniformi di caratteri minuscoli o maiuscoli, di punti, di virgole, di parentesi; pagine di segni *allineati fitti fitti come granelli di sabbia* rappresentano lo spettacolo variopinto del mondo in una superficie sempre uguale e sempre diversa, come le dune spinte dal vento del deserto. (*Lezioni* 98; my emphasis)

> Still, all "realities" and "fantasies" can take on form only by means of *writing*, in which outwardness and innerness, the world and I, experience and fantasy, appear composed of the same verbal material. The polymorphic visions of the eyes and the spirit are contained in uniform lines of small or capital letters, periods, commas, parentheses, pages of signs, *packed as closely together as grains of sand*, representing the many-colored spectacle of the world on a surface that is always the same and always different, like dunes shifted by the desert wind. (*Six Memos* 99; my emphasis)

After reading this quotation, students usually realize how in the very first paragraph of "Memories of a Battle" Calvino is calling attention to the writing process, to the material by which memories are constructed—in other words, to the grains of sand as metaphor for the letters of the alphabet and for the linear and logic sequence implied in the act of writing and reading a text. He is trying to bring to the surface of memory a specific day, more precisely the "moments between dark and light at the dawning of that day" (*Road* 77). What is the source of the tension between dark and light? How does it relate to the writing process? Through these questions students comprehend that the representation of the past for Calvino is difficult and partial not only because of oblivion but also and above all because the memories re-created through writing and the necessary but artificial alphabetical ordering can give only an opaque, distant, and obscure vision of the past.

The author's recollection moves on to focus on the moment when a group of partisans wakes up and begins marching to fight near Baiardo. Calvino makes clear that he has no visual memories of that moment, because it was a moonless and starless night. More important, he does not want to tell the story of that morning according to a retrospective logic. For these reasons, he transforms the text into a "memory exercise" that highlights the otherness of the past and the difficulty of transforming his memory into a present focused on the writing process and the present moment:

> Molte cose dovrei ancora aggiungere per spiegare com'era questa guerra in quel luogo e in quei mesi, ma anziché risvegliare i ricordi tornerei a ricoprirli con la crosta sedimentata dei discorsi di dopo, che mettono in ordine e spiegano tutto secondo la logica della storia passata, mentre adesso ciò che voglio riportare alla luce è il momento in cui abbiamo piegato per un sentiero. (*Strada* 79)

> I would have to add all kinds of things to explain what the war was like in those months, but rather than awakening memories this would bury them again under the sedimentary crust of hindsight, the kind of reflections that put things in order and explain everything according to the logic of past history, whereas what I want to bring to light now is the moment when we struck off along a path that winds downwards around the village. (*Road* 82–83)

The reference to "now" and the immediacy of the moment of writing helps make the reader appreciate the distance between the present reality and the past experience as well as writing's inability to fully express the completeness and urge of the experience. Calvino insists on what he wants to bring to light *now*; he explains how this attempt is meant to prevent the kind of historical, retrospective, and totalizing interpretation that—filling all the gaps in his memory with narrative—would sound false. The only possible narrative has to be analogical and resort to many magnified details of the past, including the feeling of the ground under the soles of his feet, the twinges from chestnut husks and wild thistles, and so on (80; 84). With written exercises and theoretical readings on narrative and memory, I help students understand the meanings and implications of this narrative strategy. I ask them to identify and describe a similar narrative approach in Calvino's other autobiographical writings included in *The Road to San Giovanni*, such as "Dall'opaco" ("From the Opaque"). In addition, I assign to students the writing of a memory and ask them to motivate their narrative strategy along the lines of what Calvino does in "Memories of a Battle."

The experience of writing involves the emergence of philosophical questions concerning past events and calls into question the individual and historical dimensions of personal memory. Calvino remembers what he has touched, felt, or heard of, yet, instead of being interested in the content of his remembrance, he becomes fully absorbed in its process and asks himself why the broken net of memory holds some things and not others (81; 84). In this manner, the doubts of Calvino the writer meet the doubts of Calvino the partisan. The consciousness and sense of identity of the partisan gradually fade to the point of not realizing whether he wins or loses the battle. Likewise, the writer asks himself whether he is destroying or saving the past. Calvino's "Memories of a Battle" concludes by discussing the emptiness of memory and the dilatory reality of the present moment. This moment, inevitably crystallized in the writing process, is embedded in the opaqueness of memory's threads, from which at last a traumatic event can emerge: the death of a comrade named Cardù.

> Tutto quello che ho scritto fin qui mi serve a capire che di quella mattina non ricordo quasi niente, e ancora più pagine mi resterebbe da scrivere per dire la sera, la notte. La notte del morto nel paese nemico vegliato dai vivi che non sanno più chi è vivo e chi è morto. La notte di me che cerco

> nella montagna i compagni che mi dicano se ho vinto o se ho perso. La distanza che separa quella notte di allora da questa notte in cui scrivo. Il senso di tutto che appare e scompare. (*Strada* 85)

> Everything I've written so far serves to show me that I remember almost nothing of that morning now, and there would be other pages to write to tell of the evening, the night. The night of the dead man in the enemy village watched over by the living who no longer know who is living and who is dead. My own night as I search for my comrades in the mountains to have them to tell me if I have won or if I have lost. The distance that separates that night then from this night I'm writing in now. The sense of everything appearing and disappearing. (*Road* 89)

The death of a friend or comrade is an important feature of the autobiography of survivors of wartime. The survivors decide to speak and write their accounts to recall the names of the dead. Since Calvino's autobiographical perspective is focused on a subject inevitably open to the presence of the other, it confirms the ethical nature of the author's testimony and his idea of subjectivity.[4] The conclusion of "Memories of a Battle" leads the reader back to the idea presented in the opening paragraph—namely, to the writing process and the material by which memories are constructed. Calvino's final sentence reinforces the idea that the memories re-created through writing can give only an opaque vision of the past. The emphasis is on the obscurities of the two nights that merge while the author remembers the past. Thus the obscurity of the night in which he was fighting becomes the darkness of the night in which he is writing.

After students complete the textual analysis, I solicit a class discussion on memory, narrative, and writing by asking them to read a theoretical essay. The most effective and appropriate is Ricoeur's "The Reality of the Past." Calvino's "Memories of a Battle" moves from a past conceived within the sameness of the present to an idea of the past as otherness, without preventing the analogical dimension of the fictive narration. Ricoeur upholds precisely the necessity of keeping a connection among these three approaches to the past that students learn to appreciate in Calvino's autobiographical memory.

The Path to the Spiders' Nests *and the Emptiness of Form*

Students realize the importance of Calvino's reflection on memory and writing when they understand that his approach is not purely deconstructive. His ethics of writing alludes not only to the impersonal, neutral, and undecidable text as such but also to the awareness that the meaning of the text and the subjectivity involved in it are ultimately defined by the writing process. That is, the acknowledgment of the lack of foundation of literary writing does not lead Calvino to celebrate the relativism and spuriousness of a human practice founded on darkness and nothingness. On the contrary, the absence of foundations highlights both the power of writing and its weakness as two moments that are inextricably linked.

At this point it is helpful to lead students to appreciate the relevance of Calvino's reference to the notion of emptiness in Taoism. In the notes to *Six Memos for the Next Millennium*, Calvino points out the importance of the Taoist notion of emptiness as an indispensable principle of being, of everything that is (qtd. in Calvino, *Saggi* 2: 2972). Emptiness is a prominent figure in the *Tao Te Ching*, although the term is rarely used. Valuing the empty is a concept similar to valuing the submissive, an idea that signifies a desire to hold firmly to a passive way, or "[t]urning back is how the way moves" (40.88). To "turn back" means to return to one's roots, to the submissive and weak condition of childhood. The notion of turning back is also at the core of Calvino's *The Path to the Spiders' Nests* and is summarized in the Taoist principle of *wu wei* ("without action"): "The way never acts yet nothing is left undone" (37.81). This is the paradoxical idea of a "passive action" that may be more effective than what is accomplished by the strong, powerful, or wealthy.[5]

The usefulness of turning back becomes apparent for people who are struggling for survival or dealing with the extreme situations that occur during wartime. This idea came about in China during a turbulent time, when the different Chinese states were constantly engaged in wars of increasing scope and ferocity. Survival was a real and pressing problem, to which much of the wisdom of the *Tao Te Ching* was a direct response (xxvi–xxvii). In this ancient work one still finds precepts to help common human beings survive in perilous and dramatic situations. These precepts, which are ethical and political, help students understand Calvino's ethics of writing and the main idea at the core of his notions of autobiography, history, and knowledge—namely, that the writing process can recognize the complexity of human life only by acknowledging the emptiness and limits of symbolization.

Calvino was concerned with the future of literature in the technological era. At the core of *Six Memos*, he emphasizes the unique and specific role played by literature in our society:

> [L]a funzione della letteratura è la comunicazione tra ciò che è diverso in quanto è diverso, non ottundendone bensì esaltandone la differenza, *secondo la vocazione propria del linguaggio scritto*.
>
> (*Lezioni* 45; my emphasis)

> [T]he function of literature is communication between things that are different simply because they are different, not blunting but even sharpening the differences between them, *following the true bent vocation of written language*. (*Six Memos* 45; my emphasis)

His memories from the Italian Resistance do not propose any myth or antimyth. I emphasize that these memories were written not to produce a political community but to develop a higher consciousness of history. They teach us that the people from the past do not need to be remembered for the glory that they left or for the opinions they held about themselves. Only a consciousness higher and more thorough and universal than the one that was available to the people who lived those events can provide new insights on history without dissolving its complexity into a narrative of res gestae, of supposedly pure facts. Only through an ethics of writing can the human subject acquire a kind of consciousness that is not prisoner to its own assumptions and remains open to the multiple facets of a reality that cannot be reduced to any ideology. This is the fundamental lesson of *Six Memos*, which I usually have students read along with "Memories of a Battle" and Calvino's 1964 introduction to *The Path to the Spiders' Nests* (Introduzione).

The Path is his debut novel, first published in 1947, in which he recounts his war experience from the point of view of a child who conveys his inability to fully understand the violence that he experienced then. Here one can appreciate an instance of what in Taoist terms might be considered turning back. In the 1964 introduction, Calvino reveals how much the reflection on writing affected his creative process. He wanted to create a narrative deeper than ideology and admits to not having been able to reach this goal because writing "diventa subito un diaframma tra te e l'esperienza" 'becomes a partition between you and experience' (Introduzione xxiii; Preface 28). In a passage that maintains the flavor of a philosophical, Platonic meditation, he comments on the destruction of experience and its memory that occurs in writing:

> Di questa violenza che le hai fatto scrivendo, la memoria non si riavrà più: le immagini privilegiate resteranno bruciate dalla precoce promozione a motivi letterari, mentre le immagini che le hai voluto tenere in serbo, magari con la segreta intenzione di servirtene in opere future, deperiranno, perché tagliate fuori dall'integrità naturale della memoria fluida e vivente. La proiezione letteraria dove tutto è solido e fissato una volta per tutte, ha ormai occupato il campo, ha fatto sbiadire, ha schiacciato la vegetazione dei ricordi in cui la vita dell'albero e quella del filo d'erba si condizionano a vicenda. (xxiii)

> Your memory will never recover from this violence you have done it in writing: the favored images will be consumed by their premature promotion to literary themes, while the images you wanted to keep in reserve, perhaps with the secret intention of using them in future works, will wither, because they are cut off from the natural wholeness of vital, flowing memory. The literary projection, where all is solid and fixed for good, has now occupied the field, has faded and crushed the vegetation of memories where the life of the tree and that of the blade of grass are reciprocally conditioned. (24)

This reflection on writing becomes an integral part of the novel and has to be read along with it. Its tone anticipates that of "Memories of a Battle" and of the late novels. Calvino insists on the importance of the emptiness of the form, of what is left out of the creative and writing process:

> [E] tutto è lontano e nebbioso, le pagine scritte sono lì nella loro sfacciata sicurezza che so bene ingannevole, le pagine scritte già in polemica con una memoria che era ancora un fatto presente, massiccio, che pareva stabile, dato una volta per tutte, l'*esperienza*, – e non mi servono, avrei bisogno di tutto il resto, proprio di quello che lì non c'è. Un libro scritto non mi consolerà mai di ciò che ho distrutto scrivendolo. (xxiv)

> [A]nd everything is distant and misty, and the written pages are there, in their shameless confidence which I well know is fraudulent, the written pages already arguing against a moment that was still a present, which seemed stable, given once and for all, *experience*—and they are no use to me. I would need all the rest, the very things that are not there. A written book will never console me for what I destroyed writing it. (24–25)

The temporal gap between past and present is accentuated in writing. Writing leads the author to select through a sort of alphabetical logic fragments of his life. What is crucial for Calvino is not what appears in the written text but what is discarded. The privilege given to the empty spaces is justified by the fact that what is not written cannot be reduced to text. Moreover, as he emphasized in "The World Written and the World Not Written," a James Lecture given in 1983 in English at New York University, the writer realizes that the process of giving life to human subjectivity is always incomplete and partial.

"La poubelle agrée"; or, Rubbish as Autobiography

Finally, I ask students to read "La poubelle agrée" to show them how Calvino's earlier works shaped his approach to autobiography. In "La poubelle agrée," Calvino holds that writing one's autobiography is a "rito di purificazione" 'rite of purification,' the abandoning of the detritus of the self that he compares with the daily act of putting the rubbish in a pleasing garbage can approved by the community (*Strada* 97; *Road* 103). Since he wrote this text in 1974–76, when he was living in Paris, he names the garbage can in French. He concludes this text by alluding to the idea of rubbish as autobiography and of throwing away as complementary to appropriating. At the center of this reflection, there is an idea of writing: "Scrivere è dispossessarsi non meno che il buttar via, è allontanare da me" 'Writing, no less than throwing away, involves dispossession, involves pushing away from myself' (115; 125). As in his other autobiographical works, he points to the importance of emptying oneself and to the emptiness of form, thereby making the reader aware of the incompleteness and necessity of human subjectivity, which finds a constitutive element also in what is (or will be) left out from the memories of the past.

In a course such as Autobiography and History in Italo Calvino, instructors, in addition to the three texts I have introduced here, may wish to use the other "memory exercises" included in *The Road to San Giovanni*: "The Road to San Giovanni," "Autobiografia di uno spettatore" ("A Cinemagoer's Autobiography"), and "Dall'opaco" ("From the Opaque"). Other texts to include in this course would be *The Path to the Spiders' Nests* and the trilogy *I nostri antenati* (*Our Ancestors*), which includes *Il visconte dimezzato*, *Il barone rampante*, and *Il cavaliere inesistente* (*The Cloven Viscount*, *The Baron in the Trees*, and *The Nonexistent Knight*). These three fantastic short novels, although open to different interpretations, can be read in allegorical terms as Calvino's autobiography and Italy's collective biography in the years immediately following World War II. Finally, to provide a full perspective on Calvino's most important autobiographical texts, instructors can include in the syllabus *Eremita a Parigi. Pagine autobiografiche* (*Hermit in Paris: Autobiographical Writings*).

I conclude my course on Calvino by emphasizing how his autobiographical texts do not communicate any complete and final meaning but do reflect on literary discourse and the way in which meaning is produced. By meditating on the writing process, he overcomes the binary opposition between the search for an absolute meaning and the assertion of the undecidability and open-endedness of interpretation of the text. I call this strategy the ethics of writing to convey his idea that the function of literature is to communicate the distance of what is different and remains different, of what speaks of a reality that is never completely present to itself. This communication, which appears to be simply self-reflexive, senseless, without foundation and purpose, leads literature to play a crucial and distinctive role, an ethical function in human culture. Thus a great work of literature, as Calvino writes, "is a book that has never finished saying what it has to say" (*Uses* 128), a book that—even though it does not necessarily teach us anything we did not know before—becomes, when we read it, ever fresher, more unexpected, and more marvelous than we thought.

To help students develop a final reflection, I ask them to discuss Calvino's idea of the classic work of literature developed in his "Why Read the Classics?" In this essay Calvino replies to those who believe that literature does not provide any definite knowledge and therefore is not worth the effort that reading demands. He recalls an episode from Socrates's life. As the hemlock was being prepared for him, Socrates was learning a tune on the flute. "What good will it do to you?" they asked. His answer was simple: "To know this tune before dying" (*Uses* 134).[6] By referring to Socrates and to the origins of Greek and Western philosophy, Calvino makes clear that literature, like philosophy, has an important value in itself, regardless of whether it provides any positive or ultimate knowledge. Literature, like philosophy, can only allude to a kind of knowledge and truth that it does not possess but that it must seek in the ethical dimension provided by the writing process. Finally, the conclusion triggered by students' reflections on "Why Read the Classics?" is that Calvino himself is a classic of our time.

NOTES

[1] According to Lao-tzu's *Tao Te Ching*, when we, as human beings, fashion clay into vessels, we focus on the vessels as final products, as artifacts of use and importance (11.27). By so doing, we tend to forget that the use of the vase depends on its hollowness, emptiness, or bareness. Such traits do not imply nihilism but do have crucial ethical implications in Taoism.

[2] Often there is little or no time to focus on this secondary material, since the close and direct reading of Calvino's texts, along with class discussions, takes most of the time available in a term.

[3] Calvino chose this name to pay homage to the suburb of La Havana, Cuba, where he was born in 1923. In the battle of Baiardo he was part of a detachment of partisans belonging to the division of the Garibaldi Brigade called Felice Cascione. Calvino recalls Gino and Olmo, the commanders of these military units, in "Memories of a Battle."

[4] In my course Literature and Testimony, I read Calvino's wartime memories along with the testimonies of Primo Levi and other survivors of the Shoah. See Lollini for a study of the theoretical implications of this ethical view on autobiography.

[5] The classic example of the pine and the willow in heavy snow helps students understand this paradox: the pine branch, being rigid, cracks under the weight of the snow, but the willow branch yields to the weight, and the snow drops off (Watts 76).

[6] This episode is quoted by Calvino from Émile Cioran. The English translation misunderstands Socrates's answer by maintaining that it is part of the question. The original reads: "Mentre veniva preparata la cicuta, Socrate stava imparando un'aria di flauto. 'A cosa ti servirà?' gli fu chiesto. 'A saper quest'aria prima di morire'" (*Saggi* 2: 1824). The English translation adds a question mark to the title of this essay that is not present in the original Italian ("Perché leggere i classici").

Readerly Expectations: Identification and Fantasy in Calvino's Experimental Fiction

Robert Rushing

I usually make no secret in class of my admiration for Italo Calvino and his writings, so, to encourage discussion and put all opinions on the table, I typically begin a lesson by talking about what there is in him to *dislike*, why students might have a hard time with his writing or find it unappealing. One has to be careful here, as always in classroom discussions, to make it clear that while there are good critical reasons for disliking a writer, some objections may apply to an individual reader ("boring" is the most common objection, "too hard" a close second) but not to readers generally. In particular, I have found that Calvino's more experimental writing (certainly *Invisible Cities* and *If on a winter's night a traveler*, as well as the "cosmicomic" stories in *Cosmicomics* and *T Zero*) can generate frustration and confusion in students, a frustration that in turn interferes with productive discussion about other issues.

I have found, for instance, that assigning *If on a winter's night a traveler* to undergraduates with no warning about its curious structure provoked a good deal of frustration, annoyance, and even anger—the feeling that they were being cheated, that they must have misunderstood something (a few students thought they had received a defective copy of the book). This response is perfectly appropriate: the reader of *If on a winter's night* is being deliberately cheated by the author. One way to address this difficulty is to turn it into an assignment. In the class session before students begin reading *If on a winter's night*, I take time to describe the unconventional structure of the novel and ask them to consider how this might interfere with our normal enjoyment of a novel. Are there other kinds of enjoyment offered as compensation? Why would an author want to interfere with our enjoyment in the first place? How is this disruption of the reader's enjoyment dealt with in the plot?

Unconventional structure is not the only reason readers might dislike Calvino. His writing is cerebral, intellectually distant, and at times mechanical, and in many works he eschews a whole series of conventions that are typical of the realist novel and form the horizon of undergraduate expectations: *Invisible Cities* is essentially bereft of plot; *If on a winter's night* relentlessly blocks the forward movement of traditional narrative; and nearly all Calvino's works (with the exception perhaps of *The Baron in the Trees*) favor flat characters over ones with psychological depth.

A series of questions about the Calvinian character type can set the stage for productive discussion: How are these flat characters like or unlike the characters of popular fiction, such as an Agatha Christie novel or the Harry Potter novels? Why would a writer deliberately generate flat characters when we normally perceive them as a flaw or weakness? What really constitutes a character in the first place? These questions are particularly well suited to a discussion of Calvino's cosmicomic stories, since one of the first things that students notice are the curious characters that populate them. In fact, the apparently trivial question of character names is almost invariably the first issue raised by students. The protagonist of the stories is Qfwfq, and most of the other characters have equally odd names: Lll, Wha, Professor Oo, and the unforgettable and especially unpronounceable Mrs. Ph(i)Nk$_0$. When the cosmicomic stories are taught, it is a challenge to get the class to agree on a convention for pronouncing these names: does one spell out the name of the protagonist each time (Q-f-w-f-q) or attempt a kind of rapid consonantal explosion (*kuhffwuhffk*)? Whatever the consensus, no solution seems to be sufficient to the guttural contortions of the name Mrs. Ph(i)Nk$_0$. There are further questions. Why would an author present his readers with such impossible consonant clusters? Why write stories that, in a very literal sense, are difficult to discuss out loud? Could Calvino not want us to discuss them? In short, are there psychoanalytic issues behind the cosmicomic stories? At this point, one could examine Calvino's satire of literary criticism in *If on a winter's night* (note that Calvino specifically targets psychoanalysis as a methodology), but one could just as easily remain with the cosmicomic stories and ask how they work to create distance—or two kinds of distance: between the author and the text and between the text and the reader.

One way to approach this distance is to suggest that Calvino's texts are rigorously depersonalizing. On the one hand, they work to erase the figure of the author, as when Calvino notes in *If on a winter's night* that the author "Italo Calvino" lacks an "inconfondibile accento" 'unmistakable accent' and generally posits the author as an unreachable figure who is not responsible for the text the reader enjoys anyway (9; my trans.). On the other hand, his narratives interpose a series of structures that interfere with the reader's enjoyment. So I ask my students what depersonalizing strategies are at work in the cosmicomic stories. They are usually quick to point out the names that resemble mathematical formulas and the absurd scenarios that are quite impersonal, even inhuman. Examples in *Cosmicomics* are Qfwfq as an infinitely small mathematical singularity in "All at One Point," as a dinosaur in "The Dinosaurs," and as a mollusk in "The Spiral." Often students will use the word "identify," as in, "I couldn't really identify with this story" or "How am I supposed to identify with a dinosaur?" It is helpful to remind them that identification is precisely what is at stake here. Often a brief explanation of *identification* will provoke them to recognize other ways that Calvino resists reader identification. The scientific premise for each story suggests that the stakes are impersonal or that the individual is transcended. Qfwfq is inconsistent, claiming, for instance, to have been present at the birth of the moon on more than one occasion—and it is a completely different story each time.

In the context of the traditions and conventions of Western literature, it becomes apparent that Calvino is taking the idea of the character developed by previous writers and the convention of identification developed by previous readers and detonating both. One can speculate whether this detonating reflects modernist alienation or postmodern skepticism toward metanarratives. In a close-reading context (say, a small seminar), however, it is convenient to wait until we have fully established the ways that the cosmicomic stories resist identification and then ask, What's so great about identification, anyway? This moment is often revelatory, since even students who most object to Calvino's impersonality are also able to articulate good critiques of identification in literature. The ploy of identification is fundamentally deceptive, since readers find themselves assuming the guise of a fictional character who is, after all, not any reader and may even be radically unlike any reader. The reaction can be ideologically charged if readers are encouraged to identify with characters who represent ideological positions alien to them. Or the identificatory scenario can be criticized as unrealistic, because it encourages a fantasy relation to literature through a series of ideal characters. Most students have no trouble hypothesizing about social and economic motivations for Calvino's depersonalized, anti-identificatory view. In short, the traditional postmodern suggestion that "we just can't believe in it anymore" can lead to a discussion about alienation and atomization in contemporary society.

At this point in the discussion, if not earlier, students will object (or the instructor should) that they have understood Calvino in exactly the opposite sense. Take the question of character names in the cosmicomic stories. The point of these abstract and mathematical names is to offer an identity equally open to all readers—men, women, readers from different linguistic traditions, and so on. Far from a detonation of the traditional Western convention about deeply drawn, complex, and individual characters, this identity is the ultimate version of the everyman that students learned about in high school English, the character with whom anyone can identify. Could the whole point of the contrast between the cold and impersonal scientific introduction and the story that follows be precisely Calvino's insisting on the possibility of personalizing our impersonal, alienated world? After all, in *Cosmicomics* Calvino manages to tell humorous stories about such topics as the big bang ("All at One Point") and Einstein's understanding of the deformation of space-time by mass ("The Form of Space"). A sustained examination of the stories can demonstrate that they return again and again to topics that are decidedly personal, even if Calvino prefers to deal with them abstractly or in a formulaic key that highlights topics such as desire, loss, rivalry, and love. Just as every erotic attraction in *If on a winter's night* reveals itself to belong to a romantic triangle, the cosmicomic stories return obsessively to the same structure of male subject or spectator (Qfwfq), female object of desire, and male rival (e.g., "All at One Point," "The Distance of the Moon," "The Form of Space," "The Dinosaurs," and "The Aquatic Uncle"). Likewise, there is an obsessive insistence on loss and grief, as if Calvino could not help greeting every new world, each new order in the universe, with a sense of regret for everything that was lost along the way. Desire, jealousy, loss, nostalgia—all these qualities speak of personal, easily identifiable traits.

It is useful to leave this contradiction unresolved. One should emphasize, however, that issues of impersonality are important because they exert a powerful conditioning effect on both ordinary readers (who typically prefer their literature with personality and identification left intact) and critics. Calvino worked hard to cultivate the image of a coolly detached observer dedicated to Enlightenment rationality and science. This image is reinforced by his constant use of irony and playful self-effacement (as in *If on a winter's night*). His personality—or, rather, his apparent lack of personality—has colored the criticism of his work, leading particularly to a dearth of psychoanalytic approaches. Yet the assumption of the cool, impersonal, and rational author overlooks the way that he returns repeatedly to the same decidedly personal and psychoanalytically charged topics, especially those of desire and loss. This conditioning effect has ramifications in the classroom as well.

There is another element in Calvino's writings, however, that affects how we read them. Most of his work bears the mark of the fantastic: the animated suit of armor in *The Nonexistent Knight*, cities suspended on spiderwebs in *Invisible Cities*, or the science fiction stories of *Cosmicomics* and *T Zero*. Critics have typically counterpoised this tendency to his realism, often in his works that demonstrate a clear political engagement (e.g., *The Path to the Spiders' Nests* or *Marcovaldo*). This opposition has been particularly true in Italy, where Calvino's supposed turn from realism to fantasy was generally regarded with suspicion or disapproval—the turn away from realism seen as tantamount to political disengagement. Here one might ask students what the function of fantasy in literature is: Why do authors make use of the fantastic? Does Calvino use it for the same reasons? Should we disapprove of the expression of wish fulfillment in literature, as we tend to do in the real world?

The disapproval of fantasy stems from a conception of it as wish fulfillment or escapism. American students, despite their generally pragmatic character, tend to view escapism as a positive value in literature. When asked why we read literature, they often stress its value as entertainment, a relief from the pressures of the real world. It is not too early to show how this discussion of fantasy and realism is related to the questions of identification and character discussed earlier: both identification and the traditional understanding of fantasy as wish fulfillment work to encourage readers to lose themselves in the text. The Slovenian psychoanalytic theorist Slavoj Žižek suggests a definition of fantasy that might allow us to understand its role in literature in a different light, working against a notion of fantasy as fundamentally escapist. He writes:

> Fantasy is usually conceived as a scenario that realizes the subject's desire. This elementary definition is quite adequate, on condition that we take it *literally*: what the fantasy stages is not a scene in which our desire is fulfilled, fully satisfied, but on the contrary, a scene that realizes, stages, the desire as such. The fundamental point of psychoanalysis is that

> desire is not something given in advance, but something that has to be constructed—and it is precisely the role of fantasy to give the coordinates of the subject's desire, to specify its object, to locate the position the subject assumes in it. It is only through fantasy that the subject is constituted as desiring: *through fantasy, we learn how to desire.* (6)

In class, I offer the introductory chapter of Žižek's *Looking Awry* (3–20), especially the section entitled "Goal and Aim in Fantasy" (6–8), to read along with some of the cosmicomic stories. This selection is particularly pertinent because Žižek makes his point about fantasy largely through a reading of science fiction, and his manic energy and sense of humor make him appealing, if not entirely comprehensible, to undergraduates. How can we understand these stories not as wish-fulfillment fantasies but as fantasies in Žižek's sense—stories that stage desire, that teach us desire? "All at One Point" depicts the universe before the big bang, saturated by desire (all the characters appear to be equally enamored of the sensual and maternal Mrs. Ph(i)Nk_0), a universe in which, in a far cry from wish fulfillment, desire appears to be predicated on the inaccessibility of the object of desire. Because the whole universe is still just an infinitesimal dot, in which all the characters are not only touching but copenetrating one another, Mrs. Ph(i)Nk_0 is both absolutely open to all the male characters who love her and totally off-limits, because, as an infinitely small point, she cannot be penetrated. The only way to resolve this impossible scenario is with the birth of normal space—but space means distance, and the moment the universe begins, Mrs. Ph(i)Nk_0 is lost. This loss might seem like a contingent accident (that is, she could also have been not lost), but it happens so consistently in *Cosmicomics* ("Without Colors," "The Origin of the Birds," "The Aquatic Uncle," "The Distance of the Moon") that it begins to appear as a formal rule. This sort of exercise is ideal for group work: I assign each group a story and the task of reporting on how it describes desire or, to use Žižek's language, how it "[gives] the coordinates of the subject's desire, [specifies] its object, [and locates] the position the subject assumes in it."

Can students link this notion of fantasy to the earlier discussion of Calvino's impersonality? After exploring the various ways in which the cosmicomic stories describe and construct desire, can one understand better why Calvino might want to reject conventional ways that readers identify with characters? In short, identification is already a kind of wish fulfillment, something that obscures the mechanisms of desire. After all, identification allows a text to construct the reader's desire, determine its coordinates, and specify its object, without the reader's being aware of it. This is the basic structure of the fetish: students know very well that their desire is being manipulated, that its operations are being obscured, but, all the same, they prefer such realist narratives. Perhaps it is precisely through Calvino's explorations of desire, then, that we can learn about our own desires, particularly as readers.

Reading Calvino's Women

Carol Lazzaro-Weis

Feminist literary theory arose alongside a feminist politics that privileged women's voices and was committed to theorizing and seeking to resolve women's subservient social position. While some feminist critics studied male writers' canonical works to unveil strategies of oppression in the patriarchal narrative of femininity, others asserted a countercanon of women's writings, giving rise to debates over whether women wrote to subvert the canon or to speak exclusively to one another. Both critical stances claimed to produce new insights into the reading of literature that were related to politics and dedicated to producing social change.

Although the success of the political goals of feminist literary theory is difficult to assess accurately, feminist literary critics have certainly produced changes in the literary canon. Hostile resistance—typified by Harold Bloom, who feared that the countercanon identified by feminist literary criticism threatened Western civilization—has not entirely disappeared, although it has abated (Rooney 74). Feminist literary theory joined with other new critical methodologies and literary movements, such as poststructuralism and postmodernism, to question the possibility of neutrality and truth in literature and to examine the relation of ideology to representation. Ideology, according to Louis Althusser, is a system of beliefs that determines all representations of the real and the imaginary and reveals itself through society's discursive and cultural practices. Although powerful and unavoidable, it is not just propaganda foisted on the unsuspecting and the powerless. Our interaction with ideology is what determines our subjectivity and allows us to take our place in the world as subjects. We interpret ourselves and the world around us, but our viewpoints vary by our historical situation, our knowledge, and our divided consciousness.

My goal in class is to get undergraduate students to look at feminist theory as one of many critical tools that can be used to explicate how a text and its author participate in various literary, historical, and social contexts. Although second-wave feminism enabled feminist literary theory, students are often critical a priori of feminist theory, viewing it as an ideologically driven attempt of a radical, self-serving, and now outdated movement. For them, reading as a feminist means reading through a narrow optic that looks for ways to attack men and the male writer. To put to rest the uninteresting question they think we will be answering, "Can a women write or think like a man?," I quote Berthold Schoene-Harwood, who, like Judith Butler, describes the process by which we acquire an identity in language as "impersonation." Writing and reading as a male are not determined by gender; rather, they derive from a rhetorical performance, and individual impersonations of masculinity are "precarious, tragically unstable and ultimately detrimental identity constructs that, instead of conducing to a man's quest for autonomous self-identification, rigidly circumscribe it" (Schoene-Harwood 4). I emphasize that we will be reading texts not to determine if or how novels distort or reflect the biological differences between the sexes but to discover the strategies by which the text produces forms of masculinity and femininity for the characters and for their readers. And since these strategies interact with historical and literary contexts, we learn to read these subtexts as well.

I include Calvino in a course that deals primarily with Italian women writers and their use of diverse genres to express their individual and communal protests and desires. By reading Calvino, we can begin the discussion of what it means to write as a male or female and to qualify the functions of the social, cultural, and literary limitations placed on the writer. Our focus is the effect of genre on gender. We read portions of *The Path to the Spiders' Nests* and explore its relation to the historical literary movement neorealism. Calvino's parody of Ariosto's romance *Orlando furioso* in *The Nonexistent Knight* breaks from postwar neorealism. These works introduce students to the genres of epic, romance, folktale, and the neorealist novel in their Italian context.

Calvino is one of the few Italian writers after Dante, Petrarch, and Boccaccio to receive international renown and acclaim. His works, all of which have been translated into English, are taught in comparative literature classes and address narrative structure, genre, and pleasure and desire in reading—universal themes for the universal reader. At the same time, however, his writings derive from Italy's literary traditions and from debates on the value and status of writing. For him, literature should enable readers to understand their place in history, and most of his works can be linked to the political movement they allegorize. *The Cloven Viscount*, for example, symbolizes divided Germany, and *The Baron in the Trees* and *The Nonexistent Knight* reflect Calvino's concern as an intellectual with his relation to the Italian Communist Party in the 1950s. Characterization is strongly influenced by myth and caricature; characters are usually divided in their desires if not their physical selves, as they are in *The Cloven Viscount*, where the divided self functions as a trope for the divisions in Calvino and his authorial self. The folktale had an enormous influence on his production, and its structure permits him to effect specific social critiques and explore the general human condition (see Benson). Calvino has also written extensively on the use and meaning of literature. Literature produces rather than reflects knowledge in a complex interplay between reader and writer and in the storyteller's use of finite forms in infinite variations. The Calvinian paradox operates like the paradox of Zeno, the mathematician who set out to disprove spatial finitude. Calvino, in the introduction to his *Italian Folktales*, reaffirms the power of the aesthetic over "committed" literature to critique real society as well as the storyteller's presence and importance in the narrative:

> [T]he storyteller, with a kind of instinctive skillfulness, shies away from the constraints of popular tradition, from the unwritten law that the common

> people are capable only of repeating trite themes without ever actually "creating." Perhaps the narrator thinks he is producing only variations on a theme, whereas he actually ends up telling us what is in his heart. (xxxi)

Although *The Path to the Spiders' Nests* and *The Nonexistent Knight* predate second-wave feminism and the birth of feminist theory, they introduce the various issues we will take up later. Calvino began writing in a tradition influenced by Marxist views of literature as a direct representation of a specific ideology by a committed writer, stricter Marxist views of literature than those espoused by Althusser and Pierre Macherey.

Many considered his partisan saga, *The Path to the Spiders' Nests*, the classic of a new genre that represented the people of the Italian postwar republic. I have my students read the chapter focusing on the character Kim, the commander of the partisan brigade, a chapter Calvino claims to have inserted to make sure he was conforming to political neorealism's ideology, and ask them to discern its ideological components and to compare its aesthetic structure with those in other chapters. The novel's realism is heavily structured by the influence of writers such as Charles Dickens and Robert Louis Stevenson. But *The Path to the Spiders' Nest* also includes many of the folktale motifs found in the rest of Calvino's writings. Seen through the eyes of Pin, an adolescent searching for companionship, the partisan saga foregrounds the themes of alienation, nature, and maturity. The depictions of the partisans are far from heroic. They reflect Calvino's malaise concerning the role of the intellectual and writer—as well as the role of literature—in the new consumer society. Through this debunking of the myth of heroism, Calvino also calls into question the value of fiction when it is read or written as a direct representation of the real.

We also discuss here representations of women, invariably a secondary theme for most students, who prefer to identify with Pin and his archetypal search for integration into society. Students quickly become aware that women are depicted as dangerous, incomprehensible, and destructive figures who need to be eliminated, like the destructive goddess figures on whom they are modeled. Calvino follows models found in other contemporary Italian writers, such as Alberto Moravia and Cesare Pavese, who also portray women grotesquely. Women are part of nature, but on a lower level (like the frogs they are usually compared with), and are dangerous to mankind. These negative portraits are an essential part of Pin's *Bildung* and Calvino's depiction of the impossibility of heroism in Italian life. But they are also literary: fairy-tale motifs and functions such as the absence of parents, appearance of helpers, and magical spaces define women's roles and their actions. Martin McLaughlin, among other critics, classifies this work as a "small-scale" epic, since epics are stories of "le Donne, i cavalieri, le armi, gli amori" 'Women, knights, arms, and loves' (31). After we isolate several themes and characters from the two literary genres, we discuss Calvino's own disappointment with his first work, voiced in his 1967 preface to the novel.

Here Calvino apologizes for his exaggerated depictions of sex, violence, political ideology, and stereotypical characters, which he attributes to overdoses of realism and ideology, and writes that he wants now to represent "rounded adult characters [and] genuine female characters" (qtd. in McLaughlin 34).

His fantastic trilogy indeed shows that he preferred structuralist to Marxist theory and that he never accepted the reduction of literature to a finite number of functions, themes, and motifs that produced unchanging meanings. He also was a critic of the neo-avant-garde movement in Italy that proposed to demystify bourgeois literature with obscure experimental texts. Second-wave Italian feminist writing arose in reaction to this movement, embracing the confessional mode to give a direct representation of reality. The neo-avant-garde did not believe that literary discourse was capable of generating or uncovering values (Re 125), whereas Calvino, while refusing a paternalistic approach, thought literature should serve as a model for the production and transference of meaning. In many of his works, characters as readers have complex relationships with the storyteller. They often challenge him in ways to test or negate his reliability.

The Calvinian paradox is often fueled by a love triangle, and Calvino writes in *If on a winter's night a traveler*, "there is no novelistic discourse without a Female Third Person" (141). What, then, is the role of women in the paradox? As Marilyn Schneider notes, the erotic male-female relationship "functions to elaborate a quest for wholeness rather than to develop a love story" ("Calvino's Erotic Metaphor" 94). Key to Calvino's depiction of man's frustrated and frustrating search for wholeness is the depiction of women in the long tradition of negative stereotypes. Calvino's erotic male-female relationship allegorizes the elemental life forces of male and female as opposing forces of inorganic (male) matter and (female) nature (94). Male characters, authors, and readers in his texts try endlessly to satisfy women's desires as a way to make themselves whole. Herein lies the rub. Calvino's archetypal woman can be read as reified desire (male lack) or a means to effect a criticism of male or society's fantasies. His thematic of "travel as quest without attainment" is replayed endlessly in stories of missed encounters between male and female (de Lauretis, "Calvino" 70). Teresa de Lauretis, in her well-known essay on *If on a winter's night*, writes as an angry feminist and purports to reveal Calvino's game. In his highly experimental text, she writes, a male reader pursues a female reader by endlessly trying to find the book she wants to read. Although most male critics are in agreement that the woman is running the show here, de Lauretis sees the work as the ultimate expression of postmodernism's manipulation of woman as merely a function and a repeat of "the absent Woman, the one pursued in dreams and found only in memory or in fiction, that serves as a guarantee of masculinity, anchoring male identity and supporting man's creativity and self-representation. Similar to Flaubert's declaration Madame Bovary c'est moi" (82). De Lauretis argues that Calvino's woman reader is passive and has no interest in writing, thus the authorial function, however questioned, must and will remain male.

Not all critics would agree with de Lauretis's well-argued attack on Calvino's woman. Angela Jeannet attempts a more complete view of the feminine in Calvino. If most critics concentrate on the Amazon and the reader in Calvino, she introduces the "bambina," the mysterious girl, like the Blue Fairy in Pinocchio, who is empowered because she can protect her own space (159). Yet despite her different reading, Jeannet agrees in content, if not in tone, with de Lauretis. Calvino was a critical but still faithful heir of portraits of women in the Italian literary tradition, and his women embody men's awareness of their vulnerability—their desire for tenderness—and thus evoke men's greatest anxiety. The female character is confined to unmasking the male's impotence.

As we turn to *The Nonexistent Knight*, we engage in a humorous account of Calvino's theories of the roles of writer and reader and images of the feminine. Students compare this work with *Shrek* and readily identify with Calvino's critiques of hypocrisy and the characters' search for honor and justice. Epic and romance mix with fairy tale in this parodic rewrite of Ariosto's *Orlando furioso* (1532). In our critical reading, we discuss scholars who have theorized romance as the expression of a universal desire. Northrop Frye argues that romance's quest and love story illustrate desire as an internal psychic force and a way of perceiving reality, the search of the libido or desiring self for fulfillment that will ease tensions resulting from the anxieties of reality (*Secular Scripture*). Adriana Cavarero claims that the myth of the universal, when unmasked, is male (49–50). I also introduce students to the situation of Italian women writers in the Renaissance, as well as that of Ariosto, using the series editors' introduction to the University of Chicago–University of Toronto series The Other Voice in Early Modern Europe (King and Rabil).

As "the fullest embodiment of the authorial persona in Calvino's fiction," the character Bradamante stands alone in Calvino's work (Schneider, "Calvino's Erotic Metaphor" 97). She is ostensibly his parody of Ariosto's female warrior Bradamante. Valeria Finucci, in her study of women in *Orlando furioso*, deftly demonstrates how the narrative presents this empowered woman and then proceeds to domesticate her and turn her into the least threatening and most marriageable of all women. The construction of femininity in Bradamante is a long process; Ariosto gradually assigns her the proper feminine characteristics, putting an end to her masquerading as a man and her ability to defeat men and molding her to take her place as the beginning of a new dynasty, the Este family at Ferrara, for whom he wrote this foundational myth. Bradamante comes to display beauty, femininity, powerlessness, and emotionalism (*Lady* 240). She also learns to read the tapestry that appears at the end of *Orlando furioso* and replaces the design on another woman warrior's shield. The moral of this ekphrasis is that women need to control their emotions to take their proper place in society (250–53).

Moderata Fonte's *Floridoro: A Chivalric Romance* (1581) is an answer to Ariosto's romance. Fonte, the author of several polemical works on women's role in society, all part of the long-enduring *querelle des femmes*, wrote *Floridoro* as an original tale for the new dynastic union of Florence and Venice. She dedicated her work to Francesco de' Medici, who had just married the Venetian beauty Bianca Capello. Ariosto's romance was written in the turbulent period of the late Italian Renaissance. Calvino's romance is also written at a time when "world conditions were still confused" (Finucci, *Lady* 33). Most important here for our purposes, Fonte's youthful work and the commentaries on it have significant parallels with Calvino's work. *The Nonexistent Knight*, however, is not a foundational epic for a noble family but the story of modern man's desire to refashion himself as a unified social being, a desire that is mediated by a series of quests for the desired woman. We learn at the beginning of the chapter 4 that a nun named Teodora is writing the story. Although Calvino may have chosen a woman as his storyteller simply to conform to folktale convention, having a woman write the story can function for us as a way to test not only the universality of the text but also ourselves as readers.

Teodora claims writing is hard because she is a woman. How is she to describe certain events like love and war when, as a secluded nun, she has no firsthand experience of such things? Fonte's contemporaries criticized Italian women writers for their inability to "universalize" their experiences, however authentic and touching, and dismissed their writings as derivative and incomplete—and certainly not literature. Teodora tells us her only experience with knights was when they raided convents for booty, and she is not writing about those incidents. She breaks her writer's block by calling on her experience, however limited, of serving men meals to produce a series of stylized portraits of the miles gloriosus in literature. She frets over how she will get all these characters separated and then reunited, using the reversals expected in romance. Thus she consults maps and reads other stories so as not to insult the reader's intelligence. She is both a writer and reader of literary traditions, including the one she claims keeps her writing: her quest (and desire) to be rescued by a knight, since she is getting bored with the contemplative life. Eventually Teodora writes Agilulf out of the book and brings Raimbaut to rescue her, and we find out that the woman warrior Bradamante and the author-nun Teodora are one and the same.[1]

Both Fonte's and Calvino's narratives have a women writer at the helm who writes men in and out of her narrative of desire. Fonte's has twin and contrasting heroines. The female warrior, here named Risamante, has an identical twin sister, Biondura, the damsel in distress whom knights fight to save. But neither woman, unlike the women in Ariosto, inflicts disorder in the narrative and needs to be tamed. Instead, as Finucci points out, Fonte's women have agency and are never reduced to being simply exchangeable commodities in the marriage marketplace ("Moderata Fonte" 11).

Calvino follows a tradition of female-authored chivalric romances as a result of his belief in literature's paradoxes. The main character in his story originally is Agilulf, a nonexistent knight who is only the armor he inhabits. He exists through sheer willpower and represents, in McLaughlin's terms, "organization-man in consumer society" (44), the man who believes that following the rules will ensure his stable and complete identity. Agilulf is mind over matter; he is directly contrasted not to a natural woman but to his alter ego, Gurduloo, who is so natural he keeps mistaking himself for all matter. Eating is difficult for Gurduloo, who cannot determine what should be eaten or who should be eating, and for Agilulf, who has to fake hunger as well as most natural desires. The other knights do not question Agilulf's strong identity, mysterious to all but himself, since he performed the task needed to enter the knighthood when he saved the virginity of Sophronia, the daughter of the King of Scotland. But when another young knight, Torrismundo, claims Sophronia is his mother, Agilulf and Torrismundo embark on a quest to find her. Their quest begins with a hilarious reversal of Boccaccio's story of Alibech, the hermit who seduces a naive young woman by renaming the devil and hell according to the male and female anatomical parts. To serve God, they need to put the devil in hell at every possible opportunity. Eventually the hermit, whose diet consists of various herbs, can no longer keep up with the lady's "religious" desires. In contrast, Agilulf convinces the sensual Priscilla—a medieval Circe who, by faking to be a damsel in distress, seduces errant knights and then reduces them to beggars—that they are having a sexual encounter unlike any other since it is based on unrequited desire and a lot of imagination.[2]

Agilulf is the first love of Bradamante, the periwinkle knight, who has saved Raimbaut in battle. Thrown from his horse, "Raimbaut must now die now that he knows the world exists" (*Nonexistent Knight* 43), but being saved by another knight allows him to postpone this moment. Discovering that Bradamante is a woman gives Raimbaut a reason to continue living. His quest to avenge his father is replaced by his quest for Bradamante's love. Yet Bradamante falls in love only with men who do not want her, for "if a man followed her in utter abandon, lost his self-control, she at once fell out of love or went searching for a temperament more adamantine" (63).

Calvino's divided selves derive as much from existentialism as they do from theories of the postmodern. In *Le deuxième sexe* (*The Second Sex*), Simone de Beauvoir applies existentialist philosophy to the situation of women and finds that both existence and essence are denied to women. Her novel *Tous les hommes sont mortels* (*All Men Are Mortal*), published two years before *Le deuxième sexe* and dedicated to Jean-Paul Sartre, attempts to put existentialist theory into critical action and to function as an eye-opener for writers, readers, and critics. It recounts the story of the doomed searches for wholeness and immortality of two narcissists: Fosca, who drinks a potion in an Italian town during the Renaissance wars to become immortal and change the world, and the actress Regine, whom he meets in the twentieth century and who is determined to make him love her so she too can become immortal. When Bradamante challenges Raimbaut to an archery competition, it almost seems as if Beauvoir is writing:

> Thus does a young man always hurry towards his woman? But is he truly urged by love of her and not by love of himself? Isn't he looking for a certainty of existing that only a woman can give him? A young man hurries, falls in love, is uncertain of himself, happy, desperate, and for him his woman is the person who certainly exists, oh which only she can give proof. But the woman too either exists or not. There she is before him, also trembling and uncertain. How is it the young man does not understand that? What does it matter which of the two is strong and which is weak? They are equals. But that the young man does not know, because he doesn't want to. What he yearns for is a woman who exists, a woman who is definite. She on the other hand, knows more things, or less, anyway things that are different. What she is in search of is a different way of existing. (64)

Falling in and out of love and desiring a different way of existing are not the only problems Teodora, Beauvoir, and the Italian women writers we will study have in common. Teodora and Fonte find writing and its stereotypes difficult. As for Teodora's alter ego, Bradamante, writing is not the transference of knowledge but an ongoing search for its production: "So of love as of war I shall give a picture as best as I can imagine it. The art of writing tales consists in an ability to draw the rest of life from the nothing one has understood of it, but life begins again at the end of the page when one realizes that one knew nothing whatsoever" (6). Language is not just a communicative tool but also a symbolic system that structures and gives meaning to the cultural and individual imagination.

My students are now ready to read as well as write as informed gendered subjects. Calvino's women introduce us to the Italian literary tradition against or in which Italian women writers situate themselves. We can determine differences in their writings depending on what lack or desire the woman writer aims to represent or fill or what situation, public or private, she wishes to decipher. Like Teodora/Bradamante, students are divided into reading and writing selves. In Calvinian fiction this division is often expressed in terms of the opposition between the active and contemplative life. And like these writing women, students are not being asked to choose but to insist on following all roads to knowledge. As Bradamante says when she gallops off with her new love, "Sometimes I gallop over battlefields after adventures of duels and loves, sometimes I shut myself up in a convent, editing and jotting down the adventures that have happened to me, so as to try and understand them" (140).

NOTES

[1] Fonte's uncle, the Venetian historian Nicolò Doglioni, expresses his wonder that his niece, "this inexpert young woman (*verginella*) enclosed within constricting walls [Fonte had originally only a convent education] sings perfectly of all of the above to the amazement of those around her and of nature itself" (qtd. in Finucci, "Moderata Fonte" 1).

[2] But if Agilulf dupes Priscilla from taking his imaginary manhood, he literally disintegrates when, after saving Sophronia from the Muslim sultan who abducted her, she loses her virginity to Torrismundo after they find out they are not related.

CLASSROOM CONTEXTS

Why Read Calvino? What We Tell Our Italian Language and Literature Students

Natasha V. Chang

This essay, directed at those who teach Calvino in Italian at the undergraduate level, shows how Calvino's metafictional work can help instructors achieve two common goals of upper-level Italian courses: familiarizing students with the academic discipline of literary studies and refining language skills. As teachers of literary texts in their original language, we often struggle to integrate these competing goals. On the one hand, we want students to become familiar enough with narrative structures, literary genres, literary history, and basic literary theory that they can construct an intellectually sound critical analysis. On the other hand, we want to foster advanced reading, writing, listening, and speaking skills in the target language. Furthermore, it becomes especially difficult to reconcile such distinct goals when students—who have become increasingly pragmatic in the face of rising tuitions and employment anxieties—may very well privilege the acquisition of a language skill over what they perceive to be the less functional acquisition of the skills of literary analysis.[1]

This essay is situated at the crossroads of three disciplines: literary studies, the teaching of writing, and foreign language pedagogy. Using *Se una notte d'inverno un viaggiatore* (*If on a winter's night a traveler*) as a touchstone text, I give concrete suggestions that show how one can, and why one should, use this novel in upper-level undergraduate Italian courses to teach literary studies and advanced language skills—not as separate or contingent bodies of knowledge but as interdependent practices. I also show how literary studies and language teaching can be brought together using the pedagogical tools of teaching writing, or composition and rhetoric—that is, the methods of first-year courses in writing-across-the-curriculum programs common to many universities. Many of the principles I discuss here are relevant to teaching similarly self-reflexive texts, such as *Le città invisibili* (*Invisible Cities*) or *Le cosmicomiche* (*Cosmicomics*).

For nonnative speakers, the work of analyzing *Se una notte* in Italian transforms the normalized activities of reading and critiquing literature into an activity that is as strange, as new, as foreign as the target language itself, because the novel explicitly asks readers to think critically about linguistic and literary production. Calvino's novel is as much literary theory as literature. It shifts the object of discussion to the modalities of literary production and opens a space for the discussion of how the target language is more than a tool and how literature in the target language is more than a means of acquiring that tool: both are complicated polysemous systems that work in delightful and surprising ways.

Constructing Textual Meaning: Calvino's Critique of Convention

When students first approach this or any other novel, they bring a set of expectations to their reading without knowing it. I introduce *Se una notte* with an activity designed to make students aware of their unconscious set of narrative expectations. I provide them with a handout listing the opening sentences of five unidentified novels. After we discuss the examples, I reveal the title and author of each and briefly give a bit of background. We then talk about what these first sentences reveal about different genres and discuss the importance of the first words of a piece of writing. What might a novel called *Se una notte d'inverno un viaggiatore* be like? How might one finish the title's unfinished sentence? Who might the main characters of the novel be? Where might the novel be set? Next, I ask students to write the first paragraph of the novel, read their paragraphs aloud, and compare them with those of their peers. Finally, we read aloud the first paragraph of Calvino's novel and compare it with what the students have written.

This exercise shows students that their expectations of Calvino's text are formed from narrative conventions they have already learned. I ask them what implicit rules of narration they felt Calvino broke by directly addressing the reader, by referring to his own text, and by referring to himself. With its opening words, this novel breaks with the traditional narrative convention that most readers have naturalized, putting on display the mechanics of the literary and linguistic apparatus—in short, it belongs to the genre of metafiction.

Students speak, write, and think about the material before they have even read it, and as a consequence they confront their expectations of the text before confronting the text itself. Later, after they have completed "Capitolo primo," I ask more questions: Who is "Italo Calvino" in this text, the actual author, a fictional character, or both? Who is "tu," an ideal reader or the student? My goal is not to reach a definitive answer to these questions but to put them on the table for development in further classes. Most important, though, I tell students that this exercise points to some of the key issues that I will explore with them when reading *Se una notte* and also when reading their own writing—namely, how different words make different impressions, what effect on the reader different narrative techniques may have, and how a reader can actively engage with a text. This exercise models reading and writing as a process that entails several stages: brainstorming, drawing on past knowledge, informal writing, discussion, and reevaluation or rewriting.

When first approaching *Se una notte*, even as students begin to understand the set of narrative expectations they bring to the novel, they are often still not aware that they draw on many codes of signification to make sense of the text. Students often have a restrictive concept of what a text is, and so, in the beginning stages of reading Calvino's novel, I give them a second exercise to help them see and understand the organizing structures of the text from a visual point of view. After they read "Capitolo primo" and "Se una notte d'inverno un viaggiatore," I have them form small groups and draw a picture that recognizably depicts the levels of textual narrative, accounts for the major events of the plot, and shows the main characters. They may use any representational strategies they like, but they must show the relations among events, characters, and narrative levels of the text. Inevitably students draw on codified modes of visual representation in their work—framing, *mise en abyme*, horizontal and vertical alignment, relative size, and so forth. I use their drawings to talk about how they decode the text: Did they show themselves or Calvino in the drawing? Where do they position the real world in relation to the fictional world, and what does such a position imply? How do they represent time? What are the levels of narration represented? How do the drawings differ from one another? Using the drawings as a point of departure, I focus especially on the semiotic codes students use to produce meaning about the text and, if appropriate, draw structural connections between visual and narrative codes (such as in the figure of *mise en abyme*). I then turn that language back to the text and, eventually, to their own writing.

These initial exercises lay the foundation for a poststructuralist exploration of *Se una notte*. Selections from Umberto Eco's writing on the "open work" (*Opera aperta*) provide an especially productive gloss on this novel, but I do not introduce them until after students have written their first formal paper, to encourage them to develop an autonomous critique, independent of what they will view as an authoritative critical text. If Eco's writing can be seen as a type of reader-response theory, then we must also think of the author. To this end, Roland Barthes's essay "The Death of the Author" and Michel Foucault's

"What Is an Author?" are also useful to read with *Se una notte*. But working through such articles may not be necessary, since Calvino's text enables students to grapple with many of the same questions presented in such theoretical writing. Ultimately, as a literary text that raises questions from within about its function and status as literature, *Se una notte* not only prepares students for the often counterintuitive leap necessary for studying literary theory later on but also provides them with a literary context for serious critical inquiry.

Making Meaning as a Writer: How Good Readers Make Good Writers

The first formal paper I assign links the acts of reading and writing in the foreign language and shows students that good readers are more often than not good writers. Addressing the question of textual authority in Calvino's novel, the assignment asks students to argue that either the reader or the author is empowered in the text. I usually assign this paper as they are reading "Capitolo quarto" and "Senza temere il vento e la vertigine" and ask them to use and synthesize the issues we have brought up in class discussion. Through writing in Italian about *Se una notte*, the interdependence of language learning and literary studies is apparent. On a practical level, there is a clear homology between the types of questions that students must address when reading and the types of questions that they must address when writing. As they write their essay, I ask them to think about word choice, about the effects and effectiveness of their argument, about the meaning implicit in a sentence, and about their own critical bias. It is essential to reinforce this homology in class through a rigorous, sentence-level discursive analysis of the literary text. Take, for example, the following sentences from the opening of "Capitolo terzo":

> I piaceri che riserva l'uso del taglia carte sono tattili, auditivi, visivi e sopratutto mentali. L'avanzata nella lettura è preceduta da un gesto che attraversa la solidità materiale del libro per permetterti l'accesso alla sua sostanza incorporea. Penetrando dal basso tra le pagine, la lama risale d'impeto aprendo il taglio verticale. . . . (47)
>
> The pleasures derived from the use of a paper knife are tactile, auditory, visual, and especially mental. Progress in reading is preceded by an act that traverses the material solidity of the book to allow you access to its incorporeal substance. Penetrating among the pages from below, the blade vehemently moves upward. . . . (*If on a winter's night* 42)

A close reading of this passage opens the question of the gendered metaphors that dominate Calvino's text. A parsing of the text will bring to light topics such as the problematic relation between the principal reader as a male reader and the text as a female body, or the differences between *il lettore* and *la lettrice* as types of readers (see de Lauretis, "Calvino"). Students can apply these same close-reading skills to their own writing and can question, for example, the extent to which they draw on gendered metaphors or other narrative techniques.

Because this first paper topic generates an oppositional set of theses, debate is the most useful postwriting activity. I divide students into two teams according to the position they took in their paper, either pro-author or pro-reader. They read and discuss the papers of their team members beforehand and then support their positions during the debate using arguments and information from their peers' papers as well as from their own work. After the debate, they talk about whether (and how) hearing the arguments of the other side influenced their thinking. This paper assignment and subsequent debate construct a false binary (author/reader) that students can later deconstruct as they put their voices together, as they hear contrasting opinions, and as it becomes evident that there is neither a clear right nor a clear wrong answer to the questions they have posed in the reading and writing process.

But it is not only that good readers make good writers—good writers make good readers. My second formal writing assignment builds on the first and strives to take students' reading of the text to another level by pointing out the ideological implications of Calvino's critique of narrative convention. This second essay asks students to consider how—in blurring the line between fiction and criticism and in critiquing narrative convention—literary criticism emerges as a focal point of the narrative. They must go beyond their understanding of Calvino's critique of narrative convention as pro-author or pro-reader and point out the ways in which the text dismantles the traditional ideas of both author and reader.

The second writing assignment once again reinforces the interdependence of writing and reading in the target language through the link of critical thinking. For students, writing, but not necessarily reading, involves critical thinking. In fact, most will tell you that the pleasure of the text depends on how entertaining it is. But in Calvino's text, the pleasure lies in thinking critically, for this is not a text that is easily digested. To write well, students will have to read well, and they will have to find a way to negotiate their difficulty in comprehending the text. Like the first assignment, the second should be written in stages, but this time I ask students to critique one another's writing through peer review.

The third essay is half critical writing and half creative writing and is designed to point to the interconnectedness of creative and critical work that, by now, has emerged as a major theme in Calvino's novel. I ask students to write the ending of *Se una notte*, before having read it, and to include a critical explication of the narrative choices they have made. This assignment brings them full circle, returning to the same issues touched on in the very first in-class exercise. I ask students to consider the ways in which their perspective about the text and about literature as a whole has evolved: How does describing something contribute to its creation? What is the rapport between writing a text and reading it? What is the rapport between fiction and its criticism? After having completed the assignment, students read their endings aloud to the class, and their peers ask critical questions about the endings as if they were interviewing the author himself, thus facilitating a communal dialogue about students' writing in relation to Calvino's. This third essay, in addition to building on the critical issues raised in class, is one of the most enjoyable because students have the liberty to conjure up fantastical and entertaining endings and in so doing make the text their own.

Transparency and Teaching

I conclude by returning to the challenge of familiarizing students with an academic discipline while refining language skills. Advanced students are far beyond the review of grammar rules in the classroom, yet they have certainly not perfected their language skills; indeed, many who have yet to go abroad may have reached a learning plateau. It is at this point that students must stop thinking of language as a communicative tool—something that can help them find an apartment when they go abroad—and start thinking of it as a symbolic system that structures and gives meaning to cultural imagination. They must understand that the sharpening of language skills cannot be subordinated to the cognitive process or vice versa. For many, this is a difficult lesson to learn, but the learning process can be facilitated if the professor adopts a transparent pedagogical approach. When students understand why they are being asked to do something, they can apply that same reasoning to many different types of intellectual activities. *Se una notte* elucidates the modalities of literary and linguistic production and opens space for a discussion of how literature can illustrate that language works in ways they never imagined. Learning to see language as a system of signifiers and signifieds can be a liberating experience for them that gives new meaning even to nonliterary language—the language of advertisements, body gestures, and all other cultural codes both in the target culture and in their own.

So what do we tell our students when they ask us, "Why read Calvino?" First, we can tell them that *Se una notte* will allow them to see the political and ethical *impegno* ("commitment") of reading and writing. Second, because this text disrupts a series of classical binaries such as reader/author, reality/representation, and fiction/criticism, it can shake the foundations of thinking about narrative that students have been dependent on; they may begin to understand the ideological layers on which their knowledge is constructed. And, perhaps finally, we can tell them to read *Se una notte* because it is a classic, not in the traditional sense but in the sense that Calvino outlined in his definition of the term: "un libro che non ha mai finito di dire quel che ha da dire" 'a book that has never finished what it has to say' (*Perché* 13; my trans.).

NOTE

[1] Several scholars discussed the declining value of literary studies in the *PMLA* forum "Why Major in Literature—What Do We Tell Our Students?" (Berman).

Reading, Writing, Desire, and Closure: Teaching Calvino to Undergraduates in Italian

Julia M. Cozzarelli

Calvino said, "La letteratura è uno degli strumenti di autoconsapevolezza d'una società" 'Literature is one of a society's instruments of self-awareness' (*Pietra sopra* 291; *Uses* 97). Self-awareness through literature is at the heart of my approach to teaching Calvino. I focus in this essay on the use of his texts as the capstone of an upper-level undergraduate literature course taught in Italian, Nineteenth- and Twentieth-Century Italian Literature: Shifting Identities and the Voice of the Narrator. It not only explores definitions of readers, writers, and narrators but also enables students to examine their assumptions about literary forms and the desire for closure. Because the concepts of self-awareness and identity permeate all aspects of the course, I use a student-centered teaching method and also draw additional inspiration from Calvino with the infusion of a sense of play.

Nineteenth- and Twentieth-Century Italian Literature is an elective for students majoring in Italian studies, but, because of the makeup of our student body, it tends to include a large proportion of Italian minors and nonmajors. The course is primarily discussion-based and relies on a format with maximum opportunities for active learning. Course enrollment is restricted to fifteen students, and the class meets three times a week for fifty minutes. The relatively open course title allows for the inclusion of a wide range of works, but I prefer to limit the number of authors discussed and to read the works closely and in chronological order. The first part of the course incorporates several selections that fit its narrower subheading, with an emphasis on the works of Luigi Pirandello. The study of Calvino begins in the second half of the course, with a selection from *Il sentiero dei nidi di ragno* (*The Path to the Nest of Spiders*), several stories from *Le cosmicomiche* (*Cosmicomics*) and *Ti con zero* (*T Zero*), and small passages from Calvino's critical writings. *Se una notte d'inverno un viaggiatore* (*If on a winter's night a traveler*), with its encyclopedic convergence of literature and theory, is ideal for closing the course, and we read it in its entirety. Calvino's works are well received by students, and the activities and methods described here could easily be adapted to a monographic course on the author.

My strategy is to guide students to discover through practice what they often perceive as abstract theory in lecture. While each class incorporates minilectures on the key features of the authors, texts, and related historical periods, most of the class session is devoted to student-driven interactions and collaborative learning. This method relies in part on the physical arrangement of the classroom. Seating position cannot be fixed because students are regularly required to move from place to place. Student participation and active learning are maximized through activities such as role playing, creative writing, illustration, and performance, making open floor space a frequent requirement.

In preparation for each class session, students complete reading assignments while looking for particular concepts or patterns. Before a discussion on identity and definitions of self inspired by *Le cosmicomiche*, for example, they read the stories "Tutto in un punto" ("All at One Point") and "Senza colori" ("Without Colors"), making note of the language (or lack thereof) that the narrator Qfwfq uses to refer to himself and to his physical and emotional characteristics, as well as of how Qfwfq portrays himself in relation to others. Students write their observations for such assignments in a journal that they bring to class.

We warm up with basic questions, often personalized, that stimulate conversation and serve to check comprehension. Students may be asked to elucidate a story's setting, for instance, and then relate it to a place they remember seeing. Ironically, the unpredictability in content and structure that makes Calvino's texts a source of delight can also make them perilous for inexperienced readers, especially those who are not fluent in Italian. Thus I devote a portion of each class to overcoming linguistic insufficiencies or strengthening language skills and comprehension. In a sense, the course can be treated as being on one end of the continuum between basic language learning and traditional literary analysis; although its focus is literature, the basic principles of the language classroom still need to be applied.

After reviewing comprehension together, the class splits into small groups to discuss the topic at hand. I vary the format of the discussion questions: some require individual replies, others pair or small-group work, and still others are designed for larger groups. In the lesson following the above assignment on Qfwfq, I ask students to reflect on their individual experiences. They write a brief paragraph describing themselves and then discuss what they have written with a partner and conduct a close reading of the paragraph's language and content. When defining themselves, do they gravitate toward terms that describe their physical selves or their psychological and emotional selves? Do they define themselves by comparing or contrasting themselves with others? When did they first become aware of themselves as separate entities from those around them? The pairs or small groups are then asked to consider Calvino's narrator, using their notes from the homework assignment and then answering additional questions about Qfwfq. Where, for example, does he begin and others end? Does Qfwfq change? How does he change? How does he convey a sense of awareness? What are his desires? Does he yearn for knowledge? Finally, how do the students' self-presentations align with or diverge from that of Qfwfq's self-presentation? The students genuinely enjoy small-group or pair activities, and ultimately such activities both illustrate and evaluate the themes discussed in class.

Our discussion of *Le cosmicomiche* continues as students are asked to sketch Qfwfq using the story descriptions as a reference. This activity forces them to confront the paradox of attempting to define what the author has deliberately left undefined. It also allows a presentation of relevant topics that include reader presuppositions about the narrator and his role.

Theory can be introduced more formally in the minilectures that are woven into the fabric of each class session. This integration should appear seamless to the students and requires careful planning by the instructor and projections about the direction the discussion should take. Most class sessions conclude with an interactive exercise. Students may create their own topics for debate, expand the themes or fictional events under discussion into their own lives, find particular motifs or meanings in certain portions of the text, produce written works inspired by or extending from the selections under discussion, or even role-play, a particularly rewarding activity when done spontaneously. They can be challenged to adapt one of the tales to film, paying particular attention to the transition from literary imagery to visual and auditory imagery. Can the spirit of the original tale, including its language and tone, be maintained?

Se una notte d'inverno un viaggiatore is a particularly thought-provoking text and requires that students again examine their preconceived notions about the reading experience. Tying into the course subtitle's focus on defining identity, the novel shifts between second- and first-person narration while providing ample opportunity for students to examine their conceptions of readers, writers, and narrators. In addition, we explore two other themes through this novel: reading and its connection to desire and the expectation that literary works will have concrete and satisfying conclusions.

I first approach the role of desire in *Se una notte* by asking students to discuss the two main characters as both models of sexual desire and allegorical representations of the reading process. We then focus on the essential question of the reader's relation to literature. The desire that motivates Calvino's text is not only that of the Lettore ("Reader") and Ludmilla but also that of the living individual who is reading the novel. The use of the second-person pronoun to refer to the Lettore draws students' attention to themselves and to their act of reading. This in turn focuses attention on the boundaries between fiction and reality. In preparation for a possible discussion, students describe the Lettore while highlighting the limitations of his reading process. This assignment is then personalized by asking them to compare themselves with the model reader that they have constructed.

Students come to realize that Ludmilla and the Lettore represent two different types of reading. The Lettore is object-oriented, consumed by the desire to bring a definitive conclusion to two quests: the romantic pursuit of Ludmilla and the search for the continuation of the interrupted tales that he has encountered as a reader. Ludmilla, on the other hand, is process-oriented. She is concerned not with completing texts but with continuing the pleasurable act of reading in all its diversity and infinite potential. She is not, however, a passive reader. We come to learn that it is she who determines the events in the novel since the unseen writer follows her unspoken dictates.

Once these major categories are covered, we investigate other representations of readers and writers in *Se una notte*. Calvino defines a variety of types at the end of the novel through the words of several readers, each one representing a different version of the reader-writer paradigm. I ask students which commentary best reflects their stances as readers. Some relate to the reader who mirrors the Lettore's search for closure, lamenting that he will never find peace until he knows how an unfinished story ends. Others are drawn to the reader who questions traditional assumptions about literature, assumptions most students usually share.

The discussion of desire in *Se una notte* leads to a topic ideal for the conclusion of the course: closure. Both traditional and postmodern approaches to closure in the novel can be examined through a creative writing activity. It is useful to prepare the students by drawing attention to how Calvino's text has repeatedly instructed the Lettore (and the readers) to be aware of the dangerous trap into which he constantly stumbles. The Lettore has been drawn into the stories only to be left hungering for a finished tale he will never find. Students look carefully for the word *trappola* ("trap") and its synonyms and note their relevant contexts. One prominent example is the "romanzo-trappola" 'trap novel' referred to in chapter 6, which is created from a series of interrupted novels in translation (*Se una notte* 125; *If on a winter's night* 125).

With the thirst for a conclusion sparked likewise in the minds of my students, we embark on our class activity, an experiment in literary closure. Either in pairs or small groups the students write original endings to one of the incomplete stories in *Se una notte* and then read their stories aloud and confront the feelings that are evoked by this process. This activity is not only entertaining for the students but also remarkably effective in enhancing their understanding of the issues discussed throughout the course. It forces them to confront two complicated subjects: first, thwarted desire and the paradoxical and unsettling dissatisfaction experienced after desire attains its ultimate goal; second, the feelings aroused by the writing activity and its ability to alter the meaning of the original text.

The endings that the students write for the incomplete tales usually leave them with a sense of dissatisfaction. When asked afterward if similar endings would have improved Calvino's incipit texts, most respond with a resounding no. This reaction foreshadows their disappointment with the apparently flippant conventional ending of the novel. The readers' feelings of anticipation have been building throughout the text in a desire for closure, but the conclusion is inherently dissatisfying. This in-class writing experiment highlights, on a small scale, the ultimate trap against which Calvino has warned his readers. This trap, situated at the point where the novel's web of intersecting lines converge, is the ending itself. When the students are finally presented with a conclusion, they often realize that it was the act of reading that had been the object of their desire and not the search for an ending.

This creative writing project also causes students to reassess their definition of what constitutes a complete text and their place within that text. By attempting to fulfill their longing for a conclusion, they are left uneasy with the process and, paradoxically, more readily accept Calvino's partial stories as written. Indeed, after this reading-writing experience, students are nearly unanimous in the belief that the unfinished stories are complete as they stand. This attitude reflects a change in their perception of them from incipient novels to self-contained short stories. But that shift raises even more questions. This activity can be disconcerting: although it is enjoyable and helps enhance the themes in *Se una notte*, students begin to question whether their fictional endings might violate Calvino's original text. This awareness can spark further discussion and additional critical exploration.

The structure, style, and content of my approach to teaching Calvino are not limited to the classroom experience. The spirit of the course is carried through to the elements on which I assess students. Students are graded on participation, papers, quizzes, and a presentation. They write two formal papers for the course, usually centered on an aspect of the texts as they relate to the topics covered in class. I also assign individual creative writing projects modeled on the text. Students may be asked, for example, to choose another genre and to write the first pages of an eleventh incomplete novel for *Se una notte*. The presentation is a student-led class session, a useful and essential experience in the active learning process. The student-led classes must be in keeping with the overall style of the course: students are required to give a minilecture on a topic of their choice (discussed with the instructor in advance) and to furnish several discussion questions and creative interactive activities. In the past, students have focused on subjects ranging from related historical events to Calvino's real personal relationships and have created quizzes, questionnaires, and even puzzles for their classmates. Although the level of sophistication of the presentations may vary, they are always productive, engaging, and entertaining.

By the end of the course, students realize that they have traveled far since their first day of class. Calvino's writings have led them to reexamine themselves; their awareness of their own identities; their definitions of readers, writers, and narrators; and their former assumptions about literature. Their admiration for the author and his work, together with their realization that the act of reading can be a source of pleasure and desire, illustrates their transformation. The student response to the course is usually overwhelmingly positive, and for the instructor the experience is both edifying and rewarding.

Teaching *Il castello dei destini incrociati*: An Intuitive Approach

Rita Gagliano

Metafiction is often overlooked as possible reading material for the advanced Italian classroom, perhaps because it may be too complex for students still struggling to master the target language. Yet the introduction of such texts in upper-level courses is crucial for furthering the courses' core goals: to hone students' communicative and critical skills and their skills as readers of literature. Among the Italian writers who have popularized metafiction, Italo Calvino is the author best suited for the undergraduate classroom, since he combines a clear and precise use of the language with a complex exploration of questions of meaning. Moreover, in my experience, of all the texts I have taught in upper-level courses, those penned by Calvino receive the most attention from students, inspiring the fiercest and most beneficial debates. His writing comprises philosophical insight, apprehension, and, most often, a sense of the absurd that alternately stimulates, entertains, and openly challenges the students, forcing them to explore and reassess their expectations of the texts. Calvino's rejection of the conventions of traditional literature leads them to reassess what they might demand of the text, a first step toward critical thinking that forces them to look for patterns and motivations not only in the story but also in that virtual space beyond literature, that of intellectual inquiry. The text thus becomes a pretext for exploring and broadening students' ability to think critically about literature.

Like all works of metafiction, *Il castello dei destini incrociati* (*The Castle of Crossed Destinies*) allows a critical reading of the text that goes beyond the plot—that is, breaking with the students' tendency to invest in the characters and their stories (the who and what) and directing them instead to think critically about central issues in the study of literature (the how and why). Students learn to set aside their desire for a quick answer and spend time carefully exploring the issues at hand, never reaching a final answer but enabling a dialectical relation with the text crucial to a critical discussion. As a result they become self-aware readers as well as better writers.

In teaching *Il castello*, I move fluidly from the text to practical examples, from immediate awareness of the complex issues explored in the text to their application in the realm of the everyday. I aim to facilitate and demystify critical thinking by moving beyond the methodological restrictions of theory, instead drawing insights of critical theory, such as advances in structural linguistics and in poststructuralist theory, directly from the text. I devise class activities and assignments that lead students from intuition to analytic thinking, so they can master the text's internal workings without feeling intimidated or frustrated by its complexity. Ultimately this "intuitive leap" allows them to own the text, enjoy its particular mechanics, and, most important, learn about the potential of language (Bruner 13).

I require students not only to read the primary text but also to keep a guided reading journal, basing their entries on prereading questions that support class discussion and on broad postreading questions that stimulate further reflection on the implications of the topics discussed. Students also maintain a vocabulary list, which keeps track of the difficult words they encounter, supports vocabulary building, and encourages precision of expression in discussions of the text.[1]

The first class is a kind of brainstorming session in which students engage in a guided discussion of the title of Calvino's work as well as of the symbolic charge of the two main settings of the story: the forest and the castle. I provide them with a handout that includes brief excerpts from Dante's *Commedia*, *Il novellino*, the *Decameron*, and popular fairy tales and ask them to draw comparisons among the disparate texts. Not surprisingly, Calvino's choice of a fantastic register gives immediate access to the content of the text. A discussion on the fantastic also allows me to address basic concepts of rhetoric and reader reception. After introducing suspension of disbelief and allegory, I invite students to apply these two concepts to their reading experience of Calvino and to reflect on how their individual attitudes differed when reading fictional versus nonfictional material.

Since *Il castello* contains reproductions of the Visconti Tarot, I use the cards as props in the discussion of language as a code made up of minimal units of meaning, in keeping with my intuitive learning imperative. The cards also served as material support for the questions of creativity and meaning production that permeate the book. Such practical exercises build awareness in students who might understand a complex concept at a visceral level and are then able to explore and appreciate its nuances through guided class discussion.

To re-create the basic premise of the narration—a group of characters are rendered mute and can communicate only by way of a tarot deck—and to explore its implications, I replicate this paradoxical situation in the classroom. I divide the class in three groups and give each group a different sentence to convey to the rest of the class without using language and with the following limitations: the first group can only use pictorial representation; the second, mimicry; and the third, the tarot cards. This exercise helps students recognize how much we rely on language to communicate. It also makes them aware of the many nonverbal ways in which we can be expressive. We discuss the communicative difficulties each group encounters in its task and identify the specific potential and limitations of each method of communication. The difference between language-based and image-based messages proves especially significant.

The level of approximation needed for the message transfer makes some students uncomfortable. In moving a message from the original written format to a code made up of different signifying units, something is always left out. Students recognize that a similar gap is also implicit in the narrator's attempt to reproduce linguistically a message that is pictorial in origin. I ask them to reflect in their journal on what statement Calvino might be making about the creative process, to get them to see the problem of approximation, or issues of "implicature," inherent in interpretation (Grice, "Utterer's Meaning" 225).[2] In a follow-up exercise, I give students a short paragraph in which central words are blacked out. They must read the paragraph carefully, fill in the blanks with words they deem appropriate, and then read the resulting text. Each group's production of a different text using the same contextual clues demonstrates the importance of speaker intent and of reader interpretation and the possible discrepancy between the two.

Building on previous class activities, I give each student four tarot cards (one major arcana, one court card, and two minor arcana) and ask students to find the cards' divinatory meaning and use it, along with ideas sprung from the pictorial representation, to create a brief narrative similar to those in *Il castello*. This exercise leads them to explore further the gap, or connection, between pictorial and linguistic codes while inviting them to extrapolate the tropes and narrative patterns reproduced in their stories. Reading these stories in the next class prompts a discussion of recurring narrative patterns, such as the difference between male and female characters, the archetypes of the journey and of transgression, and betrayal.[3] Students also see that even a closed symbolic system like that of the tarots cards can be a catalyst for an infinite number of narratives.

Tarot-based exercises make possible consideration of literary interpretation and meaning production, where meaning is no longer self-evident but constructed by a subject who affects the final outcome. Such exercises also permit students to move from their pragmatic experience of reading to the abstract world of theory without sacrificing the direct understanding of complex concepts. Comparing and contrasting Ferdinand de Saussure's definition of a code and the poststructuralist responses to it lead to fierce debates on language as a closed or open code.

Il castello, like all works of metafiction, presents students with difficult and at times paradoxical issues while instilling in them new competencies. Such works may greatly contribute to their learning process, for it is the perplexity of metafiction that at once challenges and engages readers. The open-ended debates these tests inspire on such topics as creativity, meaning production, and interpretation are central to the study of literature. Though the open-endedness of these texts initially frustrates students' desire to find a fixed and sensible meaning, discussions regarding precisely this open-endedness ultimately introduce students to the pleasures of critical thinking.

NOTES

[1]I advise students to use *Microsoft Excel* to build an open glossary of terms in alphabetical order.

[2]Grice has argued that the meaning of words is a derivative function of what a speaker means in individual instances of uttering it and sees the universal meaning as mere abstraction ("Utterer's Meaning" 225; see also "Logic").

[3]I use excerpts from Campbell's study on myth to support the discussion on archetypes.

Calvino, Translations, and Translatability

Giulia Guarnieri

The title of my course Italo Calvino: Translations and Translatability summarizes the approach I use to teach the works of Calvino. That which renders the translatability of Calvino into English problematic also makes him singular and exceptionally challenging. Toward this end, I have developed a three-module teaching strategy that is particularly useful in helping students understand Calvino's poetics.

Module 1: Calvino and His Existential, Cultural, and Literary Background

The versatility and polyvalence expressed in Calvino's texts are connected with their ability to narrate the social and historical context in which they were written. Because of his militant political commitment, Calvino knew how to grasp the unease of his time. At the beginning of the course, I underscore his cultural background so that students, before dealing with the translations of his works, understand the specificity of his poetics. I focus their attention on aspects that, from a linguistic point of view, appear to be most problematic, such as his use of allegory and metaphor to mirror the illness of contemporary society and his use of the fairy-tale register as a criterion of order.[1]

I have found that the knowledge of Calvino's poetics, his personality, and his personal life allows students to develop the necessary sensitivity to remain faithful to the translation of his works. The intricacy of the themes underscored is strictly linked to the complexity of his language, which uses different registers and makes continuous use of metaphors, neologisms, and allegories, as well as the complexity of the sociocultural context. I find that this plurality of thematic, stylistic, semantic, and lexical levels creates no small challenge for the translator of Calvino's texts. As one of his main translators, William Weaver, states, "what you lose is not the meaning, but poetry" (85).[2] This module is taught by lecturing and does not account for more than fifteen percent of the whole course.

Module 2: Theory of Translation: Major Authors

In the second teaching module, dedicated to an analysis of the most important theories of translation, students should learn the theoretical, conceptual, and methodological tools used in analysis and translation. This module accounts for about twenty percent of the course time. I begin by introducing different types of translation, including free, literal, technical-scientific, semantic, and idiomatic. I then apply these styles by using relevant authors to offer students an overall vision of the discipline. I introduce theoreticians such as Peter Newmark,

Eugene A. Nida, and Lawrence Venuti, each of whom concentrates on a particular aspect of the translation process. Newmark is particularly useful since he creates practical and conceptual categories (e.g., over- and undertranslation) that are especially pertinent tools in translating Calvino.[3] Nida is interested in methodology, and his approach is valuable when describing the grammatical, syntactic, and lexical categories of a text (Nida and Taber). Venuti can be used to investigate the ethical aspects of translation that are linked to issues that include faithfulness of translation. The so-called equivalence effect is an aspect that comes from the critical and hermeneutical activity that assigns a creative role to the translator. According to Venuti, the translator should not remain invisible, a mere anonymous linguistic instrument, but should vindicate his or her subjectivity, both professionally and legally. These issues are not only interesting to students but also vital to their success as future translators.

The ideas put forward by Newmark are particularly useful in translating Calvino's texts since they offer a clear methodology for confronting the most challenging aspects of his prose. In addition, Newmark supplies a glossary with definitions of the different types of translation problems and solutions: cultural equivalency, compensation, nonequivalent words, false friends, and interference, among others. This glossary provides students with a concrete framework for making choices, thus offering more security in the work of translation.

To introduce the practical aspect of translation, I begin by distributing short passages taken from technical magazines or specialized journals that need to be translated into English. To make the activity more appealing and rewarding, I usually choose texts that discuss painting and architecture. Next, I ask students to apply the theoretical and methodological notions learned from the authors examined in class. I choose passages from Italian authors who present lexical challenges similar to those of Calvino, such as Pier Paolo Pasolini, Carlo Emilio Gadda, and Giorgio Manganelli, whose prose is saturated with neologisms, jargon, dialect, and cultural terminology. Experiencing firsthand the difficulties of translation, students realize that it is not a purely technical operation. Very seldom do literal translations work; translating requires knowledge of the context in which the text was produced and sensitivity to the author's intentions.

Module 3: Translating Calvino's Texts

After working with the theoretical and methodological aspects of translation, both in theory and in practice, students analyze the existing translations of Calvino. The third module, which accounts for the remaining sixty-five percent of the course, treats the translatability of Calvino's novels and prepares students to translate passages of his narrative. We analyze existing translations, point out specific problems that arise in translating Italian cultural nouns, and examine an aspect of the translation process specifically linked to gender studies (see Cixous; von Flotow).

Analysis of Existing Translations

Weaver, an American, is undoubtedly the best known of Calvino's translators, but there are numerous others: Archibald Colquhoun (the first to translate his works), Tim Parks, Martin McLaughlin, George Martin, Patrick Creagh, Louis Brigante, Sylvia Mulcahy, and Peggy Wright. To highlight the different choices, I start with the comparative analysis of works for which we have several versions, such as *Favole italiane* (*Italian Folktales*), written in 1956 and translated first by Brigante in 1959, then by Mulcahy in 1975, and then by Martin in 1980. Two other very interesting texts to examine are the translations of *Il sentiero dei nidi di ragno* (*The Path to the Nest of Spiders*): Colquhoun's 1956 translation and McLaughlin's 2000 revised and corrected version of Colquhoun's translation. Calvino revised his first novel several times (in 1947, 1954, and 1964) to eliminate passages he considered too offensive and violent. He replaced these parts with others more in tune with the sensitivity of the times. All the changes made to *Il sentiero*—by Calvino, as well as by the two translators—create a rich comparative analysis. Students notice the active roles of the translators in updating and modernizing the novel and customizing its vocabulary to the changed mentality of the times.[4]

In this module, the practical work takes priority over the theoretical analysis, and I begin with exercises of comparative analysis. I propose using two or more translations of a single text so that students notice the different choices made by the translators when dealing with Calvino's language. The short story "Giovannin senza paura," taken from *Favole italiane*, has three English translations, by Brigante, Martin, and Mulcahy, and I present them all to students, asking questions that stimulate their analytic abilities. Why, for example, are there three translations of this story, which is certainly not one of Calvino's best-known works?

For the comparative analysis of the translations, we begin with their titles: "Giovannino the Fearless," "Dauntless Little John," and "Little John the Fearless." I ask students why the first name is not left as it appears in the Italian, Giovannin, and if there is a loss in the change. In most cases they grasp the gap between the Italian version and the translations, and they point out that in all the solutions adopted for the title, there is a loss of the provincial flavor of the original, inspired by the regional Italian fairy tale. Calvino's altering of the name to Giovannin is the first of a series of diminutives found throughout the story, in words such as *ragazzetto*, *porticina*, *scaletta*, and *pietruzza*. The word *ragazzetto*, for example, becomes in the English translations "young lad" (Brigante), "little boy" (Martin), and "little John" (Mulcahy). Other questions I ask students include the following: Which of these versions is the best translation? How would you translate the title? What is lost in translating these diminutives into English?

In the analysis of this text, students encounter rather simple phrases that in translation seem to stray from the original unnecessarily. Brigante, for example, translates the phrase "Girava per il mondo" (11) as "One day while traveling through the country-side" (3). I ask students why Brigante might have opted for this unfortunate choice. The story in which Giovannino is requested by the giant man to follow him into the palace offers another example of unfaithful translation. The original Italian is the following: "Allora l'uomo passò lui e una stanza dopo l'altra traversò il palazzo con Giovannino dietro che faceva lume. In un sottoscala c'era la porticina" (15). In his translation, Brigante transforms the dynamic of the events and of the places: "So the giant went first. Passing from one room to another, they walked up and down through the palace until they came to a hallway where there was a small door" (9). Students notice that there are elements missing from the original (the light that Giovannino is holding, the back of the staircase) and that there are scenarios added ("walk[ing] up and down through the palace").[5]

For exercises on the translatability of the vocabulary, I divide students into groups of three or four. Their assignment is to analyze an original text and its translation, paying particular attention to the challenges posed by the vocabulary, such as the jargon and dialect, diminutives, augmentatives, and pejoratives that are typical of Calvino's style. Particularly useful for this task is a story from the *Gli amori difficili* (*Difficult Loves*), "Furto in una pasticceria" ("Theft in a Pastry Shop"), which has been translated by Weaver, by Colquhoun, and by Wright. The three main characters of the story, Dritto, Gesubambino, and Uora-Uora, have very unusual, symbolic names, especially Gesubambino ("Baby Jesus"), who recalls, among other elements in the story, the Christmas festivities. The English translations retain the names Dritto and Uora-Uora but change Gesubambino to Baby, a name that nullifies the moral and ironic charge of the plot, which finds Gesubambino as a thief of pastries during the Christmas holidays. When I ask students to find a more appropriate way to translate this name, most decide to use Baby Jesus. The class proceeds to translate other cultural terms, most of which are related to Christmas food: *panettone*, *torrone*, *meringhe*, *croccante*, *pan di spagna*, *crafen*, *brioche*, *savoiardi*, *cannoli*, *amaretti*. These words are often translated using an undertranslation ("almond cake" for *croccante* and *torrone*) or with a circumlocution ("sugar-coated buns" for *panettone*). I point out that these Christmas cakes can be left in Italian since they are now generally understood in the United States.[6]

Proposals of New Translations

I ask students to form groups to work on translating cultural terminology. The challenge is to translate certain phrases using a more culturally inclusive approach that is in tune with today's sensitivity toward expressions that denigrate minorities and women. In *Il sentiero*, for example, Calvino refers to a woman with "capelli da negra," which Colquhoun translated as "black hair." Some students still consider this remark denigrating and propose an alternative solution such as "Afro-American hair." Although this solution remains very generic, it does not carry any racist undertones.

The most significant challenge for Calvino's translator, however, is the terminology that derives from the cultural context of the author. Often these expressions turn out to be rather obscure for students and necessitate a historical-social explanation, something far beyond the literal translation of a word or phrase. The word "cornuti," in *Il sentiero*, has a different cultural meaning in the United States and in Italy and thus requires an introductory explanation. "Cuckolds," the translation proposed by Colquhoun, communicates the sense of betrayal and is perceived by readers as something severe but not dramatic. In Italian, at the time the novel was written, this word was used as a severe form of personal offense, an act against human dignity. Then, there existed a customary machismo, according to which a wife's betrayal indicated a serious affront to a man's dignity—and indeed was punishable by the penal code as a felony.[7] I explain that in Italy today, even though marital betrayal no longer constitutes a crime or carries the cultural and moral connotations of the 1940s and 1950s, it is common to make a hand gesture that replicates horns when one wants to insult an adversary during a confrontation.

Another popular cultural term worth discussing is "terrone," also in *Il sentiero*, which Colquhoun rendered as "despised folk from the South," a translation that carries the degrading value that it carries in the Italian. I also discuss the translation of common Italian places such as "osteria" and "carrugi" with neutral descriptive words like "tavern" or "alley." This practice offers another instance of Newmark's undertranslation, because the English words are less specific and lack information conveyed by the Italian original. Students also find the translation of historical terms problematic; words such as "fascio" and "balilla" are left in the Italian in McLaughlin's and Colquhoun's translations of *Il sentiero*, without a translation or footnote. Yet a footnote is present for acronyms and words such as "G.A.P" or "Todt," although the information given is insufficient to render fully the historical and political reality of those years.[8]

Gender in Translation

The final part of the module, which is structured as lecture, discussion, and practical exercises, addresses Calvino's portrayal of women, often depicted as negative and exemplified by passive figures associated with images of danger, punishment, and irrationality (see Frasson-Marin). In my lecture on this topic, I refer to Luise von Flotow's *Translation and Gender: Translating in the "Era of Feminism"* and Sherry Simon's *Gender in Translation: Cultural Identity and the Politics of Transmission*. Both authors view the translator as a re-creator of meaning, therefore the translator's subjectivity and positionality are crucial in generating and constructing cultural values. Their studies also suggest that the translation act can accentuate the misogynous connotation of an author, thus actively contributing to the circulation of discriminatory ideas. After this preliminary segment, I introduce the 1981 translation of *Se una notte d'inverno un viaggiatore* by Weaver, in which he translates "Lettore" and "Lettrice" as

"Reader" and "Other Reader." Students find that the translation of "Lettrice" as "Other Reader" loses every feminine attribution and becomes neutral. "Other" does not mention the sex of the reader, whereas the Italian has the feminine connotation indicated by the suffix *-trice*. Some students suggest that Weaver could have rendered the term with "female reader," and we speculate that he opted for an implicitly misogynous choice that, according to some critics, is in line with Calvino's preference. Of course, students realize that it is objectively difficult to translate gender from Italian into English since Italian (like other Romance languages) uses specific terms and suffixes to distinguish male from female. Von Flotow points out the lack of gender indicators in the English language and (except in a few cases) suggests that it is up to the translator's ethics to resolve the issue by using more politically correct forms (75). Stefano Tani suggests using the terms "She-Reader" and "He-Reader," which he sees as are more faithful to the original (114).

The choice made by Weaver has negative connotations for women and also subtly modifies the image of the female character. The translation of "Lettrice" as "Other Reader" works to increase the prejudices against the female gender, since the term "other" signifies different from the norm and contrary to what is right and just. I share with students the translator's response to the accusation of implicit misogyny. Weaver does not attribute any importance to this criticism, stating that "one cannot write a novel where the characters are a Female and a Male Reader" (84).[9] According to him, "other" does not have any particular implication. "I did not find something better, and I used it. It is a solution made out of desperation. Before I thought of naming the characters Reader One and Reader Two; but this instead is offensive for the female character."[10] In his answer, Weaver reveals his lack of sensitivity to gender and does not see that other solutions are achievable.

As part of their research regarding gender, I ask students to translate the most problematic pages of *Se una notte d'inverno un viaggiatore*, in particular the passage in the first chapter where the female reader makes her first entrance and the students get to know her name, Ludmilla. I urge them to find innovative solutions for the translation of "Lettore" and "Lettrice," to create a more politically correct term and to translate according to the translation theories regarding gender we have covered in class. Among the most original solutions are the neologisms "Readher" and "Readeress." These terms visibly differentiate the female from the male. Some students suggested using "Male Reader" and "Female Reader"; others preferred to use the personal pronouns "He" and "She," completely eliminating the term "Reader." Still others proposed keeping the terms in Italian and explaining this choice in the preface or with a footnote.

Among the methodological objectives stated earlier, my course accomplishes a rather implicit one, that of informing the students that the success of a novel in a foreign country is partly due to the work of translators. Venuti, in *The Scandals of Translation*, emphasizes that the work of a translator is often underappreciated, underpaid, and invisible. With my lessons, I demonstrate to students how the work of a translator is relevant and demanding and responsible for the accuracy and potential enjoyment of the translated piece.

NOTES

[1]Other topics are man's relation to technology and its pervasive penetration into our lives; Calvino's appreciation for literary experimentation; and his interest in the relation between order and chaos, which gives Calvino an understanding of reality.

[2]The interview quoted from here, although published in English, was conducted in Italian; Weaver's response was, "ciò che si perde non è il senso, ma la poesia."

[3]Newmark gives the following definitions for the terms in his *Textbook of Translation*: "*Over-translation*: when the translation gives more detail, often a more specific word. *Under-translation*: when a translation gives less detail and is more general than the original" (285).

[4]McLaughlin, in the preface to his translation of *Il sentiero dei nidi di ragno*, explains the changes made to the first translation by Colquhoun in 1956, based on Calvino's first edition of *Il sentiero* (1947). McLaughlin starts by explaining his changing the title from *The Path to the Nest of Spiders* to *The Path to the Spiders' Nests*, to be more faithful to the plural *nidi* but also to eliminate the echo in English of the expression "nest of vipers," which, in his view, produces contempt. In addition, McLaughlin states the importance of updating Colquhoun's translation by eliminating small errors and reinserting passages that were previously eliminated by either the editor or the translator. McLaughlin also adds in his translation the parts that were changed by Calvino in his last revision of the novel (1964).

[5]This story is also useful for vocabulary purposes. The expression "riappiccicò," for example, is translated by Brigante and by Mulcahy as "attached" (9; 4) and by Martin as "stuck" (11). Generally students see how these translations can be classified as examples of over- and undertranslation and how they lose the informal tone of the story.

[6]We take the same approach with jargon and informal terminology like "piluccare," "piluccarsi," "impiastricciati"; common idioms such as "fare il palo" and "vetro sinistrato"; or diminutives like "faccino" and "baffetti."

[7]Article 599 of the Italian penal code stated that female adultery was punishable with up to two years of prison time. This law was declared unconstitutional with sentence 126 in 1968 and sentence 127 in 1969.

[8]McLaughlin defines several terms in footnotes to his translation: "G.A.P: *Gruppo Azione Patrioti*. The smallest unit of the Italian partisan organization, usually in towns" (Calvino, *Path to the Spiders' Nests* 40); "Todt: The German Todt organization was responsible for building defences, and Italian workers in it were exempt from military service" (63); "Sim: *Servizio Informazione Militare*—Military Intelligence Service—a term that could apply to either side" (65).

[9]"Non si può scrivere un romanzo dove ci sia un female ed un male reader."

[10]"Il significato di Other non ha nessuna connotazione particolare, siccome non trovavo di meglio l'ho adottata. È una soluzione nata dalla disperazione."

Teaching Calvino in Creative Writing Classes

John Domini

To work with the fiction of Italo Calvino in a creative writing course—whether one teaches his short stories or his novels, in an undergraduate or a graduate class—requires a pedagogy different from what one would use in literature or cultural studies courses. Creative writing has established itself as a component of the liberal arts curriculum in American colleges and universities; students and professors now work toward mainstream academic goals and objectives as well as toward less clearly defined artistic aspirations. These dual purposes shape my essay, which considers assignments both creative and analytic and is guided by the two curricular considerations while addressing choices for reading and points commonly raised during student-teacher interaction.

In the process, I look first at what Calvino teaches fiction-writing students about prose style, in particular the uses of complex syntax and abstract language. Second, I examine how his stories and novels use modes of narrative either entirely new or still little-known to Americans in college. Understanding those modes, therefore, becomes another teaching objective. Finally, I show how both questions—the alternative models Calvino presents in style and in storytelling—help illuminate the general investigation into the liberal arts. That is, in looking at Calvino as apprentice writers, students can better define the postmodern culture around them.

Open-System Analysis: Literature as Process

Creative writing, to a greater degree than most courses of study in the humanities, depends on what teachers of foreign languages call active learning. Students engage with the subject as a practice, and a lot of the course work must be participatory; indeed, *workshop* remains the defining term for this discipline. All creative writing courses involve an in-class critique of student manuscripts. Usually this critique takes the form of discussion by the whole class, combined with written comments seen by only the student-writer and the professor. All the variations on the pedagogy, however, emphasize literature as a process, a series of informed choices. Workshop leaders show students how their creative activity comes down to such choices, and this hermeneutic guides even the examination of published work by dead authors. Workshops often interrogate a text in a roundtable discussion, to define the internal tensions of a piece and how they relate to one another. That is, instead of identifying a metaphor and its meanings, students may be asked to consider different language or situations in which the metaphor may be couched. "Open-system analysis" serves as a shorthand expression for how a creative writing class considers published work. Such analysis instills means of criticism appropriate to a workshop with apprentice texts, themselves very much open to adjustment.

Thus a fantasy about Qfwfq at the dawn of time, from Calvino's *Cosmicomics*, will be assessed as if the artist wrote in the same language as the students, so that his stylistic choices can be more readily grasped. And the workshop leader will call attention to the arrangement of narrative, so that the flatness of the characters or the ambiguity of the climax will seem less fantastic. It is not that a creative writing teacher should never lecture or prescribe—the class requires a definition for "flatness of character," certainly—but that Calvino's fiction tends to serve students best when introduced later in the term. The workshop needs first to have reached consensus on basic elements of fiction. It needs a grasp of the realist tradition, the predominant mode of English and American fiction, which has shaped student notions of narrative literature. Within this tradition or mode, plot is not just the events (grounded in recognizable, sensual data) but also the change those events cause in the main characters (with whom we can identify). After students have achieved an understanding of these classic definitions, Calvino's work provides a concrete embodiment of what's "experimental," an otherwise nebulous term, and also allows the teacher to define *fabulist*, *metafiction*, and even *postmodern*. I generally provide a two- or three-minute biography as well, bringing out how different the author's background is from that of nearly any younger American.

Still, critical vocabulary arises from discussions of how the stories work. When students note the fairy-tale quality of "The Distance of the Moon," in *Cosmicomics*, for example, the professor can then make the connection to fabulism. In the same way, ideally the students will first bring up Qfwfq's recurring vertiginous leaps into the contemporary at the conclusion of each short narrative, at which point the workshop leader can help them consider the implications. Two issues need to be addressed regarding Qfwfq's ambiguous final status: the difference between genre fantasy or science fiction and what Calvino's doing, which is considerably more complex and subtle, and the contingent condition of the narrator, who dwells at once in the story's past and the reading's present. That condition defines metafiction: the drama concludes when it enters our own.

These two issues have points in common and can be usefully explored together, in small groups of students who then make brief presentations. The metafictional irony is a signature device for Calvino and is extraordinarily apropos to the open-system analysis of literature in creative writing. In an early work like *The Baron in the Trees*, the narrator, Biagio, embodies the same paradox, ending his pseudo-memoir by imagining his "thread of ink" will burst into new arboreal life (217).[1] The late work *Mr. Palomar* does without the sort of narrative that sustains *Baron*, but it has a remarkably similar closing. *Palomar*'s eponymous thinker expires just as he arrives at a refutation of linear time: "each instant, when described, expands so that its end can no longer be seen"

(126). Calvino may involve readers in a story with characters or in the intriguing development of metaphors, yet he always calls attention to the artificiality of that involvement. He creates new story forms only to repudiate the closure of a story. Thus even after students have turned to their own texts in the workshop, whatever Calvino they have read will make a highly useful reference in discussion, because of the questions his work raises about the philosophy of narrative.

Further Reading: Story and Catharsis, Teacher and Sensibility

For secondary sources that confirm Calvino's pertinence to creative writing, I recommend beginning with John Barth's "The Literature of Replenishment," first published in 1979 and collected in *The Friday Book*. The essay addresses *Cosmicomics* in particular and its author's importance to postmodern storytelling in general and makes excellent supplemental reading for advanced undergraduates and MFA candidates. It demonstrates how an innovative fiction writer can assess the project of another and so provides a model for assignments such as the reader-response essay or presentation.

For such assignments in a creative writing workshop, unlike in a literature course, students must emphasize technique. Technique includes the chosen mode of storytelling, and so they must be able to define the self-reflexive aesthetic Calvino chose. The best analyses will distinguish the approach of *Cosmicomics* from that of, say, James Joyce in *Dubliners*. This distinction between fabulist metafiction and psychological realism is just the sort of essential grounding even graduate students may lack. Far too many arrive at the workshop knowing only that, in this art form, quality work generates an emotional affect. They know that a good drama delivers catharsis, but they need the workshop leader (perhaps with the help of Barth's essay) to explain how Calvino achieves catharsis without the structures of our agreed-on reality. Indeed, when approaching a later fiction such as *If on a winter's night a traveler*, students will have to grapple with the possibility that Calvino eschewed catharsis altogether. That grappling may occur in a response essay, but it also proves valuable in a one-on-one conference or as part of a workshop. Apprentice fiction is always in some way unrealized, exploring a situation without cohering as story; Calvino's fiction, the later work especially, demonstrates how such exploration defines the art—and may be itself the story. In a workshop, then, purposes can be clarified through a comparison of students' writing with an experimental novel like *If on a winter's night*. In a conference, should a student's attempts to embody the passions stubbornly take the form of empty signifiers, the remedy may lie in assigning, and later discussing, *Invisible Cities*.

A workshop leader need not share Calvino's sensibility to use his fiction. Few writers, indeed, take the same approach to fiction as Calvino, but even so markedly different an author as Joyce Carol Oates uses two entries from *Invisible Cities* in the text derived from her Princeton course, *Telling Stories*. The more illuminating pedagogical example, regardless of a teacher's personal aesthetic, comes from T. C. Boyle. Boyle has worked extensively with Calvino, from *The Nonexistent Knight* and *The Cloven Viscount* to *If on a winter's night*, and he selected four passages from *Marcovaldo* for his anthology *Doubletakes* (Boyle and Kavashy-Boyle). His introduction to the excerpts calls attention to two qualities in particular: the "straightforward charm and lyricism" of the prose and the sympathy generated for the characters despite the "imaginative range" (89). That second quality, the cathartic identification created despite unlikely settings, clearly owes much to the first, the highly charged but accessible style. Both points seem central to teaching Calvino in a creative writing course.[2]

Syntactical Niceties: Against the Concrete

When it comes to word choice and sentence construction, to prose rhythms and the visual affect of the printed page—in Calvino's case, a page often brimming with a single long paragraph—that is, when it comes to what the creative writing curriculum generalizes as style, the Italian fabulist tends to strike young Americans as an exception to the rule of their required reading; for Calvino composes his ironies, and the quandaries into which they lead his protagonists, in language like the sort I am attempting to emulate in this sentence: a language prolix until it verges on florid and embracing all manner of syntactic niceties and linguistic flourishes as a means of getting across strange worlds in fascinating ways. He uses high rhetoric yet keeps his materials accessible. More remarkably, he relies on abstractions.

Most of the fiction that students have read and analyzed depends on its manipulation of sensory data, what Anglo-American realists call the concrete. A much-quoted passage on this point comes from Flannery O'Connor, who argues in "The Nature and Aim of Fiction" that fiction's "least common denominator" is "that it is concrete" (67). Likewise Janet Burroway, in her widely used text *Writing Fiction*, insists that "concrete, particular details . . . are the life of fiction" (75). Yet Calvino brings off one of his masterpieces, "A Sign in Space" from *Cosmicomics*, without pausing to develop a single physical detail.

When using "Sign" in class, I challenge students to find such a detail, and at once we need to address the paradox developed on the first page. Qfwfq's original "mark" is invisible (because "who had eyes to see with?") and calls up no adequate comparison ("there were no things to copy, nobody knew what a line was" [31]). Yet, all across the galaxy, the sign is impossible to miss. It is the only one out there. Students seeking more tangible materials move to the long closing list of signs, in which Qfwfq searches for his original as the millennia rush past. But those details come and go during a twenty-six-line sentence that ends in ellipsis, slips in and out of several semicolons, and includes lengthy parallel parentheses on the philosophical distinction between signs created by nature and signs made, like Qfwfq's, as signs. The rhetoric overwhelms whatever is concrete within it. With little recourse to the senses, the story nonetheless gets across the narrator's desperation and tragedy. The exercise can draw out one other example, in the metaphor that precedes the closing list: "the Galaxy turned like an omelet in its heated pan." But this detail is imaginary, after all, and again it takes us to emotion; "and I was frying," the passage concludes, "with it, in my impatience" (46).[3]

I find students learn the most from Calvino's glancing engagement with the physical through an imitation assignment. I ask workshop members to imitate fifteen lines or so of a distinctive stylist. Generally I give the assignment twice a term, and I begin with an author who prizes the concrete, such as Ernest Hemingway or another realist students are likely to have studied before coming to creative writing. Thus two or three weeks later, when they try to write like Calvino, the experience opens them to a different manner of expression, highly sophisticated and no longer dependent on sensory input. Still more instructive is my requirement that each page of imitation is accompanied by a page of analysis, in which they must identify and define at least three points of style, or three of the devices by which an author creates his affect. In this way, students come up with their own understanding of how Calvino maintains a syntactical instrument that is refined and yet full of feeling.[4]

Thought Experiments: The European Contract and the American

Boyle is hardly the only writer to marvel at how such strange work as Calvino's nonetheless engages the passions. Anyone who teaches *Invisible Cities* or *If on a winter's night* struggles with his seeming absence of Aristotelian drama. But even protagonists in Calvino's earlier works, like Baron Cosimo from *The Baron in the Trees*, present an idiosyncratic variant on identification and catharsis. The baron makes for an interesting class discussion or paper on "round characters," as developed by E. M. Forster in *Aspects of the Novel*. Cosimo has a certain roundness, a distinct personality, but he is also predictable in the way of flat characters. I sometimes assign a compare-contrast paper—one that, as always in this discipline, emphasizes technique over theme—in which students oppose either Qfwfq or Marcovaldo to someone like O'Connor's Misfit, from "A Good Man Is Hard to Find." Calvino's figures are nebulous in many regards, yet always easy company, with sunny natures we can count on; O'Connor's man, however, may be explicitly outfitted with childhood trauma and a professor's spectacles, but he is finally impenetrable and chilling. The distinction takes learners to the authors' philosophical underpinnings: the one Rabelaisian in his embrace of new possibilities, the other monkish in her rejection of the world.

But the same character-based study will not work with the books Calvino wrote after the 1960s. These fictions supplant psychological and social probing with thought experiments, and many Americans who take creative writing (including some graduate students) will have little preparation for such narratives. For them, one place to begin is a generally appreciative review of *If on a winter's night* by John Updike, in which he claims the novel "manages to charm and entertain the reader in the teeth of a scheme designed to frustrate readerly expectations" (470–71). This assertion, pointing to an implicit agreement between reader and writer, can be the basis for fruitful discussion or for a written response. Learners develop fresh critical vocabulary as they articulate the alternatives to watching recognizable characters go through familiar changes.

Such alternatives, unfortunately, have been given short shrift in most of the teaching texts for creative writing, an oversight in keeping with the emphasis on the concrete. Burroway, for instance, acknowledges the value of "an intensely created fantasy world" (199), but the stories included in her collection are almost exclusively representations of orthodox Anglo-American realism. Although such works certainly deserve a place on a creative writing syllabus, effective pedagogy demands a thorough investigation of Calvino's aesthetic as well. Not long before Hemingway wrote his first stories, Franz Kafka made his extrapolations from Jewish nightmare and Marxist economics; not long before O'Connor set loose the Misfit, Jorge Luis Borges imagined the world eradicated by an encyclopedia. The latter sorts of stories, the European and Middle Eastern tradition out of fable and myth, which tends to reduce the importance of individuals, remain largely unknown to American students exploring literature as a creative act. Yet workshop members have as much to learn from the fabulist's approach as from the realist's, and the most revealing distinctions may turn up elsewhere than in Calvino's syntactic style. Not that the distinctions do not turn up at the level of syntax. The imitation assignment can be adapted, for instance, to compare Calvino's writing with that of Aimee Bender, a fellow professor of Boyle's at the University of Southern California. Bender is something of a fabulist herself, and so the exercise quickly establishes that American work in this vein relies far more on conversational plainness. The contrast takes the workshop to discussion of cultural differences, to questions beyond style.

But the most significant difference, beyond Calvino's way with words, remains his treatment of identification and catharsis. Students are puzzled by how such satisfying work, especially the books after *Cosmicomics*, can break so radically from ordinary storytelling. In the workshop leader's initial defining of key terms, a designation like "fiction of ideas" supplies a useful characterization for students who are not writing majors or MFA candidates. However the professor frames Calvino's approach, one exercise that allows students to explore the way it works is what I call the tool assignment. In this exercise, students write descriptions of some man-made tool and its use and develop their descriptions, over three or four pages, into an analogy for some recognizable transition or revelation. For example, the way a boy bounces a tennis ball off the garage door could express his emotional state on the evening he learns his parents are divorcing. The point of view must be third-person, outside the main characters, and emotions must be expressed not in dialogue or external summary but through the central metaphor. The best exercises become extended extrapolations, fluid allegories that coin fresh meaning out of their elements, just as Calvino does in his later fiction. My rules for this assignment therefore also exclude two tools, the book and the computer; these devices are themselves composed, as it were, of metaphors.

Of course the tool assignment will be most useful during the period when the class is reading Calvino, and likewise his challenge to psychological and social realism is better understood when placed with others in the same mode. Kafka's "hunger artist" or Borges's dreamer in "The Circular Ruins" make illuminating companion figures for Calvino's Mr. Palomar or Marco Polo. An American or two also belongs in this part of the reading list, perhaps Boyle or Bender, perhaps Donald Barthelme or Ursula K. Le Guin. Since many students will be new to this kind of narrative, part of their education will come in learning the differences between authors from different cultures. Yet even in this company, the Calvino of *Invisible Cities* or *If on a winter's night* can stand apart. The fiction offers less humor than Barthelme, less plot than Le Guin. In exploring how the Italian author nonetheless manages to move and entertain, the workshop leader always has the option of falling back on traditional explication. I have introduced students to the Fibonacci sequence and demonstrated its application to *Invisible Cities*; the mathematics sets up expectations that drive the reading. But such explorations are never entirely one-sided. More than one student, for instance, has pointed out how Marco Polo's ostensibly dispassionate list of stopovers comes to embody a conflict, one that on page 98 erupts into an actual scuffle between the explorer and the emperor. In speaking of this conflict, students also grasp the point that neither man wins. No sooner does Kublai Khan declare the world an empty chessboard than Polo begins to repopulate the board. He creates a metaphor within the larger metaphor of content versus form, namely, the "rafts laden with logs" (132). Yet while Polo dreams up content, loading down his rafts, he does not alter the book's balance between the container and the thing contained—a kind of suspense, actually.

Energy from Meaning: The Play of Known and Unknown

Calvino's imaginative investigations into form versus content have occupied many critics and thinkers, but my conclusion must emphasize their impact on students. In this fiction of ideas, apprentices come to realize, the ideas are what generate narrative energy and satisfaction. Among the shorter works, "A Sign in Space" and "The Dinosaurs" rely on a character surrogate, the central consciousness of Qfwfq, to move toward opposite ideological poles; "Sign" dramatizes a triumph for form, whereas "Dinosaurs" insists on some immutable intrinsic value. In coming to appreciate such interplay, students learn how a story can depend on something other than psychological problems acted out in arenas defined wholly by the five senses.

More interesting still, the investigation into alternative narrative means can also call attention to another sort of give-and-take, one between bizarre surfaces and old-fashioned structures. *Invisible Cities*, for all its strangeness, reveals a classic novella typology: it has a recurring central incident, twin lead characters, and thematic dualities, all earmarks of the mid-length form (e.g., any novella by Henry James). Similarly, *If on a winter's night* owes much of its appeal to its skillful forays into genre fiction, and nearly all the stories in *Cosmicomics* have a sturdy dramatic framework, first a ground situation and then a change agent. At best, students understand that this mode depends not solely on nonstop invention—although Calvino's inventions are fascinating—but also on the tension between innovation and tradition.

To comprehend such storytelling, at once playful and erudite, is especially instructive for the undergraduate who comes to creative writing simply to fulfill a humanities requirement. For students with no particular vocation in the literary arts, Calvino prompts cross-disciplinary insight into postmodern culture; his fiction sets them thinking about both the fairy tales they know from childhood and the bodiless encounters that occur online. But whatever a student's commitment to the discipline, what students gain from Calvino is repeatedly borne out in the final sessions of the term, when they use him as a reference in their written evaluations of stories by their peers. I grade these evaluations, and I let everyone know I am looking for evidence of what they have learned from their reading. Few authors come up as often as Calvino in those comments.

Ultimately, what Calvino has to offer a workshop is his profound idiosyncrasy. Creative writing is the branch of the liberal arts in which a student can most benefit from the encounter with the unknown. Calvino himself took his greatest liberties with dramatic form after he joined a workshop, the group Oulipo. Clearly Oulipo gave him the sort of permission students in creative writing receive from a good seminar: it enabled fresh developments of his vision and craft. Insofar as his experience proved beneficial, it allowed him to notch one or two signs in his fin de siècle space that proved the continuing existence of aesthetic bliss. Insofar as my students succeed in their confrontation with Calvino, the class helps them raise critical questions about what, in their moment rather than his, constitutes such bliss.

NOTES

[1] All quotations from *The Baron in the Trees* are from Colquhoun's 1959 translation.

[2] Both points came up in the editorial deliberations for the *Northwestern Fiction Reader* developed in 1998–99 for the Northwestern University undergraduate writing

major. The surprises of Calvino's style and his questionable catharsis—the qualities Boyle highlights—justified the inclusion of work from *Cosmicomics* in the reader.

[3]Calvino's minimal engagement with the physical can also be seen in stories other than Qfwfq's, even in a relatively down-to-earth piece like "The Argentine Ant" (in *"The Watcher" and Other Stories*).

[4]Calvino's unencumbered sense of style has not gone unnoticed by teaching poets either. Lauren Haldeman, for example, recently used *Invisible Cities* in her poetry writing course at Iowa, highlighting the dominant stylistic device, also used at the end of "A Sign in Space," of many details folded into a situation-setting list, selected and arranged to generate intensity.

Using *Mr. Palomar* to Question Received Truths in a General Education Course in the Humanities

Joseph Francese

For each semester over the past ten years, I have taught The Modern World: Focus on Knowledge: What and How We Know, a four-credit, advanced general education course in the arts and humanities. The course is taught in English to a broad cross-section of students at a very large (approximately 45,000 students) public institution. Classes of fifty students meet twice a week. The students and I examine how we receive, develop, and communicate knowledge in the contemporary world. The required readings all serve to question socially constructed perspectives on a shared reality that was digested in childhood as factual and natural. Specifically, we explore common sense, or the conventions, assumptions, and inherited knowledge that condition our views. Put simply, we interrogate our ideologies. The questioning of commonly held perspectives about science, history, perception, storytelling, identity, and gender enables and encourages students to forge independent meaning and fosters their capabilities for abstract thought. Ultimately, the goal is to explore how a personal ethics might be fashioned not out of metaphysical truth(s) but out of uncertainty.

One of the required readings is Italo Calvino's *Mr. Palomar*, not an easy text for undergraduates. Yet its complexity is precisely what attracts students to the novel; it provides many with a welcome challenge. Students indicate very clearly in their course evaluations that they appreciate the opportunity to honestly discuss as adults the complex ideas and relevant issues raised by the required readings. *Mr. Palomar* figures in class discussions that take place approximately two-thirds into the semester, as part of a unit in which we question the objectivity of scientific perception.

While this course meets many educational goals, one of them (and not the least important for an Italianist) is that the use of texts such as *Mr. Palomar* can serve as the vehicle for introducing undergraduates to important aspects of modern Italian culture and history. Thus *Mr. Palomar* is an integral part of a context to which students might not typically be introduced in the undergraduate curriculum, such as Primo Levi's *The Periodic Table* or Antonio Tabucchi's *The Edge of the Horizon*, which figure in discussions of questioning the objectivity of perception and of questioning the objectivity of historiography, respectively. Discussion of the culture of Italy, which resembles but is quite distinct from that of the United States, dovetails with the theme and structure of the course, the interrogation of received knowledge (common sense), when it allows students to step outside themselves and see what they know about themselves and their culture, from a less subjective, alien vantage point.

In the research assignments, designed to reinforce the course goal of helping students become more familiar with ways of knowing in the arts and humanities and become more knowledgeable and capable in a range of intellectual and expressive abilities, they are encouraged to choose research topics that will enable them to engage critically with their society, history, and culture(s) or to learn more about the history and culture of other societies. This sort of inquiry is at the core of *Mr. Palomar*, whose protagonist's thought process reflects that of a research project. Therefore I advise students to choose research topics that will allow them to focus on key ideas in human experience, to appreciate the roles of knowledge and values in shaping and understanding human behavior, to emphasize the responsibilities and opportunities of democratic citizenship, to see the importance of language and the value of the creative arts, and to think about important issues that occur and reoccur among peoples in an increasingly interconnected, interdependent world. Of course, all papers will not accomplish all these objectives, but these goals figure into faculty-student discussions of possible topics. Parenthetically, I discuss topics with each student for two additional reasons. First, it helps us identify a topic that is relevant to the student, one that is at the intersection of the course topic and of his or her major. Second, such discussion lessens the possibility of plagiarism. To close the parentheses, I suggest to those who choose to write on *Mr. Palomar* that they use the text to interrogate how our subjectivity conditions what we think is objective perception and then to question all truths that we as individuals and as a society hold to be self-evident.

To enhance their capacity for critical thinking and self-interrogation, I ask students to question Calvino's popularity in the anglophone world. What affinities do they and his broad reading public in the United States feel for his characters? Why do Americans buy and read translations of Calvino instead of other Italian writers? In other words, what makes him marketable? For the most part, students respond very well. They are anxious for real-world experiences, and Mr. Palomar's intellectual distress does not remind them of any textbook situation ever encountered during their academic career.

Required courses in the humanities must help students improve their understanding of themselves as individuals, which will also expand their capacity to understand and interact with others (a capability that I hope they will continue to refine long after they have left my classroom). To that end, group discussions often concentrate on our belief systems. I encourage students to share and explain their opinions, but, because they often personalize their interventions in class, I also instruct them on how to civilly disagree with one another, on how to develop the ideas of others (even those with whom they are not in agreement), and on how to listen. Since Mr. Palomar struggles with finding the proper method for gathering information, he serves as a model for interactions with diverse, antagonistic points of view.

Indeed, Mr. Palomar is an integral part of an ongoing conversation between the students and me. We begin the course by analyzing the starting point for knowledge, the one thing students believe they know with absolute certainty, what we refer to in class as the center of our Ptolemaic universe, the self. The metaphor is not casual: the goal is to enable students to see themselves and the United States society as members of a Copernican, planetwide system of interrelated and overlapping human consortia. In other words, our goal is to see ourselves not as the center of the universe but, like Mr. Palomar, in relation to diversities in our society, to other societies, and to the shared natural environment. This perspective is a fundamental point of arrival for the course, which begins with discussions centering on Luigi Pirandello's relativistic conception of individual identity. We read works by Pirandello such as *It* Is *So! (If You Think So)* and *Each in His Own Way* (61–138; 277–361). Readers of these plays must juxtapose, compare, and contrast the characters' self-images and the perceptions other characters have of them. This exercise leads students to question the subjectivity or objectivity of the social bond—how we see others and how others see us. Subsequently, they are quick to grasp the consequences of Mr. Palomar's failure to begin his journey of understanding with necessary introspection: only by knowing ourselves (*nosce te ipsum* reverberates in the first chapter of Levi's *Periodic Table*) can we begin to understand the other. Indeed, the dialectic of self-knowledge and the ability to deal with the other as another self subtends and informs Tabucchi's *The Edge of the Horizon*.

We spend a week with *Mr. Palomar* during the section in which we question the objectivity of visual perception, a topic that dovetails with a discussion of ideology, our class's verbal shorthand for received belief systems and how they shape our views. This section of the course enables the group to interrogate the objectivity of the so-called hard sciences. To this end, we use works such as Levi's *The Periodic Table* and selected chapters from Thomas Kuhn's classic text in the philosophy of science, *The Structure of Scientific Revolutions*.

As for *Mr. Palomar*, we do not approach the novel through a close reading because this is a not a traditional course in literary appreciation. Rather, we use the same strategy here as with all the other texts. We extract the concepts and ideas that plague Mr. Palomar and attempt to make them relevant by discussing them within the context of our lives. Students enjoy his persistent, head-on confrontation with our contemporary condition—his clumsy attempts at understanding old and new phenomena, of keeping himself abreast of the goings-on in the worlds of politics, science, and society while maintaining a politically correct posture that reflects his interest in the humanity of others. Of course, his convoluted quest for certainty ends in frustration, a situation my students understand very well. Mr. Palomar, they tell me, just does not get it, but they admire his perseverance. Thus we are able to underscore a very important concept: the quest for knowledge does not end with a college degree. It is a lifelong process wherein each answer reached unavoidably raises new questions and reveals new lacunae in what we know.

The first of the two class sessions (each lasts two hours) devoted to *Mr. Palomar* serves as an introduction; during the second we examine the text. My primary goal in the introductory session is to draw students into the topic. To that end I discuss Calvino—his biography, his oeuvre, and the broad context of Italy in the second half of the twentieth century—before situating *Mr. Palomar* on that wide canvas. Thus students who major in the hard sciences are attracted to Calvino by Qfwfq, the hero of his "cosmicomic" stories; in fact, many choose to pursue this aspect of Calvino's writings in their research projects. In contrast, philosophy and literature majors are fascinated by the theoretical issues with which the narrating voice grapples. Students in foreign affairs are encouraged to integrate the writer's youthful involvement in the Communist Party into material from courses they have already completed. Others are attracted by Calvino's commitment to causes larger than himself and are encouraged to relate the writer's rethinking of his political stances in the late 1950s to their own youthful quest for a life path. As a result, students write, using *Mr. Palomar* as the point of departure, on a wide array of topics, such as how our identity is conditioned as much by others' views of us as by who or what we think we are; how place and historical period determine who we are, how we live, and what we become; how our subjectivity conditions what we think is objective perception; and how the media shape our perception of reality.

When we turn to the text in the second session, we first consider Mr. Palomar's attempt at imposing order on a chaotic, infinite universe: the table of contents wherein he would embrace all reality while confining it within a three-dimensional system of Cartesian coordinates, a finite totality. This attempt raises a vital issue that surfaces throughout the course: abstract thought, or how we are often called on to make sense of amorphous masses of data (an instructional goal of all majors across the curriculum). In this way, we stress the fact that the capability to think abstractly is a cornerstone of college education; the ability to gather information and process it into a cogent narrative (which ultimately may contradict our previous notions on a topic), developed and honed through the writing of research papers, is an essential part of career training, no matter what the field of study.

After emphasizing this point, we inspect the divergent ways of knowing tested by Mr. Palomar, following more or less the diegetic progression of the text. He considers the self, then society, in conjunction with the nonorganic universe. His intellectual distress centers on questions highly relevant to our course material. They regard the self and observation: Is it possible to observe the world objectively? If so, how is this vantage to be reached? He attempts to reduce the world's complexity by isolating and looking at minimal units, the narrative tesserae that constitute the chapters, and he attempts to induce from them a general pattern or design. He concerns himself only with what can be seen, a strategy that is consistent with Calvino's later prose fictions, which tend to discount the psychology of the characters. Indeed, the awareness that the moon does not need him to exist allows Mr. Palomar to contemplate a world that will go on without him, just as the gecko and the albino gorilla remind him that the evolution of life on this planet may have followed other paths that would have forestalled the development or dominion of Homo sapiens. Ultimately, he would like to intuit a harmony among nonhomogenous harmonies (the self, society, the environment), but he is confronted with the awareness that he must first be at harmony with himself, the strategy he rejected at the outset.

By the end of the second session we come to see that, to assume a posture of objective detachment from which to understand the harmony of the universe, Mr. Palomar eschews subjectivity because it is too relativistic. That is, he discards introspection and knowledge of the self, the form of knowing that the students and I used as our starting point when we discussed Pirandello. When Mr. Palomar seeks to remove the self from his calculations—when he seeks absolute truths and certainties without considering interrelatedness—his project falls asunder. The novel fits perfectly with other required readings that stress the importance of understanding the self and its reflection, the diverse other selves (who make up the society that places constraints on our individuality), as they interact within the determining and conditioning context of the materiality that surrounds us. Thus Palomar's final, unsuccessful attempt to move beyond agency and achieve sublime detachment (he would learn how to be dead) underscores for the class the importance of incisiveness within and interaction with a social consortium. His ultimate understanding that death does not endow a life with a final meaning, because the individual is subject to redefinition by posterity, makes clear that there must be a future in death.

Calvino's text transmits values that are grounded in intellect and reason and that reflect his lifelong interest in utopias. Nonetheless, there is a limit to this view: Calvino, for all his interest in the act of observation, does not go beyond an almost voyeuristic observation of the other in *Mr. Palomar*. Because he would assume an objective point of observation, far above the fray, he views the world and society not as a participant but as an outside observer. He observes and thinks about life but does not live it. Students usually come to see that there are shortcomings to this approach. Indeed, it seems to many that *Mr. Palomar* is lacking in humanity. Mr. Palomar's enlightened intellect appears incapable of empathy for his fellow human beings and therefore of real understanding. Those with whom he comes into contact are not "other myselves" but merely others; he has not acquired the interpersonal skills and comprehension we have sought to develop throughout the course. We subsequently contrast Mr. Palomar to Spino, the protagonist of Tabucchi's *The Edge of the Horizon*, who defines himself in terms of the other. Spino's recognition of mutual determination and the necessary reciprocity of self and other make for improved and strengthened social bonds. At the same time, in acknowledging the failure of Mr. Palomar, we applaud his earnest efforts at understanding and use him to underscore the weaknesses inherent in an absolutist view of the world, one that does not admit the validity of diverse ways of being and thinking and therefore opens the door to Manichaean distinctions between good and evil, right and wrong, and their destructive consequences.

Through the Eyes of Another: Text as Visual Representation

Susan Rogers

Artists begin their studies by learning to analyze the elements that, taken together, become a work by Van Gogh or Rembrandt. In studying the brushstrokes, texture, medium, and scale of a particular painter, students are able to enter the visual imagination of the artist and learn to see the world through another's eyes. Musicians begin by analyzing strands of sound, examining composers' dynamics, tempo, orchestration, theme, and form. Thus they learn to become the composer, to hear sounds as a Mozart or a Stravinsky.

Readers need to be able to enter into the world of a particular writer, to see the world as that writer does, to enter into the realm of the text. They need to visualize this realm by interpreting the signs given to them on the page. As Guy Davenport reminds us, "when language emerges, the verb *to draw* is the same as *to write*. We can see, and to some extent read, the drawings of primitive man" (64). The same creative impulse compels both artist and writer to imagine a world, complete with rich, visual images, with a music all its own.

As a teacher, I need to be able to challenge my students to read text visually, to help them envision the writer's world and color it with sounds and images. Davenport notes that "there is the world to be seen, with its hidden harmony, and there is the poet (or painter, or composer) to perform the magic whereby we can possess the artist's vision" (193). To introduce my students to a writer who performed artistic magic, I have presented my Freshman II Writing Class with Italo Calvino's *Invisible Cities*. Calvino's writing reflects his ability to recall strong, central visual images, much like a select group of artists, musicians, and, as Arthur I. Miller informs us, scientists: "Einstein wrote that visual imagery occurred first and words followed. Einstein's statement about his mode of creative thinking bears a strong resemblance to [Miro, Picasso, and Rothko]" (431). The striking visual images in *Invisible Cities* appeal to my students because of the connections they find between the book's subject and their respective majors—at my polytechnic university, popular majors include architecture, landscape design, and engineering. Indeed, my students would surely return to visualization in their upper-division studies, since, according to James Elkins, "statistically, science is where vision is studied, not the humanities" (86). Even with the ready appeal, they need intermediary texts and preliminary exercises to prepare them to understand such an imaginative work and negotiate its many layers.

I turn to Alain de Botton's *The Art of Travel* for help in teaching my students to both understand and appreciate the creative vision of artists, musicians, and writers. This text is the perfect accompaniment for our overarching theme, exemplified by the following quotation from Davenport: "Geography—land, seas, climates—is overlaid with the second geography of political groups, empires, linguistic conglomerates. The geography of the imagination would be a third construing of cultural divisions, showing, for instance, the areas of the portrait, the epic, the novel, the symphony" (270). To enter Calvino's vision, we need to go down the rabbit hole: starting with the "geography of the imagination," the novel; traveling down to the level of "land, seas, climates"; and moving up to politics, empires, and language. Botton's text helps students begin their imaginative travels, so that they can then navigate literary rabbit holes with increased confidence.

Beginnings

The Art of Travel details the journeys undertaken by the narrator, who travels accompanied by a work of fiction, a book of verse, or a series of paintings or photographs. The creators of these works serve as guides for the narrator, who seeks to enter into the world of the artists, follow their journeys, and see through their eyes. The selections are short and, judging by my students' reactions, rather electrifying.

I extract those chapters I feel will help my students appreciate *Invisible Cities*. I begin with the chapter for which J. K. Huysmans serves as the guide, using his duc des Esseintes, from *Against the Grain*, to introduce my students to our quarter's theme, the geography of the imagination. Usually, they resist Des Esseintes's insistence on "mind travel" as a way of escaping all that is ugly and uncomfortable about the real world. After some discussion, however, they begin to understand that the virtual worlds they inhabit in video games or in movies such as *The Matrix* or *Avatar* exemplify his vision of mind travel. After these discussions, they are able to return to the text, reading Des Esseintes as a contemporary.

Next we turn to the chapter guided by Xavier de Maistre and explore the experience of "room travel"—with him dressed in his requisite "pink-and-blue cotton pyjamas" (Botton 240)—he relates in his accounts of intrepid travels, *Journey around My Bedroom* and *Nocturnal Expedition around My Bedroom*. Joseph de Maistre wrote that his brother "had discovered a way of travelling that might be infinitely more practical for those neither as brave nor as wealthy as [Magellan, Drake, Anson, and Cook]" (Botton 240–41). I ask students, How can anyone find anything to write about, confined to his or her room? I assign them the task of going home, slipping into pajamas, and spending an evening writing about their journey. Their powers of observation usually will surprise them. In class, we travel together through their journeys, and we all see through the eyes of others and are touched by the experience.

We use John Ruskin, another of Botton's travel companions, to introduce the next phase of the class's journey. Ruskin believed that anyone is capable of drawing and that it is only through this process that we learn "to see—that is to notice rather than merely look" (Botton 217). Not only did Ruskin teach people to notice but he also asked them to write, or "word-paint." As Ruskin gave his students the tools to capture the world around them and to share their vision with others, I too help my students draw their world and also the imaginative worlds contained in books.

Envisioning Calvino

William Herschel felt that "seeing is in some respects an art which must be learnt. To make a person see with such power is nearly the same as if I were asked to make him play one of Handel's fugues upon the organ. Many a night I have been practicing to see" (qtd. in Turchi 225–26). My students need to learn to see, to become critical and imaginative readers. To that end, I have developed an approach to Calvino's *Invisible Cities* that enables them to visualize the text through the use of drawing software (depending on resources available, one can use a geographic information system [GIS] or 3-D virtual-worlds software), to turn the layers of textual meaning into visual layers of information. Reading is an introspective and private activity. Drawings that visualize the text allow us to illuminate and thus render public our reading comprehension. By drawing what they imagine, students turn surface reading into critical visual reports on reading.

To accomplish this transformation, I divide my class into seven groups and assign each group one of the following cities: Zobeide, Armilla, Valdrada, Olivia, Zemrude, Octavia, and Baucis. All students read their city description and write a synopsis whereby they would take their reader on a city tour, describing the journey through the streets of their story. Most, lulled by the short length of the reading and the realization that they can leave class after they finish this easy assignment, write breezy synopses, skipping over unknown words and difficult concepts. At our next class meeting, I ask my students to open a computer-drawing program and draw their city according to their synopsis. Believing, as James Gee does, that "in the modern world, print literacy is not enough [and that] people need to be literate in a great variety of different semiotic domains" (19), I instruct them in the use of a range of tools, from word-processing programs to drawing tools and even to advanced visualization tools such as GIS. After a short demonstration of the drawing software, students begin their projects. They soon realize that there is no way to tackle the drawing assignment on the basis of their first hurried reading.

Students usually spend the class period returning to the original text, looking up words in dictionaries, as well as searching for images online. They suddenly need to know how the dictionary defines words such as *chasm*, *fluting*, *mullioned*, and *precipice* and what sort of visual representations of those words exist. During this lesson, I am always reminded of Marie-Laure Ryan's work with visualization and the difficulties of translating text to image; whereas pictures "teletransport the spectator instantly into their space, language can afford only a gradual approach to the textual world. . . . [I]t discloses its geography detail by detail, bringing it slowly into the reader's mind. And unlike pictures, language is the medium of absence" (122). I take advantage of this teaching moment to remind my students of the way our quarter began, reviewing handouts on our course's learning-management-system site: "Critical Reading," "Critical Writing," "Questions to Ask as You Read," "Analyzing Argument." Careful rereading of the text determines the veracity of the image they draw; or, better, the text reveals the picture to be drawn.

I enjoy watching the pictures develop; making this an in-class assignment intensifies the level of attention to drawing. Everyone takes this task seriously and concentrates on bringing their texts to life. After all the students have turned in their images, I assemble a *PowerPoint* presentation, grouping the pictures by city, and, during the slide show, ask each student to discuss the joys and challenges of the project. Ryan has found that "[i]n the most complete forms of spatial immersion, the reader's private landscapes blend with the textual geography. In those moments of sheer delight, the reader develops an intimate relation to the setting as well as a sense of being present on the scene of the represented events" (122). This intimacy comes to the fore in the comments students make. Many delight in the sense of being present in their city.

Students have been working individually up to this point. Their next assignment brings them together in their groups, as they attempt to move beyond their explications and drawings to bring their cities to life. They must fully enter each cityscape to make the illusion real. I instruct the groups to answer some basic questions about their city: What would it be like to live in Baucis (for example)? What system of government functions there? How are children raised? schooled? What is the legal system like? From these questions, I progress to more challenging questions, based on philosophical musings: In Octavia, "the spider-web city," for example, what does Calvino mean when he suggests that "the life of Octavia's inhabitants is less uncertain than in other cities" (75)? How do the inhabitants of Octavia react, knowing that the net, the underpinnings of their city, will not last forever? I ask my students to think of parallel situations between the world of Octavia and our world. Living in fear of terrorist threats and natural disasters, don't we too feel that our world will not last forever?

Next, the groups work on a layering project using architectural vellum and colored pencils. Returning to our travels down the rabbit hole, I review the way Davenport envisioned constructing geographic layers: from cities to political structures to cultural works (270). Each group decides what criteria to use to visualize the layers of society for its city, and each member is responsible for one layer. Some groups work on the physical dimensions of their city and illustrate the various levels from infrastructure to the tops of buildings. Other groups prefer to work on patterns of social relationships in their city. Still others work on natural phenomena and illustrate the levels of plant and animal life that may span from below the ground up to the clouds. By holding each group of layers up to a light, we are able to see the entire structure of each city. Then I remove one layer from the bundle. The students are always surprised to see just how fragile and uncertain existence can be. Although they enjoy using simple drawing tools for this exercise, I may use 3-D visualization software in future classes; in this way, students will be able not only to manipulate the various layers but actually to bring their cities to life, much like the globes in Calvino's city of Fedora.

The last section of the project is another individual assignment. I ask students to return to Calvino's text and write an extended description of their city. The difference after a few weeks of physically manipulating drawings of their city is inspiring. Long gone is the superficiality exhibited in their first writing assignment; this time around, it is difficult to contain their enthusiasm. I usually cannot stop them from writing extended (ten- to fifteen-page) descriptions of what it would mean to live in an invisible city. I am always most impressed with the parallels they find between the cities and their lives. They will never forget the joy experienced by entering another world, in fully immersing themselves in the author's vision. My students look into the eyes of others, expand their powers of observation, and learn to draw another world.

Endings . . . and Beginnings

Adding visualization to a writing class has helped my students learn how to critically analyze texts, although our work prompts the question, Did we enter Calvino's world? William H. Gass eloquently laments:

> Marco Polo's cities were certainly invisible, as any remembered city, any sought-after city, any city rendered in words will be. Even at this moment, words are violating our vision; vision is violating our thought. The reduction of a concept to a single instance, the replacement of an individual by some generalizing name: this is an agon as old as philosophy itself. (39)

Which brings me to new beginnings, new quarters, new students, and other chances to trespass lightly upon *Invisible Cities* to give my students the necessary tools to create meaning visually—to use the resulting drawings to return to the text and to enrich their understanding of its layers of meaning, while imagining invisible geographies.

The Invisible Monster: Calvino and the Contemporary City

Dean Swinford

"The True Essence of Leandra Is the Subject of Endless Debate"

Italo Calvino's *Le città invisibili* (*Invisible Cities*) begins with a simple scenario: the young Venetian traveler Marco Polo and the aged Tartar emperor Kublai Khan sit together in a garden. As the khan ponders the size, shape, and details of a kingdom made up of distant foreign lands, he relies on Polo's accounts to make this vast kingdom tangible: "Solo nei resoconti di Marco Polo, Kublai Kan riusciva a discernere, attraverso le muraglie e le torri destinate a crollare, la filigrana d'un disegno così sottile da sfuggire al morso delle termiti" 'Only in Marco Polo's accounts was Kublai Khan able to discern, through the walls and towers destined to crumble, the tracery of a pattern so subtle it could escape the termites' gnawing' (13–14; 5–6). In the first section of the novel, Calvino clearly distinguishes the official reports of the khan's agents from Polo's accounts, which attract the khan through the mysteries they evoke.

The novel builds from this opposition of points of view. In some ways, Kublai Khan is like a mapmaker, one who sees his empire from a panoptic perspective.[1] He seeks to organize his empire and the cities it contains into a single, knowable realm. Polo, by contrast, occupies the space of the flâneur, the aimless urban wanderer venerated by Charles Baudelaire and Walter Benjamin, and disrupts this illusion of order. In Michel de Certeau's formulation of the essentially poetic practice of a pedestrian's movement, "[i]t creates shadows and ambiguities" within the order of the planned city (101). This opposition between the person who makes the map and the person who uses, or willfully discards, one also parallels the rhetorical situation of the classroom, where, as instructors, we often occupy the vantage point of the seated khan.

This essay describes a method for drawing together these opposing pairs—the planned city and the flâneur, the instructor and the student—through an assignment that joins Calvino's *Invisible Cities* with urban-planning texts, such as William Whyte's *City: Rediscovering the Center*, that draw attention to the invisible placelessness of the postmodern city. Calvino's multiperspective rendering of Venice provides a model that can enhance student engagement with postmodernism, a key concept for literary study, through his deliberate centering of description as a narrative mode.

The cities Calvino describes in the novel draw readerly attention to the unfamiliarity of the familiar. This sense of estrangement is, as Laura Chiesa contends, "emblematic and inescapable in the literary criticism of Italo Calvino" (401). *Invisible Cities* belongs to a trilogy that includes *The Castle of Crossed*

Destinies and *If on a winter's night a traveler* and privileges the estrangement enabled through the retelling of already told tales. These novels, all of which rely on "Borges' notion of a multiplied, ramified time" as "a unifying structural element" (McLaughlin 100), stress the fundamental disorientation at the heart of storytelling. In this way, these works emblematize Calvino's postmodern preoccupations. Carol P. James suggests that *Invisible Cities* reveals this postmodern influence while retaining several characteristics of high modernism: "The seriality of the cities defines the trait we shall treat as postmodern, while the framing device, the narrative of those cities which would put them into a certain perspective, relates to a modern, or in any case pre-postmodern, esthetic of a *mise-en-abyme* or 'narrative context'" (144). John Barth also sees this novel as indicative of a brief return to modernism after the postmodernism of *Cosmicomics* and *The Castle of Crossed Destinies* ("The Parallels!"); this fusion of modern and postmodern methods drives the novel and results in a sustained tension between the rationalism of modernism and the labyrinthine complexity of postmodernism. These components, however, cannot and should not be divided or set in opposition. Instead, as Tommasina Gabriele points out, Calvino's method necessitates "the prevalence . . . of contrasting elements" that cannot be resolved (18).

This tension between competing aesthetic standpoints and modalities increases through the novel as Calvino reveals that each page describes, rebuilds, and rewrites the same city, Venice.[2] The empire, like the contemporary metropolis, exists as an invisible monster; the concentrated power of its formless mass can be understood only by relinquishing the desire to see it all at once, as a totality that can be mapped. The range of its reach can be comprehended only through a consideration of its seemingly inconsequential components. Calvino seems to suggest that the city is both a real thing that shapes and determines lived experience and an imaginary context that exists only as the sum total of individual experiences in a predetermined space. It is monstrous in that it wields great power and yet ultimately has no discernible essence.

Recent studies of urbanism in the social sciences have quoted from Calvino's novel or adopted its title to describe the actual condition of lived space. JoAnn Cannon notes that Calvino has been listed, along with Philip Johnson's AT&T building, Disneyland, Monty Python, Max Headroom, and Donald Barthelme, as one of the most prominent icons of postmodernism (*Postmodern Italian Fiction* 198). In many works examining contemporary urbanism, as well as in Calvino's novel, the invisible city is an omnipresent, powerful, and discouragingly unidentifiable place, series of power relations, and economy. The concept of the invisible city also informs other artists and writers. The acrobatic street theater of Pino di Buduo's invisible cities project, for example, draws on Polo's use of "pantomime, singing and physical gestures" to reveal the "hidden dimension" of urban space (Watson 164). Gisela Heffes describes the trope of the "nonexistent, wholly imaginary" city as used by modern Latin American novelists. She points out that these writers owe at least an indirect debt to Calvino, whose "model of the city can help us to reflect both on a particular city and on all cities at once" (42). Heffes considers Calvino's influence as especially evident of an antiutopian impulse characteristic of postmodern literature, as seen by the dominance of nostalgia and memory, and not progress, as ordering principles of narrative.

Social scientists inspired by this novel also locate the modern city as a paradoxical form that both structures and destructures experience. In these texts, the city exists as a physical phenomenon and as an allegorical motif, an ideological construct that embodies the virtues and vices of a given place. The link between literary texts and critical studies of the city provides a significant learning opportunity for students of literature, since it attests to the influence of the literary imagination beyond the written page. I outline an approach to teaching Calvino's *Invisible Cities* that I have used in various sections of Survey of World Literature (1750–Present). Administered by an English department in a large public university, this survey course is open to all undergraduates and is usually primarily composed of students majoring in English and related areas of study. Recently, I have used this course to examine changing representations of and responses to urban issues. *Invisible Cities* fits quite naturally into this pairing of artistic development and social issues, since it exemplifies postmodern narrative techniques and concerns while relying on the rationalism and geometric structure of high modernism.

"Perhaps I Am Afraid of Losing Venice . . ."

Calvino's novel consists of conversations between the historical Marco Polo and Kublai Khan, but the cities described are unmistakably modern (or postmodern) in their construction. Polo recounts Mongol cities with skyscrapers, traffic, and heavy industry, creating these cities through narrative, concealing truth in lies, and revealing our own observations as illusory. Above all, his accounts accentuate the emptiness of the reports coming from Kublai Khan's agents, whose words tell the khan that "quest'impero che ci era sembrato la soma di tutte le meraviglie è uno sfacelo senza fine né forma" 'this empire, which had seemed to us the sum of all wonders, is an endless formless ruin' (13; 5). Kublai Khan's official messengers speak the language of empire. They bear dispatches detailing the collapse of enemy troops and the obsequious offers of tribute made by obscure foreign kings. The empire created through the information they provide—on "le cifre introitate dal fisco imperiale, i nomi e i patronimici dei funzionari deposti e decapitati, le dimensioni dei canali d'irrigazione che i magri fiumi nutrivano in empi di siccità" 'the revenues received by the imperial treasury, the first and last names of officials dismissed and decapitated, the dimensions of the canals that the narrow rivers fed in times of drought' (29; 21)—exemplifies both singularity and multiplicity. The messengers relate "notizie intese in lingue a loro incomprensibili" 'information heard in languages incomprehensible to them' in "lingue incomprensibili al Kan" 'languages incomprehensible to the Khan' (29; 21).

Calvino indicates that Kublai Khan's empire exists to the extent that there is an imperial treasury, as well as a bureaucracy that functions through promotion and decapitation. This empire, however, is impossible to locate. Despite the wide range of the lands called "Empire," no consensus exists on how to call it so, since the many languages used to report the business of the empire make communication impossible. Furthermore, these languages trap the khan: "solo attraverso occhi e orecchi stranieri l'impero poteva manifestare la sua esistenza a Kublai" 'only through foreign eyes and ears could the empire manifest its existence to Kublai' (29; 21). The details Calvino provides indicate that the empire is more than an ephemeral concept. The dimensions of the canals that cross the Asian plains are recorded by the khan's emissaries, but, as Polo's reports suggest, the simple compilation of details and dimensions does not produce a comprehensive totality.

While Kublai Khan listens to Polo "con più curiosità e attenzione che ogni altro suo messo o esploratore" 'with greater attention and curiosity than he shows any other messenger or explorer of his,' he also "[n]on . . . creda a tutto quell che dice Marco Polo quando gli descrive le città visitate nelle sue ambascerie" 'does not necessarily believe everything Marco Polo says when he describes the cities visited on his expeditions' (13; 5). Yet Calvino implies that the khan's initial distrust of Polo derives less from Polo's status as a European trader than from the simultaneous distrust and fascination that attach themselves to all storytellers.

Since the publication of *Invisible Cities*, many architects and urban planners have adopted the term *invisible city* to describe the urban condition spawned by modernity. For urban planners of the late 1960s and early 1970s, the social, environmental, and cultural problems of the automated city became increasingly evident: the dead center engendered a permanent underclass, urban sprawl claimed significant amounts of natural habitat and farmlands, and the invisible city effectively invalidated the human interaction implied in the etymology of the word *city*.[3]

The realization of the utopic visions of late-nineteenth- and early-twentieth-century planners of the modern city produced, paradoxically, a resignification of those visions. Fantasies of progress yielded realities such as acid rain, ranchettes, and the gleeful crackle of the drive-thru speaker. Such realities, now omnipresent, were promulgated unknowingly by both planners and other visionaries. As early as 1902, for instance, H. G. Wells speculated positively in *Anticipations of the Reaction of Mechanical and Scientific Progress upon Human Life and Thought* that, as a result of the automobile, "the whole of Great Britain south of the Highlands seems destined to become . . . an urban region, laced all together" by roads, rails, and wires (17, 19). By the 1960s, however, many planners reconsidered the overall mission of their profession by rethinking the relation of planning and development. The allegories of space produced in urban-planning texts reveal the monstrous impact of unmitigated development on modern cities. Such analysis erases the fiction that boundless development is a logical or even necessary extension of scientific progress.

Whyte's *City: Rediscovering the Center*, published in 1988, explores the shape and makeup of the contemporary city. Whyte discusses urban design issues through his presentation of the city as lived by its dwellers. In 1979, he released a video made from his research, initially entitled *The Social Life of Small Urban Spaces* and accompanied by a text of the same title published in 1980. The film consists of his narrating a condensed version of the information that resulted in *City*. The narration accompanies images culled from thousands of hours of footage compiled by him and his assistants. Many of these images also appear in *City*, which includes the chapters "The Social Life of the Street," "The Skilled Pedestrian," and "The Corporate Exodus." Through his description of the habits of pedestrians, Whyte then discusses effective design strategies as employed in specific buildings in Manhattan. The focus of his assessment of design is the corporate plaza, a borderland where the private and public meet. The success of this meeting, he stresses, indicates the overall health of an urban area.

The interlinking of Whyte's exploration of New York and Polo's exploration of Venice allows for a wide range of possible discussion topics.[4] Students can begin, as Calvino does, by evaluating the qualities of these cities in relation to the literary, artistic, and philosophical concepts underlying modernism and postmodernism. Instructors may wish to point out some of the differing estimations of the significance of the city in Calvino's writings by scholars of his novels. Michel Lafon, for instance, sees Calvino's and Jorge Luis Borges's evocation of cities the two authors have lived in as attempts to position their texts within a literary tradition as labyrinthine as the cities they describe. For László Scholz, Calvino's presentation of the city as a mechanistic structure, a composite organized like a game of chess, is intended to reflect Calvino's literary mechanisms. Cannon echoes this view and discusses the extent to which "Calvino's fictions present a variety of images of . . . form-giving structures" (*Postmodern Italian Fiction* 101). The dual tropes of the city and chessboard come together in *Invisible Cities* through the formal lattice of the novel's chapters. To this end, as Franco Ricci writes, "the invisible cityscapes (the *fabula*) are logically sequenced on the unchanging checkered pattern of the chessboard" (*Painting* 107).

The pairing of Whyte's *City* and Calvino's *Invisible Cities* highlights the opposition, noted by Kerstin Pilz, between the philosophies beneath the primary cities explored in each text, leading to significant topics in the histories of literature and art: "New York, the planned city with its grid-like layout, illustrates the ambitions of modernist thought of order, rationality and clarity. Venice on the other hand, Marco Polo's hometown that inevitably informs his descriptions of the cities he visits . . . , mirrors the topography of Calvino's hometown San Remo" ("Reconceptualising" 231). Pilz erects a fairly familiar set of dichotomies: New York / Venice, modern/postmodern, rational/labyrinthine.

These oppositions do not exist in isolation, despite Barth's classification of *Invisible Cities* as "modern" ("'Parallels!'"). As Simonetta Chessa Wright notes, the image of the labyrinth conveys an entire range of associations that easily transcends any modern-postmodern dichotomy: "il labirinto diventa strumento magico, che permette di organizzare il caos, lo spazzio, il tempo e la comunicazione del messagio poetico" 'the labyrinth operates as a magical instrument, which permits the organization of chaos, space, time, and the communication of the poetic message' (37; my trans.). In adding Whyte and Calvino to the discussion, however, I ask students to compare not only two equally artful evocations of the city but also two sets of circumstances that determine and suggest (or prohibit and elide) specific modes of presentation. This fusion of materials works particularly well in a survey course and entails an examination, by student and instructor alike, of the value of these dichotomies to effectively describe aesthetic practice.

"Cities Also Believe They Are the Work of the Mind or of Chance . . ."

Using the city as an organizing component of my course Survey of World Literature, I divide the semester into units based on the stages of Western urban development and cultural reactions and responses to this development. In a fifteen-week semester, we explore four units: "Romanticism: The City of Nature," "Realism: The Industrial City," "Modernism: The Total City," and "Postmodernism: Beyond the City." In each four-week unit, the class covers a selection of literary texts, planning texts, and visual art. I begin each unit with a section from a planning history text such as Peter Hall's *Cities of Tomorrow*. Then, during class, I work with students to identify the chief areas of concern that Hall covers. For example, students can better appreciate T. S. Eliot's evocation of an "unreal city" in *The Waste Land* (55) after learning about concerns of disease and overcrowding and perceived mechanization of professional life through the increased implementation of inventions like commuter trains and clocks.

Calvino's *Invisible Cities* fits into the final unit, an exploration of the postmodern city. In this unit, I supplement readings from Hall with selections from Rem Koolhaas's *Delirious New York* and James Howard Kunstler's *The Geography of Nowhere*.[5] I also have students read excerpts from Whyte's *City* and watch clips from *The Social Life of Small Urban Spaces* as part of our discussion of the lived reality of the postmodern. With Calvino in particular, I find that this fusion of multidisciplinary responses to similar problems helps illustrate the immediacy of the social in literary texts that seem to eschew reality, daily life, and realistic representation.[6]

After covering planning concepts and historical trends pertaining to the development of the city, I move to issues of literary genre, narrative, and representation associated with the period. The introductory essays from the *Norton Anthology of World Literature* (Lawall and Mack) or an overview of modern and postmodern narrative as found in R. B. Kershner's *The Twentieth-Century Novel* clearly introduce these concepts to undergraduates. Likewise, an in-class discussion of these concepts can be easily supplemented with examples from the visual arts and images of cities—newly constructed highway interchanges, expansive housing developments, and mid-twentieth-century advertisements for the family car. To increase the relevance of the materials presented, I show photographs of local buildings, infrastructure, and design features to help students describe their personal interactions with their environments in the written assignments I include with this unit.

At the same time, I try to keep in mind that these visuals can create the illusion for students that terms used to describe literature, architecture, and art delimit aesthetic production, that only a very narrow range of practices and forms count as modern or postmodern. Students may also read certain forms of representation and urban structures as more natural than others, on the basis primarily of their experiences. For example, many may view their environment as the most natural or logical organization of space. Whyte's work provides an effective counterbalance, forcing a consideration of the practice and implementation of literary and artistic techniques and also encouraging readers to recognize the polysemous possibilities of a single place.[7] Indeed, as noted in Calvino's *Invisible Cities*, planning involves the creation of invisible cities, of "le forme che la città avrebbe potuto prendere se non fosse, per una ragione o per l'altra, diventata come oggi la vediamo" 'the forms the city could have taken if, for one reason or another, it had not become what we see today' (39; 32).

For the postmodern unit, I ask students to produce two papers. The first compares and contrasts representations of the city in Whyte and Calvino. Students may not initially see the urban issues that Calvino mentions in the novel; however, Whyte's evocation of crowding, social gathering spaces, and even the way that urban design encourages or inhibits romance aids them in their ability to detect the realism underlying Calvino's evocative, fabulistic accounts. This analysis asks students to draw on the design developments outlined by Hall and the narrative concepts detailed in the secondary readings as they examine the ways that Calvino and Whyte use very different methods to describe and comment on the city.

In the second essay, students use Calvino's method of sustained description and amplification of details to envision their own invisible city. This pairing of a traditional analytic paper and a more exploratory one encourages them to see the relevance of critical terms outside the academic arena, itself perhaps definable as a species of city. The second assignment, then, asks students to move beyond New York and Venice, or even the thorny questions of (post)modernism, as they consider the influence of the city on artistic production. For Calvino, through Polo's words, "ogni città va somigliando a tutte le città, i luoghi si scambiano forma ordine distanze, un pulviscolo informe invade i continenti" 'each city takes to resembling all cities, places exchange their form, order, distances, a shapeless dust cloud invades the continents' (145; 137). I ask students to write their own Diomiras, Sofronias, and Aglauras from the cities created by their interaction with specific places. In constructing their own invisible cities, they emphasize the ephemeral details and imaginative possibilities offered and obscured by daily reality.

The two essays are like the perspectives occupied by Polo and Khan. They are like two connected components of a map that, as Chiesa contends in her discussion of Calvino and the city, "always presupposes the idea of an itinerary and of a narrative" (403). I draw our discussion to the function of sustained description in the novel and remind students of the dominant function of setting in a work wherein "both plot and characterization are missing" (de Lauretis, "Narrative Discourse" 416). To guide this process, I provide several rules and writing restraints. First, students choose one of the city categories that Calvino uses to organize the novel, including cities and memory, thin cities, trading cities, cities and the dead, and hidden cities. Students then suggest in their description how their city fits into the category they choose. Next, they choose a limited number of objects, elements, and locations taken from their interactions with their lived environments. Finally, I ask them to model the form and content of their city on one of Calvino's. Their city does not have to belong to the category they choose; instead, the essay relies on the rhetorical practice of *imitatio* to deepen their appreciation of Calvino's narrative art. In the assignment, students produce a sustained description of an imaginary city that satisfies these criteria. I stress that they are not writing a story and thus should focus on description rather than plot.

This assignment, particularly if paired with an in-class presentation, allows students to play the role of Polo recounting the familiar in unfamiliar terms. The essays produced will construct an incredible variety of cities, allowing instructors to learn quite a bit about their students. One student, for example, used Calvino's Ottavia, "città-ragnatela" 'the spider-web city' (81; 75), as a starting point for an exploration of architecture and textual metaphors in online communities. Others have used cell phone text messaging, skateboarding, and a city conceived as the interior of an endlessly sprawling Hummer as focal points of their invisible cities.

To keep students focused on the learning outcomes of the course, I remind them that they must be able to explain and analyze their city in relation to the concepts of postmodernity and issues relevant to the contemporary city. Instructors might choose to include an essay question on the final exam that allows students to analyze their city or add an analytic component to the description of the city. This pairing of assignments encourages student creativity and analytic thinking. Another option is to assign presentations in which students, grouped by the city categories that organize Calvino's novel, present and analyze their cities.

By integrating Calvino's *Invisible Cities* with studies of urban design, I have been able to present narrative technique as a response to the lived environment. This approach has worked well in my world literature survey courses, allowing me to present Calvino's Marco Polo as a twentieth-century flâneur-planner hybrid who redesigns through reimagining. Likewise, by encouraging students to rewrite their environments through the novel's various urban categories, I have added a dimension to the presentation and discussion of problematic divisions like modern/postmodern. The projects and discussions that have resulted in my classroom continue to suggest possibilities for teaching *Invisible Cities* in relation to urbanism.

NOTES

Material from this essay originally appeared in my "Analyzing Urban Space in *Invisible Cities*" (*Academic Exchange Quarterly* [2009]: 192–97; print, Web).

[1]For more on the correspondence between cartographic and poetic means of representation, see Pietralunga.

[2]Even the relatively simple correspondence between imaginary cities and a "real" inspiration is subject to dispute. As Harold Bloom contends in *How to Read and Why*, "Though one can become dizzy keeping all these in mind, it will not do to say that each of these cities is actually the same place. Since they are all named for women, that would amount to saying that all women are one woman, the doctrine of the Spanish philosopher-novelist Miguel de Unamuno, but not Calvino's view" (63). The text suggests a single subject while preventing readers from concluding that this single subject exists.

[3]The word *city*, from the Latin *civitas*, refers to citizenship. Thus the city is the concrete embodiment of the community, and the word connotes, above all, a body of citizens.

[4]On postmodernism and national identity, see Ricciardi.

[5]*The Geography of Nowhere* offers a particularly vitriolic catalog of the negative features of a specifically American landscape. While some students may not respond well to Kunstler's indictment of the suburb, his presentation of the cartoonish and "unreal" aspects of suburbia works well with a discussion of the aesthetic considerations of the postmodern.

[6]Di Buduo's "invisible cities" project also provides an intriguing area of examination. For a description of di Buduo's transformation of environments rendered invisible by their familiarity—in this case, a bleak part of Rutgers University's Newark campus—see Saivetz.

[7]As de Lauretis reminds us, we cannot neglect the importance of both praxis and poiesis for Calvino: "Calvino had joined the partisans of the Italian Resistance in 1943 at the age of twenty, and the Communist Party in 1945 (to leave it in 1958)." She reexamines a common controversy regarding his genres, vacillating as they do between the neorealism of *The Path to the Nest of Spiders* and the fantastic qualities of *Invisible Cities*, and argues that "Calvino's works remain constantly focused on a basic vision of human activity as both praxis and poiesis" ("Narrative Discourse" 414).

"Then She Saw the Surprise": Teaching Writing with *Six Memos for the Next Millennium* and *Difficult Loves*

Douglas Basford

Memos are a consummate insider's genre, distributed to a limited audience and designed for disseminating information and for generating a set range of actions by the recipients. They are invaluable for maintaining internal coherence; to miss a memo sets one at risk of irrelevance or exclusion, and to receive a memo is to be kept in the loop. These social dynamics help in understanding what Esther Calvino says was her husband's delight at the word *memo*.[1] A memo in Italo Calvino's hands begins with the confidence of authority but remains a proposal, infused with faith that the literary values Calvino identifies will be carried into the future. Writers should read *Six Memos for the Next Millennium* and yet should not have to read it, because they ought to understand intuitively the nature of their age and ought to have already embraced "a different perspective, with a different logic and with fresh methods of cognition and verification" (*Six Memos* 15).

This spirit, Jean McGarry and I felt, perfectly encapsulated the experience we believe necessary for students enrolled in the second semester of our two-term creative writing course at Johns Hopkins University, Introduction to Fiction and Poetry. The first term, Telling It Straight, treats how writers locate and mold their subject matter, working through the memoir, realist fiction, and formal poetry of writers such as Henry James, Robert Frost, Eudora Welty, Vladimir Nabokov, and Donald Justice. We build the second term, Telling It Slant (after Emily Dickinson's famous line "Tell all the Truth but tell it slant"), around the erudite, impassioned core of Calvino's *Six Memos*: his valuation of "vocazioni opposte" 'opposite tendencies' (e.g., lightness-heaviness, quickness-slowness). His treatment serves as a way of approaching the divide between realism and antirealism, a pairing that might be said to map vaguely onto lightness-heaviness: one seeks to "make language into a weightless element," and the other tries to "give language the weight, density, and concreteness of things, bodies, and sensations" (15). Although Calvino writes at greater length about the first item in each pairing, his care not to devalue the second made this work a natural choice for inclusion in Telling It Slant. The course is divided into units, in which each Calvino lecture is complemented by illustrative work by Virginia Woolf, Franz Kafka, Francis Ponge, Russell Edson, and William Carlos Williams, as well as Calvino's *Difficult Loves*, all of which contribute to the students' attempts at antirealist fiction and free verse. We selected *Difficult Loves* for its characters. In Calvino's better-known works, such as *Invisible Cities*, *The Baron in the Trees*, *Marcovaldo*, and *Cosmicomics*, the iconic characters Marcovaldo, Mr. Palomar, and Qfwfq are mere masks of Calvino; the characters in *Difficult Loves*—the jittery Maria-nunziata, the bossy Dritto, the codger Bisma, to name but three—are far more varied, as is the range of tonality. Moreover, although our selection of *Difficult Loves* predates the current ascendency of fantasy and science fiction (à la Harry Potter, *Star Wars* prequels, and Peter Jackson's epic adaptation of Tolkein), it and *Six Memos* have proved extremely popular, persuasive, and effective correctives to the largely unsubtle moves in the genres many students are most drawn to (e.g., blue-faced hominids as aliens, good-versus-evil dynamics only slightly problematized, and computer-generated images of amassed armies and impossible aerial dogfights). At base, readers of all stripes delight in what Wolfgang Iser calls the "wandering viewpoint," the innumerable minute adjustments and "passive syntheses" of expectation and memory (108, 135). These syntheses take place regardless of the intensity of engagement in the fiction, as Calvino argues in "Levels of Reality in Literature": "the different levels of reality may be matched by different levels of credibility—or, to put it better, a different suspension of disbelief" (*Uses* 108). I think of these adjustments within the state of suspension as surprises, as a kind of recognition of a significant detail or perception followed by a "re-cognition," or a recalibration—and often enlargement—of the space of the fiction, of possibility. In the light of this dynamic, I discuss aspects of the first unit on Calvino's first "memo," "Lightness," to display our methodology, leaving readers to infer similar scenarios for the remaining units.

Our students read "Lightness" at the outset of the second term, likely their first encounter with Calvino, certainly with *Six Memos*, and very possibly with expository prose of this order—swirling, impressionistic, abstract, and extraordinarily learned. Bringing inexperienced readers around to Calvino's critical idiom requires nimble, patient Socratic inquiry and convincing illustrations. My sense is that when students have first been able to identify what is light, articulate how weight has been removed, and define lightness, they generally succeed in producing light work. Their work tends to exhibit lightness progressively, in an exact inversion of the order in which Calvino presents his three senses of lightness. Early assignments are marked with "emblematic" forms of lightness, subsequent work is drawn by narration of thought in which "subtle and imperceptible elements are at work," and their final writing ventures are suffused with a "verbal texture" that seems weightless (*Six Memos* 16–17).

Early in the discussions, students may declare that they get it, claiming that if they cannot articulate what lightness is, they will know it when they see it, and indeed they can discern how stark differences exist between, say, Federico García Lorca and the Georgian poets or, with a little less accuracy, the pair Calvino fingers as the progenitors of the light and heavy traditions, Cavalcanti and Dante. Students have the easiest time identifying emblematic lightness and so often drift into discussing what makes such images memorable. But they recognize other factors at play, understanding that something "saves" Kafka's paragraph-length tale "Poseidon" from the weight of casting the great sea god as a workaholic chief clerk and that something other than the mist in

Ponge's "Trees Disappear in a Sphere of Fog" is in operation. While attractive, the categorization of lightness as an inexpressible quality of superior writing encourages students to privilege unverbalized and unanchored intuition over the extensive and lifelong intellectual work behind *Six Memos* (as illustrated by Calvino's appeal to no fewer than forty-two creative minds—novelists, poets, dramatists, philosophers, and many others—in the first lecture alone). Faced with unfamiliar names and works, the students generally cede Calvino his due authority, but they are not discouraged, either, since his essay embraces an open, agile imagination.

Nevertheless, lightness is difficult to define beyond the terms that Calvino bequeathed to us, and students respond extremely well to working first toward what gets removed from writing to attain lightness. I have tended to ask deceptively myopic questions like, "What does Calvino mean by 'the weight, the inertia, the opacity' of the world that 'stick to writing from the start'?" (*Six Memos* 4). Of these, opacity yields answers perhaps most revealing of the students' progress. Initially they proclaim it inscrutable, milky, nebulous, and dense before arriving at how cause-effect relations are broadcast, foregrounded, obvious, and banal, how ultimately everything opaque is visible. Students begin to see how the "subtle and imperceptible elements" are what get overrun by the "ruthless energies" propelling world events and by the "flattening [of] all communication onto a single, homogeneous surface" by instantaneous, ubiquitous media like the Internet and cell phones, which Calvino did not live to see (3, 45). As immersed as students may be in these media, their contributions speak of their remarkable capacity for self-scrutiny (and self-satire) and their suddenly justified skeptical posture and responsibilities therein.

Discussing this aspect of lightness, I have found, makes students far better thinkers, but their writing improves most as they begin to absorb Calvino's first sense, that language assumes weightlessness. To begin this discussion, I have tapped into their admitted bewilderment at the "vector of information" (13). Their confusion is easily resolved by asking about the mathematical definition of *vector*, which many recall from physics or math classes: a mathematical construct, usually depicted as an arrow, visually representing measurements as direction and magnitude. Requiring more footwork is the conclusion that literature can instantaneously deliver its message and poignancy, all the while being insubstanial, nothing in and of itself. The students take far longer to perfect this quality in their writing than the "emblematic" and "imperceptible elements."

We pair an extensive elucidation of "Lightness" with discussion of two contrasting stories—one light, the other heavy—that share heavy subject matter, namely, a clash of social class: in both Calvino's "Pranzo con un pastore" ("A Goatherd at Luncheon") and Peter Taylor's "Mrs. Billingsby's Wine," a young person of little means comes alone to the house of a well-to-do family. Having been through Welty's mercurial "Why I Live at the P.O." and Henry James's saturnine early novel *Washington Square* in the previous semester, students are well prepared for the chaotic, farcical family life of the Calvino story and the Jamesian unspoken agonies and lasting insults in the Taylor story. In both stories, the mixture is explosive, although in Taylor's, Shirley absorbs insult and unobtrusively leaves. Calvino's characters, tethered to Quinto's volatile perspective, ricochet off of one another with each family member's entrance. Alliances form on the basis of unpredictable and subliminal connections and then fall away. So tenuous is each connection, no matter how grave (e.g., military service, politics), that by the time the last spurious claim of alliance comes—"us three boys fighting our war against a cruel, torturing world without being able to recognize each other as allies, full of mutual fears" (*Difficult Loves* 29)—we are not apt to subscribe to the idea of the "cruel, torturing world": the cruelty seems manageable, even harmless, if it exists at all.

Quinto's narration, infused with his self-acknowledged "awkward detachment" (26), is a veritable illustration of Calvino's marking of "that particular and existential inflection that makes it possible for Shakespeare's characters to distance themselves from their own drama, thus dissolving it into melancholy and irony" (*Six Memos* 19). Whereas Quinto is aided by his family's disconnectedness, no such relief is granted to Shirley, who seems incapable of apperception altogether, and, as a result, a heavy cloud hangs over the scene as she and Mrs. Billingsby reminisce about their town's pre-Depression past in contrast to the present (the 1950s).

"A Goatherd at Luncheon" is a showcase of Calvino's social sensibility, in which the author holds us aloft over the "things that separate people," as Quinto calls them (*Difficult Loves* 22). Yet with the exception of Giovannino's walk home, as imagined by Quinto, there are few instances of emblematic lightness such as those cited in "Lightness"—Kafka's bucket rider and Don Quixote's windmill ascent (*Six Memos* 17, 27–29). To orient the students toward the "perpetual adjustment" to the "infinite variety" of things (26), we have them read "Un pomeriggio, Adamo" ("Adam, One Afternoon") and "Pesci grossi, pesci piccoli" ("Big Fish, Little Fish") for lush settings and memorable images. In "Adam," for example, at first sight of the gardener's effeminate son, Libereso—"He was walking along the path with his watering can filled to the brim and his other arm stretched out to balance the load" (*Difficult Loves* 3)—and as he offers gifts of chafers, ants, and so on to Maria-nunziata, who nervously balks at his gifts, I see a parallel to Calvino's discussion of Perseus in "Lightness," who also lives "not in a refusal of the reality in which he is fated to live; he carries the reality with him and accepts it as his particular burden" (*Six Memos* 5).

I find it is useful to consider these similar figures in view of Michael Riffaterre's claims about the simultaneity of fictive and verisimilar threads in the fabric of fiction: "First, let us get rid of the presumed opposition between narrative verisimilitude and narrative arbitrariness" (6). Riffaterre reinterprets an example used by Gérard Genette: "*Truly arbitrary*: The marquise ordered her carriage and went to bed, for she was very capricious" (qtd. in Riffaterre 6). Riffaterre argues that connotation of the "nuclear word" of the sentence, *marquise*, "emphatically comprises semes such as *caprice*, *spoiled temper*, and indeed *arbitrariness*" (6–7). There is, however, little spoiled temper or aristocratic caprice to be found in Calvino's stories. From the first sentence of "Big Fish, Little Fish"—"Zeffirino's father never wore a proper bathing suit"—we know that violations of social decorum will be harmless, embarrassing, or worrisome only for a brief time, and, above all, that they will be inevitable (*Difficult Loves* 36). Even Zeffirino's name, derived from *zeffiro*, or Zephyr, implies a mode of behavior given not to the deliberate, "explicit motivation" in a marquise's caprice but to the equivalent in action of a shawl of light cotton (*zefir*) flapping in a gentle breeze (*zefiro*). Any number of arbitrary events might be cited—Zeffirino's father's inexplicable love of limpets, Zeffirino's inability to stay focused on a single fish, the slightest eroticism in his pursuit of the bream and gifts to Signorina De Magistris, the deus ex machina octopus attack, and the whimsical present that Zeffirino's father makes of the chopped octopus and instructions for frying it. The same goes for "Adam, One Afternoon"—the meaninglessness of Libereso's gifts, his inventive means of coercing Maria-nunziata to accept his gifts (by allowing ants to crawl all over him while she begs him to shake them off), and ultimately the "surprise": the menagerie in the kitchen. These examples constitute not haphazardness but thoughtful unpredictability, in which "the speed with which events follow one another [conveys] a feeling of the ineluctable" (*Six Memos* 33).

So convincing are the social dynamics of "A Goatherd at Luncheon" and the emblematic lightness and arbitrariness of "Adam" and "Big Fish" that when the students try their hand in the first assignment, they seem less focused on language. We ask them to write about Mrs. Billingsby and her thoughts and expectations while she decides whether to meet Shirley the third time the younger woman comes to call. We ask them to assume that Calvino is the author of the story and to infuse their prose with all possible lightness. Few students write in the first person, as Calvino does with Quinto, a choice that may reflect their reticence about assuming another voice, particularly a middle-aged Southern aristocrat. Students are also apt to include emblematic lightness in their writing, drawing from Calvino's usage—for example, gleaming shards of glass and the bouquet of perfume from a bottle that Mrs. Billingsby drops create a sensation of lightness, as does a diaphanous light in her bathroom, which also suits the flitting thoughts of someone with little to trouble her.

The second assignment has students rewrite the mountaintop scene of James's *Washington Square* in the mode of "Big Fish, Little Fish." Given the familiar territory of the two scenes and their overlapping female protagonists (the hapless Catherine Sloper and the disconsolate Signorina De Magistris), as opposed to working with their own stories and characters, and given the relative ease with which the students can identify with the desire of their "Zeffirino" to cheer up the pouting doctor's daughter, their focus intensifies on lightening up the language—even, for example, in describing how Catherine falls farther and farther behind her exasperated father as she lumbers down the trail. To maintain the level of attention on language, I have found short in-class exercises effective: rewriting heavy sentences as light ones or instead composing light sentences intended to be light but that are not light. Both these attempts produce sentences absent of the deadweight logics of clichés, which I set against proverbs and maxims, among other light and memorable sentences, for contrast.

The remainder of the semester follows much the same structure: students read each of Calvino's lectures twice, in conjunction with writings by the course's major authors, and each lesson culminates in exercises and writing assignments designed to entice students to work with the lecture's subject (quickness, exactitude, visibility, or multiplicity). Calvino never completed the manuscript for his lecture on consistency, and its haunting absence becomes more pronounced as the semester progresses. We ask the students to draw on their understanding of Calvino's modus operandi and sense of literature in the other five essays to brainstorm about what his approach to consistency might have entailed. Esther Calvino notes in her introductory statement to *Lezioni americane* that "Consistency" was to concern, at least in part, Herman Melville's "Bartleby the Scrivener."[2] This key piece of information is missing in the English translation, and so no instructor in the course has yet assigned "Bartleby" to aid in reconstructing what *consistency* meant to Calvino. It is my intention to do so the next time around.

NOTES

[1] Esther Calvino's remark about her husband's love of the word *memo* appears on the first page of "A Note on the Text," an unpaginated section of the front matter to *Six Memos*. No such statement appears in *Lezioni americane*.

[2] This mention of "Bartleby" appears on page vi of Esther Calvino's introductory statement to *Lezioni americane*.

NOTES ON CONTRIBUTORS

Douglas Basford is assistant director of composition at the University at Buffalo, State University of New York. His translations from Italian and French and his critical work have appeared in such journals as *Poetry*, *Two Lines*, *SubStance*, *Subtropics*, *Western Humanities Review*, *Atlanta Review*, *National Poetry Review*, *Hopkins Review*, and *MELUS*.

Eugenio Bolongaro teaches in the Department of Italian Studies at McGill University. He is the author of *Italo Calvino and the Compass of Literature* and has published articles on John Fowles, Boccaccio, Calvino, Bernardo Bertolucci, and Pier Vittorio Tondelli, as well as on the theory of literary genres.

Anna Botta is professor of comparative literature and Italian language and literature at Smith College. She is the coeditor of *Italo Calvino newyorkese* and *Le eccentriche. Scrittrici del Novecento*. Her areas of research are contemporary Western literary theories, modern and postmodern literatures, and Italian literature and cinema.

JoAnn Cannon is professor of Italian at the University of California, Davis. She is the author of *Italo Calvino: Writer and Critic*, *Postmodern Italian Fiction*, and *The Novel as Investigation*. She has published articles on Primo Levi, Antonio Tabucchi, Anna Banti, Italian detective fiction, and Italian film.

Rocco Capozzi is a professor of Italian studies and of comparative literature and semiotics at the University of Toronto. He is the author of *Carlo Bernari tra fantasia e realtà*; *Scrittori, critici e industria culturale*; *Homage to Moravia*; *Reading Eco: An Anthology*; and *Lettura, interpretazione e intertestualità: Esercizi di commento a* Il nome della rosa.

Natasha V. Chang is visiting assistant professor of Italian at Middlebury College, where she teaches courses in language, literature, and culture. She has published articles on Alberto Moravia, Primo Levi, and Umberto Eco and is currently completing a book entitled "The Crisis Woman: Fascism, Femininity, and the Fate of Italy's Modern Woman."

Julia M. Cozzarelli is an associate professor at Ithaca College, where she established a major in Italian studies and teaches all levels of Italian language, literature, and culture. She is interested in both literature and pedagogy, and her publications include the textbook *Sentieri: Attraverso l'Italia contemporanea* and articles on Tasso, Boccaccio, and Ariosto.

Andrea Dini is associate professor of Italian at Montclair State University, where he coordinates the lower-level language program. He is the author of *Il Premio Nazionale "Riccione" 1947 and Italo Calvino* and (with Graziana Lazzarino) of the fifth, sixth, and seventh editions of McGrawHill's *Prego!* He has published articles on Calvino and Cesare Pavese.

John Domini has taught Calvino in creative writing courses at Harvard University, Northwestern University, and elsewhere. Currently he teaches at Iowa State. He is the author of five works of fiction, including *Earthquake I.D.* and *A Tomb on the Periphery*.

His critical work has appeared in the *New York Times*, *Bookforum*, the *Believer*, *Southwest Review*, and *Michigan Quarterly Review*.

Joseph Francese is professor at Michigan State University and senior editor of *Italian Culture*. His most recent book is *Leonardo Sciascia e la funzione sociale degli intellectuali*. He has edited three volumes of collected essays (including *Perspectives on Gramsci: Politics, Culture, and Social Theory*) and is editor of a monograph series for Firenze University Press.

Rita Gagliano is an independent scholar who has taught Italian language, literature, and culture at the University of Oregon, Temple University, and elsewhere. She is the author of articles on Calvino, Gruppo 63, Tiziano Scarpa, Aldo Nove, and Isabella Santacroce and the coeditor of *Creative Interventions: The Role of Intellectuals in Contemporary Italy*.

Giulia Guarnieri is associate professor of Italian language and literature and Italian language coordinator at Bronx Community College, City University of New York. She is the author of *Narrative di viaggio urbano: Mito e antimito della metropoli americana* and of several articles on Calvino, translation studies, travel literature, and instructional technology.

Carol Lazzaro-Weis is the Catherine Paine Middlebush Professor of Romance Languages at the University of Missouri, Columbia. She is the author of *Confused Epiphanies: L'abbé Prévost and the Romance Tradition* and *From Margins to Mainstream: Feminism and Fictional Modes in Italian Women's Writings, 1968–1990*; the editor and translator (with Martha King) of *"La Signorina" and Other Stories*, by Anna Banti; and the editor of *Voyages aux Prairies Osages: Louisiane et Missouri, 1839–1840*, by Victor Tixier.

Massimo Lollini, Hatzantonis Distinguished Fellow in Italian and professor of Italian at the University of Oregon, is the author of *Le muse, le maschere e il sublime. G. B. Vico e la poesia nell'età della "Ragione spiegata"* and *Il vuoto della forma. Scrittura, testimonianza e verità*; principal investigator of the *Oregon Petrarch Open Book*; and editor in chief of *Humanist Studies and the Digital Age*.

Andrew Martino is associate professor of English and director of the Honors Program at Southern New Hampshire University. He has published articles on contemporary fiction and specializes in the contemporary novel.

Guy P. Raffa is associate professor of Italian at the University of Texas, Austin. In addition to three books on Dante, he has published articles on Calvino, Umberto Eco, and Carlo Levi, and he directs the award-winning *Danteworlds* Web site. His current project, supported by ACLS and NEH fellowships, is a cultural history of Dante's tomb and bones.

Franco Ricci is professor of Italian studies at the University of Ottawa. He is the author of *Difficult Games: A Reading of* I racconti and *Painting with Words, Writing with Pictures: Word and Image in the Work of Italo Calvino*, as well as articles on contemporary Italian fiction, and is the editor of numerous volumes on Calvino. His most recent book is *The Sopranos: Born under a Bad Sign*.

Susan Rogers is lecturer emerita at California State Polytechnic University, Pomona. Her professional research interests range from Arthurian literature and opera to William Morris and the pre-Raphaelites, from applications of the creative experience to the study of time and space. She is the author of articles on gifted education, online pedagogy, and digitally mediated visualization processes.

Robert Rushing is associate professor of Italian and comparative literature at the University of Illinois, Urbana, where he is affiliated with the Department of Media and Cinema Studies and the Unit for Criticism and Interpretive Theory. He has published on Calvino, Gadda, De Sica, and others and is the author of *Resisting Arrest: Detective Fiction and Popular Culture*.

Dean Swinford is assistant professor of English at Fayetteville State University. He is interested in the theory of allegory, the rhetoric and narrative structure of early scientific texts, and the development of the fantastic in literature and art. His book *Through the Daemon's Gate* examines the influence of the medieval dream vision on Kepler's *Somnium*.

WORKS CITED

Adler, Sara Maria. *Calvino: The Writer as Fablemaker*. Potomac: Porrua Turanzas, 1979. Print.

Alembert, Jean Le Rond d'. *Preliminary Discourse to the Encyclopedia of Diderot*. Trans. Richard N. Schwab. Indianapolis: Bobbs, 1963. Print.

Alembert, Jean Le Rond d', and Denis Diderot. "Encyclopédie." *Encyclopédie ou Discours raisonné des sciences, des arts et des métiers*. 1751–80. Vol. 5. Stuttgart: Frommann, 1966. 635–48. Print.

Althusser, Louis. "Ideology and Ideological State Apparatuses." *"Lenin and Philosophy" and Other Essays*. Trans. Ben Brewster. London: New Left, 1971. 121–76. Print.

Antonello, Pierpaolo. *Il ménage a quattro: Scienza, filosofia, tecnica nella letteratura italiana del Novecento*. Florence: Le Monnier, 2005. Print.

Austin, J. L. *How to Do Things with Words*. Cambridge: Oxford UP, 1976. Print.

Barenghi, Mario. "Note ai testi: *Il barone rampante*." Calvino, *Romanzi* 1: 1329–37.

Barenghi, Mario, Bruno Falcetto, and Claudio Milanini, comps. "Bibliografia degli scritti di Italo Calvino." Calvino, *Romanzi* 3: 1350–516.

———, comps. "Bibliografia della critica." Calvino, *Romanzi* 3: 1517–51.

Barth, John. *The Friday Book: Essays and Other Nonfiction*. New York: Putnam, 1984. Print.

———. "The Literature of Exhaustion." Barth, *Friday Book* 62–76.

———. "The Literature of Replenishment: Postmodern Fiction." *Atlantic* Jan. 1980: 65–71. Print. Rpt. in Barth, *Friday Book* 193–206.

———. "'The Parallels!' Italo Calvino and J. L. Borges." *Context* 1 (2005): n. pag. Web. 29 Mar. 2012.

Barthes, Roland. "The Death of the Author." *Image Music Text*. Trans. Stephen Heath. New York: Hill, 1977: 142–48. Print.

———. "The Plates of the *Encyclopedia*." *New Critical Essays*. Trans. Richard Howard. Berkeley: U of California P, 1972. 23–39. Print.

Beauvoir, Simone de. *Le deuxième sexe*. Paris: Gallimard, 1949. Print.

———. *Tous les hommes sont mortels*. Paris: Gallimard, 1946. Print.

Belpoliti, Marco. *L'occhio di Calvino*. Turin: Einaudi, 1990. Print.

Benedetti, Carla. *Pasolini contro Calvino: Per una lettera impura*. Turin: Borenghieri, 1998. Print.

Benson, Stephen. "The Idea of the Folktale in Italo Calvino." *Cycles of Influence: Fiction, Folktale, Theory*. Detroit: Wayne State UP, 2003. 67–114. Print.

Berman, Russell A. "Why Major in Literature—What Do We Tell Our Students?" *PMLA* 117.3 (2002): 487–521. Print.

Bertone, Giorgio. *Italo Calvino: Il castello della scritura*. Turin: Einaudi, 1994. Print.

Biasin, Gian Paolo. "The Surface of Things, the Depth of Words." *The Flavors of Modernity: Food and the Novel*. Princeton: Princeton UP, 1994. 97–127. Print.

Blanchot, Maurice. *The Writing of the Disaster*. Trans. Ann Smock. Lincoln: U of Nebraska P, 1986. Print.

Bloom, Harold. *How to Read and Why*. New York: Scribner's, 2000. Print.

Bolongaro, Eugenio. *Italo Calvino and the Compass of Literature*. Toronto: Toronto UP, 2003. Print.

Borges, Jorge Luis. *The Aleph*. Trans. and introd. Andrew Hurley. New York: Penguin, 2004. Print.

———. "The Analytical Language of John Wilkins." Trans. Lilia Graciela Vazquez. *Alamut: Bastion of Peace and Information*. Paul Perry, 1999. Web. 27 Nov. 2012.

———. *Ficciones*. Trans. and introd. John Sturrock. New York : Knopf, 1993. Print.

———. "The Library of Babel." *Ficciones*. Ed. and introd. Anthony Kerrigan. New York: Grove, 1962. 79–88. Print.

Botton, Alain de. *The Art of Travel*. New York: Pantheon, 2002. Print.

Boyle, T. C. Introduction to *Marcovaldo* excerpts. Boyle and Kavashy-Boyle 89–104.

Boyle, T. C., and K. Kavashy-Boyle, eds. *Doubletakes: Pairs of Contemporary Short Stories*. Boston: Thomson, 2004. Print.

Bruner, Jerome. *The Process of Education*. Cambridge: Harvard UP, 2004. Print.

Bucciantini, Massimo. *Italo Calvino e la scienza: Gli alfabeti del mondo*. Rome: Donzelli, 2007. Print.

Burroway, Janet. *Writing Fiction: A Guide to Narrative Craft*. 6th ed. New York: Longman, 2003. Print.

Calligaris, Contardo. *Italo Calvino*. Milan: Mursia, 1973. Print.

Calvino, Italo. *Album Calvino*. Ed. Luca Baranelli and Ernesto Ferrero. Milan: Mondadori, 2003. Print. I Meridiani.

———. *Gli amori difficili*. Turin: Einaudi, 1970. Print.

———. *Il barone rampante*. Turin: Einaudi, 1958. Print.

———. *The Baron in the Trees*. Trans. Archibald Colquhoun. San Diego: Harcourt, 1959. Print.

———. *The Baron in the Trees*. Calvino, *Our Ancestors* 77–284.

———. "By Way of an Autobiography." Calvino, *Uses* 339–41.

———. *Il castello dei destini crociati*. Turin: Einaudi, 1973. Print.

———. *The Castle of Crossed Destinies*. Trans. William Weaver. New York: Harcourt, 1977. Print.

———. *Le città invisibili*. Turin: Einaudi, 1972. Print.

———. *The Cloven Viscount*. Calvino, Nonexistent Knight 145–246.

———. *Collezione di sabbia*. Milan: Garzanti, 1984. Print.

———. *Le cosmicomiche*. Turin: Einaudi, 1965. Print.

———. *Le cosmicomiche vecchie e nuove*. Milan: Garzanti, 1984. Print.

———. *Cosmicomics*. Trans. William Weaver. New York: Harcourt, 1968. Print.

———. *Difficult Loves*. Trans. William Weaver, Archibald Colquhoun, and Peggy Wright. New York: Harcourt, 1984. Print.

———. "Ed ora siamo a zero." *Repubblica* 19 Jan. 1982: 25. Print.

———. *Eremita a Parigi*. Milan: Mondadori, 1995. Print.

———. *Favole italiane*. Turin: Einaudi, 1956. Print.

———. *La giornata d'uno scrutatore*. Turin: Einaudi, 1963. Print.

———. *Hermit in Paris: Autobiographical Writings*. Trans. Martin McLaughlin. New York: Pantheon, 2003. Print.

———. *If on a winter's night a traveler*. Trans. William Weaver. New York: Harcourt, 1981. Print.

———. Interview by Guido Almansi. *Nuova corrente* 100 (1987): 387–408. Print.

———. Interview by Gregory L. Lucente. *Nuova corrente* 100 (1987): 375–86. Print.

———. Introduction. Calvino, *Italian Folktales* xv–xxxii.

———. Introduction. *Metamorfosi*. By Publio Ovidio Nasone. Turin: Einaudi, 1974. vii–xvi. Print.

———. Introduzione. Calvino, *Sentiero* vii–xxiv.

———. *Invisible Cities*. Trans. William Weaver. New York: Harcourt, 1974. Print.

———. *Italian Fables*. Trans. Louis Brigante. New York: Collier, 1959. Print.

———. *Italian Folk Tales*. Trans. Sylvia Mulcahy. London: Dent, 1975. Print.

———. *Italian Folktales*. Trans. George Martin. San Diego: Harcourt, 1980. Print.

———. *Lettere, 1940–1985*. Ed. Luca Baranelli. Milan: Mondodari, 2001. Print. I Meridiani.

———. *Lezioni americane: Sei proposte per il prossimo millennio*. Milan: Garzanti, 1988. Print.

———. *I libri degli altri: Lettere, 1947–1981*. Ed. Giovanni Tesio. Turin: Einaudi, 1991. Print.

———. *Marcovaldo*. Trans. William Weaver. New York: Harcourt, 1983. Print.

———. *"La memoria del mondo" e altre storie cosmicomiche*. Milan: Club degli Editore, 1968. Print.

———. *Mr. Palomar*. Trans. William Weaver. New York: Harcourt, 1985. Print.

———. *The Nonexistent Knight*. Calvino, Nonexistent Knight 3–141.

———. The Nonexistent Knight *and* The Cloven Viscount. Trans. Archibald Colquhoun. San Diego: Harcourt, 1977. Print.

———. *I nostri antenati*: Il visconte dimezzato, Il barone rampante, Il cavaliere inesistente. Milan: Mondadori, 1991. Print.

———. *Our Ancestors: Three Novels (*The Cloven Viscount, The Baron in the Trees, The Non-existent Knight*)*. Trans. Archibald Colquhoun. London: Secker, 1980. Print.

———. *Palomar*. Turin: Einaudi, 1983. Print.

———. *The Path to the Nest of Spiders*. Trans. Archibald Colquhoun. New York: Ecco, 1976. Print.

———. *The Path to the Nest of Spiders*. Trans. Archibald Colquhoun. Boston: Beacon, 1956. Print.

———. *The Path to the Spiders' Nests*. Trans. Archibald Colquhoun. Rev. Martin McLaughlin. New York: Ecco, 2000. Print.

———. *Perché leggere i classici*. Milan: Mondadori, 1991. Print.

———. *Una pietra sopra: Discorsi di letteratura e società*. Turin: Einaudi, 1980. Print.

———. Preface to *The Path to the Spiders' Nests*. Calvino, *Path* [2000] 7–30.

———. *The Road to San Giovanni*. Trans. Tim Parks. New York: Vintage, 1994. Print.

———. *Romanzi e racconti*. Ed. Mario Barenghi and Bruno Falcetto. 3 vols. Milan: Mondadori, 1991–94. Print. I Meridiani.

———. *Saggi (1945–1985)*. Ed. Mario Barenghi. 2 vols. Milan: Mondadori, 1995. Print. I Meridiani.

———. *Il sentiero dei nidi di ragno*. 1947. Turin: Einaudi, 2002. Print.

———. *Se una notte d'inverno un viaggiatore*. Milan: Mondadori, 1994. Print.

———. *Six Memos for the Next Millennium*. Trans. Patrick Creagh. Cambridge: Harvard UP, 1988. Print. Charles Eliot Norton Lectures, 1985–86.

———. *La strada di San Giovanni*. Milan: Mondadori, 1990. Print.

———. *Ti con zero*. Turin: Einaudi, 1967. Print.

———. *T Zero*. Trans. William Weaver. San Diego: Harcourt, 1969. Print.

———. *The Uses of Literature: Essays*. Trans. Patrick Creagh and William Weaver. San Diego: Harcourt, 1986. Print.

———. *"The Watcher" and Other Stories*. Trans. William Weaver. New York: Harcourt, 1971. Print.

———. "The World Written and the World Not Written." James Lecture. New York U, 1983. Address.

———. *Why Read the Classics?* Trans. Martin McLaughlin. New York: Pantheon, 1999. Print.

Campbell, Joseph. *The Power of Myth*. New York: Anchor, 1991.

Cannon, JoAnn. "Italian Postmodernism and *Lezioni americane*." *Annali d'Italianistica* 9 (1991): 198–211. Print.

———. "Italo Calvino: The Last Two Decades." Ricci, *Calvino* 51–64.

———. *Italo Calvino: Writer and Critic*. Ravenna: Longo, 1981. Print.

———. *Postmodern Italian Fiction: The Crisis of Reason in Calvino, Eco, Sciascia, Malerba*. London: Assoc. UPs, 1989. Print.

Capozzi, Rocco. "*Cosmicomiche vecchie e nuove*: Keeping in Tune with the Times." Ricci, *Calvino* 65–84.

Carter, Albert Howard, III. *Italo Calvino: Metamorphoses of Fantasy*. Ann Arbor: UMI Research, 1987. Print.

Cavarero, Adriana. *Relating Narratives: Storytelling and Selfhood*. Trans. Paul A. Kottman. London: Routledge, 2000. Print.

Certeau, Michel de. *The Practice of Everyday Life*. Trans. Steven Rendall. Berkeley: U of California P, 1984. Print.

Chiesa, Laura. "Italo Calvino and Georges Perec: The Multiple and Contrasting Emotions of Cities and Puzzles." *Romanic Review* 97 (2006): 401–21. Print.

Cixous, Hélène. "The Laugh of the Medusa." Trans. K. Cohen and P. Cohen. *Reading Rhetorical Theory*. Ed. Barry Brummett. New York: Harcourt, 2000. 879–93. Print.

Coloquio Internacional: Borges, Calvino, la literatura. Vol. 1. Madrid: Fundamentos, 1996. Print.

Corti, Maria. "Le jeu comme génération du texte: Des tarots au récit." *Semiotica* 7 (1973): 33–48. Print.

———. *Il viaggio testuale*. Turin: Einaudi, 1978. Print.

Davenport, Guy. *The Geography of the Imagination*. Boston: Godine, 1981. Print.

de Lauretis, Teresa. "Calvino and the Amazons: Reading the (Post)Modern Text." *Technologies of Gender: Essays on Theory, Film, and Fiction*. Bloomington: Indiana UP, 1987. 70–83. Print.

———. "Narrative Discourse in Calvino: Praxis or Poiesis?" *PMLA* 90.3 (1975): 414–25. Print.

———. "Reading the Post(Modern) Text: *If on a winter's night a traveler*." Ricci, *Calvino* 131–45.

Deleuze, Gilles, and Félix Guattari. *A Thousand Plateaus: Capitalism and Schizophrenia*. Trans. and fwd. by Brian Massumi. Minneapolis: U of Minnesota P, 1987. Print.

Derfler, Leslie. *The Dreyfus Affair*. London: Greenwood, 2002. Print.

Derrida, Jacques. *Writing and Difference*. Trans. Alan Bass. Chicago: U of Chicago P, 1978. Print.

Dickinson, Emily. "Tell all the Truth but tell it slant." *The Heath Anthology of American Literature*. Paul Lauter, gen. ed. 2nd ed. Vol. 1. Lexington: Heath, 1990. 2925. Print.

Doležel, Lubomír. *Heterocosmica: Fiction and Possible Worlds*. Baltimore: Johns Hopkins UP, 1998. Print.

Eco, Umberto. "L'antiporfirio." *Il pensiero debole*. Ed. Gianni Vattimo and Pier Paolo Rovatti. Milan: Feltrinelli, 1983. 52–80. Print.

———. "Dictionary vs. Encyclopedia." *Semiotics and the Philosophy of Language*. Bloomington: Indiana UP, 1984. 46–86. Print.

———. "Intertextual Irony and Levels of Reading." Eco, *On Literature* 212–35.

———. *The Name of the Rose*. San Diego: Harcourt, 1983. Print.

———. *On Literature*. Trans. Martin McLaughlin. San Diego: Harcourt, 2002. Print.

———. *Opera aperta*. Milan: Bompiani, 1967. Print.

Edson, Russell. *The Tunnel: Selected Poems*. Oberlin: Oberlin Coll., 1994. Print.

Eliot, T. S. *The Waste Land*. *T. S. Eliot: Collected Poems, 1909–1962*. New York: Harcourt, 1963. 51–70. Print.

Elkins, James. *Visual Studies: A Skeptical Introduction*. New York: Routledge, 2003. Print.

Federicis, Lidia de. La giornata d'uno scrutatore *di Italo Calvino*. Turin: Loescher, 1989. Print.

Finucci, Valeria. *The Lady Vanishes: Subjectivity and Representation in Castiglione and Ariosto*. Stanford: Stanford UP, 1992. Print.

———. "Moderata Fonte and the Genre of Women's Chivalric Romances." Introduction. Fonte 1–34.

Flaubert, Gustave. *Bouvard et Pécuchet*. Trans. and pref. Mark Polizzotti. Introd. Raymond Queneau. Illinois: Dalkey Archive, 2005. Print.

Fonte, Moderata [Modesta Pozzo]. *Floridoro: A Chivalric Romance*. 1581. Ed. Valeria Finucci. Trans. Julia Kisacky. Chicago: U of Chicago P, 2006. Print. The Other Voice in Early Modern Europe.

Forster, E. M. *Aspects of the Novel*. New York: Harvest, 1956. Print.

Foucault, Michel. *The Order of Things: An Archaeology of the Human Sciences*. New York: Vintage, 1970. Print.

———. "What Is an Author?" *Language, Counter-memory, Practice*. Trans. Donald F. Bouchard and Sherry Simon. Ithaca: Cornell UP, 1977: 113–38. Print.

Frasson-Marin, Aurore. *Italo Calvino et l'imaginaire*. Geneva: Slatkine, 1986. Print.

Frye, Northrop. *The Anatomy of Criticism: Four Essays*. Princeton: Princeton UP, 1957. Print.

———. *The Secular Scripture: A Study of the Structure of Romance*. Cambridge: Harvard UP, 1976. Print.

Gabriele, Tommasina. *Italo Calvino: Eros and Language*. London: Farleigh Dickinson UP, 1994. Print.

Gardner, James. "Italo Calvino, 1923–1985." *New Criterion* 4.4 (1985): 6–13. Print.

Gass, William H. *Tests of Time*. New York: Knopf, 2002. Print.

Gatt-Rutter, John. "Calvino Ludens: Literary Play and Its Political Implications." *Journal of European Studies* 5.4 (1975): 319–40. Print.

Gee, James Paul. *What Video Games Have to Teach Us about Learning and Literacy*. New York: Palgrave, 2003. Print.

Genette, Gérard. *Figures II*. Paris: Seuil, 1969. Print.

———. *Figures III*. Paris: Seuil, 1972. Print.

———. *Nouveau discourse du récit*. Paris: Seuil, 1983. Print.

Gleick, James. *Chaos: Making a New Science*. New York: Viking, 1987. Print.

Goodman, Nelson. *Ways of Worldmaking*. Indianapolis: Hackett, 1978. Print.

Goring, Paul, Jeremy Hawthorn, and Domhnall Mitchell. *Studying Literature: The Essential Companion*. London: Arnold, 2001. Print.

Gramsci, Antonio. *Prison Notebooks*. Ed. and trans. Joseph A. Buttigieg. New York: Columbia UP, 2011. Print.

Grice, H. P. "Logic and Conversation." 1975. *Studies in the Way of Words*. Ed. Grice. Cambridge: Harvard UP, 1989. 22–40. Print.

———. "Utterer's Meaning, Sentence-Meaning, and Word-Meaning." *Foundations of Language* 4 (1968): 225–42. Print.

Hall, Peter. *Cities of Tomorrow: An Intellectual History of Urban Planning and Design in the Twentieth Century*. Cambridge: Blackwell, 1996. Print.

Harris, Paul A. "Italo Calvino: The Code, the Clinamen and Cities." *Mosaic* 23.4 (1990): 67–85. Print.

Hayles, N. Katherine. *Chaos Bound: Orderly Disorder in Contemporary Literature and Science*. Ithaca: Cornell UP, 1990. Print.

Heffes, Gisela. "Reimagining Contemporary Latin American Cities." *World Literature Today* 83.2 (2009): 42–45. Print.

Heiddeger, Martin. *Discourse on Thinking*. Trans. John M. Anderson and E. Hans Freund. Introd. Anderson. New York: Harper, 1966. Print. Trans. of *Gelassenheit*.

Huizinga, Johan. *Homo Ludens: A Study of the Play-Element in Culture*. Boston: Beacon, 1955. Print.

Hume, Kathryn. *Calvino's Fictions: Cogito and Cosmos*. Oxford: Oxford UP, 1992. Print.

Hutcheon, Linda. "Actualizing Narrative Structures: Detective Plot, Fantasy, Games, and the Erotic." *Narcissistic Narrative: The Metafictional Paradox*. London: Routledge, 1984. 71–86. Print.

Iser, Wolfgang. *The Act of Reading*. Baltimore: Johns Hopkins UP, 1980. Print.

James, Carol P. "Seriality and Narrativity in Calvino's *Le città invisibili*." *MLN* 97.1 (1982): 144–61. Print.

James, Henry. *Washington Square*. New York: Penguin, 1984. Print.

Jameson, Fredric. Foreword. Lyotard vii–xxi.

Jeannet, Angela. *Under the Radiant Sun and the Crescent Moon: Italo Calvino's Storytelling*. Toronto: U of Toronto P, 2000. Print.

Kafka, Franz. *The Complete Stories*. Ed. Nahum N. Glatzer. New York: Schocken, 1988. Print.

Kershner, R. B. *The Twentieth-Century Novel*. Boston: Bedford, 1997. Print.

King, Margaret L., and Albert Rabil, Jr. "The Other Voice in Early Modern Europe: An Introduction to the Series." Fonte xi–xxx.

Koolhaas, Rem. *Delirious New York: A Retroactive Manifesto for Manhattan*. New York: Monacelli, 1997. Print.

Kuhn, Thomas S. *The Structure of Scientific Revolutions*. Chicago: U of Chicago P, 1970. Print.

Kunstler, James Howard. *The Geography of Nowhere: The Rise and Decline of America's Man-Made Landscape*. New York: Simon, 1994. Print.

Lafon, Michel. "Borges, Calvino et la littérature." *Coloquio* 11–25.

Lao-tzu. *Tao Te Ching*. Trans. D. C. Lau. New York: Penguin, 1963. Print.

Lawall, Sarah, and Maynard Mack, eds. *The Norton Anthology of World Literature*. 2nd ed. 6 vols. New York: Norton, 2002. Print.

Levi, Primo. *The Periodic Table*. 1975. Trans. Raymond Rosenthal. New York: Schocken, 1984. Print.

Levinas, Emmanuel. *Otherwise Than Being; or, Beyond Essence*. Trans. Alphonso Lingis. Pittsburgh: Duquesne UP, 1998. Print.

Lollini, Massimo. "Primo Levi and the Idea of Autobiography." *Primo Levi*: *The Austere Humanist*. Ed. Joseph Farrell. New York: Lang, 2004. 67–89. Print.

Lorenz, Edward. *The Essence of Chaos*. Seattle: Washington UP, 1993. Print.

Lyotard, Jean-François. *The Postmodern Condition: A Report on Knowledge*. Trans. Geoff Bennington and Brian Massumi. Minneapolis: U of Minnesota P, 1984. Print.

Markey, Constance. "The Hero's Quest in Calvino." *Quaderni d'Italianistica* 4.2 (1983): 154–66. Print.

———. "The Tarot Cards as Subversive Tool in Italo Calvino." *Aspects of Fantasy*. Ed. William Coyle. Westport: Greenwood, 1986. 181–86. Print.

McLaughlin, Martin. *Italo Calvino*. Edinburgh: Edinburgh UP, 1998. Print. Writers of Italy.

Melville, Herman. "Bartleby, the Scrivener." Billy Budd *and Other Tales*. New York: Signet, 1979. 108–43. Print. Signet Classic.

Mendelson, Edward. "Encyclopedic Narrative from Dante to Pynchon." *Modern Language Notes* 91 (1976): 1267–75. Print.

Mengaldo, Pier Vincenzo. *La tradizione del Novecento: Da D'Annunzio a Montale*. Milan: Feltrinelli, 1975. Print.

Milanini, Claudio. *L'utopia discontinua: Saggio su Italo Calvino*. Milan: Garzanti, 1990. Print.

Miller, Arthur I. *Insights of Genius: Imagery and Creativity in Science and Art*. Cambridge: MIT P, 2000. Print.

Monk, Thelonious. *Blue Monk*. Recorded 1963–64. Jazz Hour, 1996. CD.

Motte, Warren F., Jr. "Clinamen Redux." *Comparative Literature Studies* 23.4 (1986): 263–81. Print.

Newmark, Peter. *A Textbook of Translation*. New York: Prentice, 1998. Print.

Nida, Eugene A., and Charles R. Taber. *The Theory and Practice of Translation*. Leiden: Brill, 1969. Print.

Oates, Joyce Carol, ed. *Telling Stories: An Anthology for Writers*. New York: Norton, 1998. Print.

O'Connor, Flannery. "A Good Man Is Hard to Find." *The Complete Stories*. New York: Farrar, 1971. 117–33. Print.

———. "The Nature and Aim of Fiction." *Mystery and Manners: Occasional Prose*. Ed. Sally Fitzgerald and Robert Fitzgerald. New York: Farrar, 1969. 63–86. Print.

Ossola, Carlo. "L'invisibile e il suo 'dove': 'Geografia interiore' di Italo Calvino." *Lettere italiane* 39.2 (1987): 220–51. Print.

Palmore, Michael J. "Diagramming Calvino's Architecture." *Forum Italicum* 24.1 (1990): 25–39. Print.

Pavese, Cesare. *"La letteratura americana" e altri saggi*. Turin: Einaudi, 1962. Print.

Perec, Georges. *Life: A User's Manual*. Trans. David Bellos. Boston: Godine, 1987. Print.

———. *"Species of Spaces" and Other Pieces*. Trans. John Sturrock. London: Penguin, 1997. Print.

———. "Think/Classify." Perec, *"Species"* 184–201.

Pietralunga, Mark. "Cartophilia and the Poetic Imagination: Map Consciousness in Italo Calvino's *Le città invisibili*." *Selected Papers from the Proceedings of the Fifth Annual Conference of the American Association of Teachers of Italian, November 18–20, 1988*. Ed. Albert N. Mancini, Paolo A. Giordano, and Anthony J. Tamburri. Spec. issue of *Italiana* 3 (1990): 237–49. Print.

Pilz, Kerstin. "Complexity: A Paradigm for 'One Culture'?" *Forum Italicum* 31.2 (1997): 423–37. Print.

———. *Mapping Complexity: Literature and Science in the Works of Italo Calvino*. Leicester: Troubador, 2005. Print.

———. "Reconceptualising Thought and Space: Labyrinths and Cities in Calvino's Fictions." *Italica* 80.2 (2003): 229–44. Print.

Pirandello, Luigi. *Naked Masks: Five Plays*. Ed. Eric Bentley. New York: Dutton, 1952. Print.

Plato. *The Last Days of Socrates*. Trans. Hugh Tredennick. Baltimore: Penguin, 1966. Print.

———. *Theaetetus*. Trans. John McDowell. Oxford: Clarendon, 1973. Print.

Ponge, Francis. *Selected Poems of Francis Ponge*. Trans. C. K. Williams, John Montague, and Margaret Guiton. Ed. Guiton. Durham: Wake Forest UP, 1994. Print.

Prigogine, Ilya, and Isabelle Stengers. *Order out of Chaos: Man's New Dialogue with Nature*. Toronto: Bantam, 1984. Print.

Propp, Vladimir. *Morphology of the Folktale*. Trans. Laurence Scott. Austin: Texas UP, 1968. Print.

Pynchon, Thomas. *The Crying of Lot 49*. 1966. New York: Perennial Lib., 1986. Print.

Queneau, Raymond. "Présentation de l'*Encyclopédie*." *Bords: Mathématiciens, précurseurs, encyclopédistes*. Paris: Hermann, 1978. 85–112. Print.

Raffa, Guy P. "'Io amo New York': Calvino's Creatively Chaotic City." *Science and Literature in Italian Culture from Dante to Calvino*. Ed. Pierpaolo Antonello and Simon A. Gilson. Oxford: European Humanities Research Centre, 2004. 276–91. Print.

———. "Walking and Swimming with Umberto Eco." *MLN* 113.1 (1998): 164–85. Print.

Ransome, Paul. *Antonio Gramsci: A New Introduction*. New York: Harvester, 1992. Print.

Re, Lucia. *Calvino and the Age of Neorealism: Fables of Estrangement*. Stanford: Stanford UP, 1990. Print.

Ricci, Franco., ed. *Calvino Revisited*. Ottawa: Dovehouse, 1989. Print.

———. *Difficult Games*. Waterloo: Bilfrid Laurier UP, 1990. Print.

———. *Painting with Words, Writing with Pictures: Word and Image in the Work of Italo Calvino*. Toronto: U of Toronto P, 2001. Print.

Ricciardi, Alessia. "Lightness and Gravity: Calvino, Pynchon, and Postmodernity." *MLN* 114.5 (1999): 1062–77. Print.

Ricoeur, Paul. "The Reality of the Past." *Time and Narrative*. Trans. Kathleen McLaughlin and David Pellauer. Vol. 3. Chicago: U of Chicago P, 1988. 142–56. Print. 3 vols. 1984–88.

Riffaterre, Michael. *Fictional Truth*. Baltimore: Johns Hopkins UP, 1990. Print.

Rooney, Ellen. "The Literary Politics of Feminist Theory." *The Cambridge Companion to Feminist Literary Theory*. Ed. Rooney. Cambridge: Cambridge UP, 2006. 73–95. Print.

Ryan, Marie-Laure. *Narrative as Virtual Reality: Immersion and Interactivity in Literature and Electronic Media*. Baltimore: Johns Hopkins UP, 2001. Print.

Saivetz, Deborah. "'What Counts Is the Landscape': The Making of Pino di Buduo's 'Invisible Cities.'" *New Theatre Quarterly* 16.1 (2000): 50–65. Print.

Salsano, Alfredo. "Enciclopedia." *Enciclopedia Einaudi*. Vol. 1. Turin: Einaudi, 1977. 3–63. Print.

Saussure, Ferdinand de. *Course in General Linguistics*. Trans. Roy Harris. La Salle: Open Court, 1986. Print.

Sbragia, Albert. "Italo Calvino's Ordering of Chaos." *Modern Fiction Studies* 39.2 (1993): 283–306. Print.

Schneider, Marilyn. "Calvino at the Crossroads: *Il castello dei destini incrociati*." *PMLA* 95.1 (1980): 73–90. Print.

———. "Calvino's Erotic Metaphor and the Hermaphroditic Solution." *Stanford Italian Review* 2.1 (1981): 93–118. Print.

Schoene-Harwood, Berthold. *Writing Men: Literary Masculinities from Frankenstein to the New Man*. Edinburgh: Edinburgh UP, 2000. Print.

Scholz, László. "La metáfora del ajedrez en Borges y Calvino." *Coloquio* 119–30.

Segre, Cesare. *Avviamento all'analisi del testo letterario*. Turin: Einaudi, 1985. Print.

Simon, Sherry. *Gender in Translation: Cultural Identity and the Politics of Transmission*. New York: Routledge, 1996. Print.

Sini, Carlo. *Etica della scrittura*. Milan: Saggiatore, 1992. Print.

Stephens, Walter E. "Ec[h]o in Fabula." *Diacritics* 13 (1983): 51–64. Print.

Tabucchi, Antonio. *The Edge of the Horizon*. 1986. Trans. Tim Parks. New York: New Directions, 1990. Print.

Tani, Stefano. *The Doomed Detective*. Chicago: U of Chicago P, 1987. Print.

Taylor, Peter. *The Collected Stories of Peter Taylor*. New York: Picador, 2001. Print.

Turchi, Peter. *Maps of the Imagination: The Writer as Cartographer*. San Antonio: Trinity UP, 2004. Print.

Updike, John. "Readers and Writers." *Hugging the Shore: Essays and Criticism*. New York: Vintage, 1984. 470–77. Print.

Venuti, Lawrence. *The Scandals of Translation*. New York: Routledge, 1988. Print.

Viano, Maurizio. "Ancora su *Il pendolo di Foucault*." *Forum Italicum* 25.1 (1991): 152–61. Print.

Vidal, Gore. "On Italo Calvino." *New York Review of Books* 21 Nov. 1985: 3+. Print.

Vila-Matas, Enrique. *Bartleby and Co*. Trans. Jonathan Dunne. New York: New Directions, 2004. Print.

von Flotow, Luise. *Translation and Gender: Translating in the "Era of Feminism."* Ottawa: U of Ottawa P, 1997. Print.

Watson, Ian. "Invisible Cities: An Interview with Pino di Buduo." *Negotiating Cultures: Eugenio Barba and the Intercultural Debate*. Ed. Watson. Manchester: Manchester UP, 2002. 159–67. Print.

Watts, Alan. "Wu-Wei." *Tao: The Watercourse Way*. By Watts and Al Chung-liang Huang. New York: Pantheon, 1975. 74–105. Print.

Weaver, William. Interview by Giulia Guarnieri. Trans. Guarnieri. *Italian Quarterly* 129–130 (1996): 77–87. Print.

Weiss, Beno. *Understanding Italo Calvino*. Columbia: U of South Carolina P, 1993. Print.

Wells, H. G. *Anticipations of the Reaction of Mechanical and Scientific Progress upon Human Life and Thought*. New York: Harper, 1902. Print.

Welty, Eudora. "Why I Live at the P.O." *Stories, Essays, and Memoir*. New York: Lib. of Amer., 1998. 57–69. Print.

West, Rebecca. "L'identità americana di Calvino." *Nuova corrente* 100 (1987): 363–74. Print.

Whyte, William Holingsworth. *City: Rediscovering the Center*. New York: Doubleday, 1988. Print.

———, dir. *The Social Life of Small Urban Spaces*. Municipal Art Soc. of New York, 1979. Film.

———. *The Social Life of Small Urban Spaces*. Washington: Conservation Foundation, 1980. Print.

Williams, William Carlos. *Selected Poems*. New York: New Directions, 1985. Print.

Woolf, Virginia. *"A Haunted House" and Other Short Stories*. San Diego: Harvest, 1972. Print.

Wright, Simonetta Chessa. *La poetica neobarocca in Calvino*. Ravenna: Longo, 1998. Print.

Žižek, Slavoj. *Looking Awry: An Introduction to Jacques Lacan through Popular Culture*. Cambridge: MIT P, 1992. Print.

INDEX

Modern Language Association of America

Approaches to Teaching World Literature

Achebe's Things Fall Apart. Ed. Bernth Lindfors. 1991.
Arthurian Tradition. Ed. Maureen Fries and Jeanie Watson. 1992.
Atwood's The Handmaid's Tale *and Other Works*. Ed. Sharon R. Wilson, Thomas B. Friedman, and Shannon Hengen. 1996.
Austen's Emma. Ed. Marcia McClintock Folsom. 2004.
Austen's Pride and Prejudice. Ed. Marcia McClintock Folsom. 1993.
Balzac's Old Goriot. Ed. Michal Peled Ginsburg. 2000.
Baudelaire's Flowers of Evil. Ed. Laurence M. Porter. 2000.
Beckett's Waiting for Godot. Ed. June Schlueter and Enoch Brater. 1991.
Beowulf. Ed. Jess B. Bessinger, Jr., and Robert F. Yeager. 1984.
Blake's Songs of Innocence and of Experience. Ed. Robert F. Gleckner and Mark L. Greenberg. 1989.
Boccaccio's Decameron. Ed. James H. McGregor. 2000.
British Women Poets of the Romantic Period. Ed. Stephen C. Behrendt and Harriet Kramer Linkin. 1997.
Charlotte Brontë's Jane Eyre. Ed. Diane Long Hoeveler and Beth Lau. 1993.
Emily Brontë's Wuthering Heights. Ed. Sue Lonoff and Terri A. Hasseler. 2006.
Byron's Poetry. Ed. Frederick W. Shilstone. 1991.
Works of Italo Calvino. Ed. Franco Ricci. 2013.
Camus's The Plague. Ed. Steven G. Kellman. 1985.
Writings of Bartolomé de Las Casas. Ed. Santa Arias and Eyda M. Merediz. 2008.
Cather's My Ántonia. Ed. Susan J. Rosowski. 1989.
Cervantes' Don Quixote. Ed. Richard Bjornson. 1984.
Chaucer's Canterbury Tales. Ed. Joseph Gibaldi. 1980.
Chaucer's Troilus and Criseyde *and the Shorter Poems*. Ed. Tison Pugh and Angela Jane Weisl. 2006.
Chopin's The Awakening. Ed. Bernard Koloski. 1988.
Coleridge's Poetry and Prose. Ed. Richard E. Matlak. 1991.
Collodi's Pinocchio *and Its Adaptations.* Ed. Michael Sherberg. 2006.
Conrad's "Heart of Darkness" and "The Secret Sharer." Ed. Hunt Hawkins and Brian W. Shaffer. 2002.
Dante's Divine Comedy. Ed. Carole Slade. 1982.
Defoe's Robinson Crusoe. Ed. Maximillian E. Novak and Carl Fisher. 2005.
DeLillo's White Noise. Ed. Tim Engles and John N. Duvall. 2006.
Dickens's Bleak House. Ed. John O. Jordan and Gordon Bigelow. 2009.
Dickens's David Copperfield. Ed. Richard J. Dunn. 1984.
Dickinson's Poetry. Ed. Robin Riley Fast and Christine Mack Gordon. 1989.
Narrative of the Life of Frederick Douglass. Ed. James C. Hall. 1999.
Duras's Ourika. Ed. Mary Ellen Birkett and Christopher Rivers. 2009.

Early Modern Spanish Drama. Ed. Laura R. Bass and Margaret R. Greer. 2006.
Eliot's Middlemarch. Ed. Kathleen Blake. 1990.
Eliot's Poetry and Plays. Ed. Jewel Spears Brooker. 1988.
Shorter Elizabethan Poetry. Ed. Patrick Cheney and Anne Lake Prescott. 2000.
Ellison's Invisible Man. Ed. Susan Resneck Parr and Pancho Savery. 1989.
English Renaissance Drama. Ed. Karen Bamford and Alexander Leggatt. 2002.
Works of Louise Erdrich. Ed. Gregg Sarris, Connie A. Jacobs, and James R. Giles. 2004.
Dramas of Euripides. Ed. Robin Mitchell-Boyask. 2002.
Faulkner's As I Lay Dying. Ed. Patrick O'Donnell and Lynda Zwinger. 2011.
Faulkner's The Sound and the Fury. Ed. Stephen Hahn and Arthur F. Kinney. 1996.
Fitzgerald's The Great Gatsby. Ed. Jackson R. Bryer and Nancy P. VanArsdale. 2009.
Flaubert's Madame Bovary. Ed. Laurence M. Porter and Eugene F. Gray. 1995.
García Márquez's One Hundred Years of Solitude. Ed. María Elena de Valdés and Mario J. Valdés. 1990.
Gilman's "The Yellow Wall-Paper" and Herland. Ed. Denise D. Knight and Cynthia J. Davis. 2003.
Goethe's Faust. Ed. Douglas J. McMillan. 1987.
Gothic Fiction: The British and American Traditions. Ed. Diane Long Hoeveler and Tamar Heller. 2003.
Poetry of John Gower. Ed. R. F. Yeager and Brian W. Gastle. 2011.
Grass's The Tin Drum. Ed. Monika Shafi. 2008.
H.D.'s Poetry and Prose. Ed. Annette Debo and Lara Vetter. 2011.
Hebrew Bible as Literature in Translation. Ed. Barry N. Olshen and Yael S. Feldman. 1989.
Homer's Iliad *and* Odyssey. Ed. Kostas Myrsiades. 1987.
Hurston's Their Eyes Were Watching God *and Other Works*. Ed. John Lowe. 2009.
Ibsen's A Doll House. Ed. Yvonne Shafer. 1985.
Henry James's Daisy Miller *and* The Turn of the Screw. Ed. Kimberly C. Reed and Peter G. Beidler. 2005.
Works of Samuel Johnson. Ed. David R. Anderson and Gwin J. Kolb. 1993.
Joyce's Ulysses. Ed. Kathleen McCormick and Erwin R. Steinberg. 1993.
Works of Sor Juana Inés de la Cruz. Ed. Emilie L. Bergmann and Stacey Schlau. 2007.
Kafka's Short Fiction. Ed. Richard T. Gray. 1995.
Keats's Poetry. Ed. Walter H. Evert and Jack W. Rhodes. 1991.
Kingston's The Woman Warrior. Ed. Shirley Geok-lin Lim. 1991.
Lafayette's The Princess of Clèves. Ed. Faith E. Beasley and Katharine Ann Jensen. 1998.
Works of D. H. Lawrence. Ed. M. Elizabeth Sargent and Garry Watson. 2001.
Lazarillo de Tormes *and the Picaresque Tradition*. Ed. Anne J. Cruz. 2009.
Lessing's The Golden Notebook. Ed. Carey Kaplan and Ellen Cronan Rose. 1989.
Works of Naguib Mahfouz. Ed. Waïl S. Hassan and Susan Muaddi Darraj. 2011.

Mann's Death in Venice *and Other Short Fiction*. Ed. Jeffrey B. Berlin. 1992.
Marguerite de Navarre's Heptameron. Ed. Colette H. Winn. 2007.
Medieval English Drama. Ed. Richard K. Emmerson. 1990.
Melville's Moby-Dick. Ed. Martin Bickman. 1985.
Metaphysical Poets. Ed. Sidney Gottlieb. 1990.
Miller's Death of a Salesman. Ed. Matthew C. Roudané. 1995.
Milton's Paradise Lost. First edition. Ed. Galbraith M. Crump. 1986.
Milton's Paradise Lost. Second edition. Ed. Peter C. Herman. 2012.
Milton's Shorter Poetry and Prose. Ed. Peter C. Herman. 2007.
Molière's Tartuffe *and Other Plays*. Ed. James F. Gaines and Michael S. Koppisch. 1995.
Momaday's The Way to Rainy Mountain. Ed. Kenneth M. Roemer. 1988.
Montaigne's Essays. Ed. Patrick Henry. 1994.
Novels of Toni Morrison. Ed. Nellie Y. McKay and Kathryn Earle. 1997.
Murasaki Shikibu's The Tale of Genji. Ed. Edward Kamens. 1993.
Nabokov's Lolita. Ed. Zoran Kuzmanovich and Galya Diment. 2008.
Works of Ngũgĩ wa Thiong'o. Ed. Oliver Lovesey. 2012.
Works of Tim O'Brien. Ed. Alex Vernon and Catherine Calloway. 2010.
Works of Ovid and the Ovidian Tradition. Ed. Barbara Weiden Boyd and Cora Fox. 2010.
Poe's Prose and Poetry. Ed. Jeffrey Andrew Weinstock and Tony Magistrale. 2008.
Pope's Poetry. Ed. Wallace Jackson and R. Paul Yoder. 1993.
Proust's Fiction and Criticism. Ed. Elyane Dezon-Jones and Inge Crosman Wimmers. 2003.
Puig's Kiss of the Spider Woman. Ed. Daniel Balderston and Francine Masiello. 2007.
Pynchon's The Crying of Lot 49 *and Other Works*. Ed. Thomas H. Schaub. 2008.
Works of François Rabelais. Ed. Todd W. Reeser and Floyd Gray. 2011.
Novels of Samuel Richardson. Ed. Lisa Zunshine and Jocelyn Harris. 2006.
Rousseau's Confessions *and* Reveries of the Solitary Walker. Ed. John C. O'Neal and Ourida Mostefai. 2003.
Scott's Waverley Novels. Ed. Evan Gottlieb and Ian Duncan. 2009.
Shakespeare's Hamlet. Ed. Bernice W. Kliman. 2001.
Shakespeare's King Lear. Ed. Robert H. Ray. 1986.
Shakespeare's Othello. Ed. Peter Erickson and Maurice Hunt. 2005.
Shakespeare's Romeo and Juliet. Ed. Maurice Hunt. 2000.
Shakespeare's The Tempest *and Other Late Romances.* Ed. Maurice Hunt. 1992.
Shelley's Frankenstein. Ed. Stephen C. Behrendt. 1990.
Shelley's Poetry. Ed. Spencer Hall. 1990.
Sir Gawain and the Green Knight. Ed. Miriam Youngerman Miller and Jane Chance. 1986.
Song of Roland. Ed. William W. Kibler and Leslie Zarker Morgan. 2006.
Spenser's Faerie Queene. Ed. David Lee Miller and Alexander Dunlop. 1994.

Stendhal's The Red and the Black. Ed. Dean de la Motte and Stirling Haig. 1999.
Sterne's Tristram Shandy. Ed. Melvyn New. 1989.
Works of Robert Louis Stevenson. Ed. Caroline McCracken-Flesher. 2013.
The Story of the Stone (Dream of the Red Chamber). Ed. Andrew Schonebaum and Tina Lu. 2012.
Stowe's Uncle Tom's Cabin. Ed. Elizabeth Ammons and Susan Belasco. 2000.
Swift's Gulliver's Travels. Ed. Edward J. Rielly. 1988.
Teresa of Ávila and the Spanish Mystics. Ed. Alison Weber. 2009.
Thoreau's Walden *and Other Works*. Ed. Richard J. Schneider. 1996.
Tolstoy's Anna Karenina. Ed. Liza Knapp and Amy Mandelker. 2003.
Vergil's Aeneid. Ed. William S. Anderson and Lorina N. Quartarone. 2002.
Voltaire's Candide. Ed. Renée Waldinger. 1987.
Whitman's Leaves of Grass. Ed. Donald D. Kummings. 1990.
Wiesel's Night. Ed. Alan Rosen. 2007.
Works of Oscar Wilde. Ed. Philip E. Smith II. 2008.
Woolf's Mrs. Dalloway. Ed. Eileen Barrett and Ruth O. Saxton. 2009.
Woolf's To the Lighthouse. Ed. Beth Rigel Daugherty and Mary Beth Pringle. 2001.
Wordsworth's Poetry. Ed. Spencer Hall, with Jonathan Ramsey. 1986.
Wright's Native Son. Ed. James A. Miller. 1997.